Fighting with the Past

THE STEVEN AND JANICE BROSE LECTURES
IN THE CIVIL WAR ERA

Rachel Shelden, editor

William A. Blair, founding editor

The Steven and Janice Brose Lectures in the Civil War Era are published by the University of North Carolina Press in association with the George and Ann Richards Civil War Era Center at Penn State University. The series features books based on public lectures by a distinguished scholar, delivered over a three-day period each fall, as well as edited volumes developed from public symposia. These books chart new directions for research in the field and offer scholars and general readers fresh perspectives on the Civil War era.

A complete list of books published in the Steven and Janice Brose Lectures in the Civil War Era is available at *https://uncpress.org/series/steven-janice-brose-lectures-civil-war-era.*

Fighting with the Past

HOW SEVENTEENTH-
CENTURY HISTORY
SHAPED THE AMERICAN
CIVIL WAR

Aaron Sheehan-Dean

THE UNIVERSITY OF NORTH CAROLINA PRESS
Chapel Hill

This book was published with the assistance of the George and Ann Richards Civil War Era Center at Penn State University.

© 2025 The University of North Carolina Press

All rights reserved

Designed by Jamison Cockerham
Set in Arno, Blaisdell, and Fell Double Pica Pro
by codeMantra

Cover art: Oliver Cromwell, courtesy of Louisiana State University Library.

Manufactured in the United States of America

Library of Congress Cataloging-in-Publication Data
Names: Sheehan-Dean, Aaron Charles, author.
Title: Fighting with the past : how seventeenth-century history shaped the American Civil War / Aaron Sheehan-Dean. Other titles: Steven and Janice Brose lectures in the Civil War era.
Description: Chapel Hill : The University of North Carolina Press, [2025] | Series: The Steven and Janice Brose lectures in the Civil War era | Includes bibliographical references and index.
Identifiers: LCCN 2025013294 | ISBN 9781469690742 (cloth) | ISBN 9781469690759 (paperback) | ISBN 9781469688107 (epub) | ISBN 9781469690766 (pdf)
Subjects: LCSH: Collective memory—United States—History—19th century. | United States—History—Civil War, 1861–1865. | Great Britain—History—Civil War, 1642–1649. | BISAC: HISTORY / United States / Civil War Period (1850–1877) | HISTORY / World
Classification: LCC E468.9 .S538 2025
LC record available at https://lccn.loc.gov/2025013294

For product safety concerns under the European Union's General Product Safety Regulation (EU GPSR), please contact gpsr@mare-nostrum.co.uk or write to the University of North Carolina Press and Mare Nostrum Group B.V., Mauritskade 21D, 1091 GC Amsterdam, The Netherlands.

To the memory of

PETER S. CARMICHAEL

CONTENTS

List of Illustrations vii

Acknowledgments ix

Introduction Making Poetry from the Past 1

1 Historical Thinking in the Nineteenth Century 11

2 The Cultural Origins of the Civil War 21

3 Legitimate and Illegitimate Rebellion 39

4 Committing to Civil War 51

5 The Language of War 69

6 The Dangers of Despotism 89

7 Ending Civil Wars 103

8 The Meaning of the Civil War 123

Conclusion Past and Present 143

Notes 149

Bibliography 181

Index 203

ILLUSTRATIONS

King Charles I   *41*

Oliver Cromwell   *79*

ACKNOWLEDGMENTS

One of the great pleasures of studying a topic outside my regular field has been the opportunity to meet new people and learn from them. I am especially grateful that, in this case, part of that learning happened in Ireland. In 2021–22, I served as the Mary Ball Washington Chair of American Studies at University College Dublin. Robert Gerwarth helped me navigate the appointment and proved flexible and generous during the uncertainties produced by the COVID-19 pandemic. William Mulligan, who led the School of History at UCD during my time there, was a wonderful host and generous colleague. I am especially grateful to Jennifer Keating, Catherine Cox, and Sandra Scanlon for welcoming me into the UCD community. Dinners with Jen and Conrad sustained us when we were far from home. Ivar McGrath suffered too many questions about the British empire in the seventeenth and eighteenth centuries and graciously directed me to readings that proved invaluable. Penny Roberts (of Warwick) and David Appleby (at Nottingham) both shared papers from a UCD conference on global civil wars that happened just before my arrival—I appreciate their willingness to share their works in progress.

Even before I arrived in Ireland, I had the good fortune to meet Damian Shiels. In addition to becoming a fast friend, Damian proved an exceptionally informed and good-natured tour guide (especially our memorable trip to Cork and the Fenian haunts of southwestern Ireland). Damian answered endless questions about Ireland, both historical and contemporary. It's hard to imagine writing this book without his help; I'll always be grateful. David

Gleeson, another native son, likewise responded to all my queries with good cheer and precision. I owe David additional thanks for inviting me to present my ongoing research at Northumbria University. Thanks to Jennifer Aston for arranging that trip and for her questions. Damian, who somehow made it in, and Patrick Andelic also asked great questions and made boon dinner companions. My deep thanks to Enrico dal Lago for inviting me to the University of Galway and for all his comments and questions (as well as for paving a pioneering trail for those of us interested in comparative history). Kevin O'Sullivan arranged the Galway trip and asked probing and thoughtful questions as did Róisín Healy and others in attendance on that rainy west Ireland day. While in Dublin, I enjoyed a friendly and very helpful conversation with Micheál Ó Siochrú. I had already learned a great deal from his essential scholarship, and his advice and thoughts on the project came at a crucial moment.

Closer to home, I leaned on many colleagues at Louisiana State University. Dean Troy Blanchard made my year in Ireland possible. I am grateful to him and to the Frey and Eaton families for the support provided through the Fred C. Frey Chair in Southern Studies. James Bishop and Zevi Gutfreund both offered me valuable guidance on the history of education in the nineteenth century. Victor Stater and Meredith Veldman patiently fielded layman's questions about British history, including queries about the Norman Yoke and other topics they would rather have not discussed but for the pedantries of nineteenth-century Southerners. Maribel Dietz answered my questions about the medieval past. Gaines Foster was, as always, supportive and thoughtful, despite how many times I disturbed his well-earned peace. He gave valuable feedback on an early version of the project, particularly in helping me think more clearly about memory. Benjamin Haines has my deep appreciation for his research help on the English attitudes question. Sue Marchand has been a sounding board throughout this project as she works on her own study of the reception of Herodotus over time. Her sage advice and questions have been consistently useful. John Bardes gamely listened to ideas and offered valuable advice as I developed the project. Steve Prince, though only just arrived at LSU, put up with frequent interruptions of his own work, including valuable last minute advice on the opening lines. I am lucky to work in a department so collegial that it is considered acceptable practice (or at least not a firing offense) to simply walk into someone's office and pose arcane questions about historiography.

Several other LSU departments have proven essential as I worked on this book. The office of Interlibrary Loan responded promptly to all my requests.

Brittany O'Neill and Hayley Johnson at LSU libraries helped me navigate databases. Professor Jim Stoner invited me to present an early part of the project at LSU's Voegelin Institute. I appreciated the attendance and questions from all the participants, especially Christine Kooi, Gaines, Cat Jacquet, and Michelle Zerba.

Within the broader field, I have acquired innumerable debts as I barraged friends with questions over the last few years. At Southerns and SCWH meetings, I have had fun and productive conversations about this project with a range of people, including Jim Broomall, Greg Downs, Andrew Fialka, Sarah Gardner, Luke Hargroder, Carrie Janney, Andy Lang, and Yael Sternhell. My thanks to them all. I am grateful to Helena Yoo Roth, who recommended Brendan McConville's book and asked excellent questions. Ian Delahanty, who has just published his own fine book on Ireland and the United States, shared sources and ideas. I'm grateful to him. Brian Schoen earned endless credit for recommending me to UCD and for all his ideas about this project and the Civil War in general. I enjoyed a delightful breakfast and conversation with Cynthia Nicoletti, who is doing her own work on the relationship between the English Civil Wars and the American conflict. Sam Watson offered valuable assistance understanding West Point and military education in general.

Back in what seems like another era (February 2020), I hosted a workshop for scholars of the English and American civil wars to gather. I intended to pursue an edited volume, but the COVID pandemic and department chair duties waylaid those plans. Still, I learned a tremendous amount from the participants. I appreciate their willingness to travel to Baton Rouge and the vibrant discussions we had over a late Mardi Gras weekend. My eternal thanks to Michael Braddick, Jason Peacey, Ann Hughes, Wayne Lee, Greg Downs, Adam I. P. Smith, and Sarah Gardner. In retrospect, it looks like I convened a panel of experts to help write my book. Although honestly not my purpose, the education I gathered over that delightful weekend made this book possible.

I enjoyed one other chance to try out arguments. My thanks to Rob Havers, president of the American Civil War Museum, for inviting me to participate in the 2023 ACWM Symposium. Kelly Hancock arranged everything with grace. My time with attendees at the event and, especially my exchanges with fellow presenters Carrie Janney, Andy Lang, Kate Masur, and Manisha Sinha, helped bring key parts of the project into focus. The remarkable ACWM facility in Richmond is an inspiring place to talk about the past.

The University of North Carolina Press staff moved with their usual precision to bring this book to completion. I am grateful to Valerie Burton, who shepherded it expertly through the production phase; to Thomas Bedenbaugh, who assisted throughout the process; to Iza Wojciechowska, who performed brilliant copy-editing work on the manuscript; and to Jamison Cockerham, who designed a superb cover and beautiful text. The Press secured two very helpful reviews of the manuscript. Both readers were generous, precise, and thoughtful in their advice and I am grateful to them.

The original invitation to pursue this project for the Brose Lecture Series came from Bill Blair, when he directed the Richards Center at Penn State University. I remember Bill and Mark Simpson-Vos patiently listening to my half-baked ideas for the lectures. Their confidence in me and the project boosted me considerably. Barb Singer proved, as always, a remarkably efficient and pleasant person to work with as I planned my visit to Penn State. I had the good fortune to deliver the first in-person Brose Lectures after the COVID-19 pandemic. Alas, Steven and Janice Brose both contracted COVID just before I arrived and could not attend the lectures in person; nonetheless, I am grateful to their sponsorship of this most special event. I enjoyed a beautiful weekend in State College while fielding insightful and supportive queries from the attendees. My conversations there helped me reconceptualize important parts of the project. Cathleen Cahill, who directed the Richards Center during the semester I visited, served as a generous host. Emma Teitelman, then the assistant director of the center, asked great questions and encouraged me to dig into the relationship between history and memory. I am grateful to them both. Rachel Shelden was enjoying her sabbatical in Washington, DC, that semester, but she nonetheless returned to State College and helped host. She has proven a steadfast supporter of the project through all its phases and I'm deeply appreciative, especially of her final reading of the manuscript. While at Penn State, I benefited from my interactions with all the faculty, especially A. K. Sandoval-Strausz, who asked good questions, and Amy Greenberg, who generously treated me to a pancake breakfast and fun conversation. Christina Snyder, Julie Reed, Mark Simpson-Vos, and Andy Graybill made a terrific group of companions during a memorable dinner while in State College.

I have subjected family and friends to what I am sure seemed like esoteric questions and ideas. I am fortunate to be surrounded by loving people who tolerate, even encourage, my interests. Kimberley Marchant asked loads of good questions during our wonderful trip around Ireland in April 2022. Johann Neem, Greg Downs, and Yael Sternhell demonstrated their boundless friendship and goodwill by reading an earlier draft of the full manuscript. They each offered me advice, which I did my best to incorporate. Whatever success I have had in my field I owe in large measure to smart and generous friends. Mark Simpson-Vos has offered his friendship and his acute editorial eye throughout this whole process. I am honored and grateful to participate in an ASD-MSV production. My brother Jon also read the whole manuscript, late in the process, offering his typical worldly insight. I owe them all. Liam and Annie helped make our most memorable family trip yet, even as I fumbled through a retelling of early modern Irish history and how it connected to the Civil War. Their thoughtfulness, humor, and adventurous spirit enrich our lives. My wife Megan tromped around Ireland with me, listened to ideas, and read the whole manuscript. She has my love and admiration.

My dear friend Peter Carmichael died suddenly as I was finishing this book. It pains me to know I won't be able to argue with him about it, as we have done for much of the last twenty-five years. Pete did not read the manuscript, but his insistence that historians have a responsibility to speak clearly about the still-relevant past inspired me. His friendship, his professional support, and his rigorous mind helped make me the historian I am today. I can't repay that debt, but I honor it by dedicating this book to his memory.

Fighting with the Past

INTRODUCTION

Making Poetry from the Past

> So we beat on, boats against the current, borne back ceaselessly into the past.
>
> F. SCOTT FITZGERALD, *The Great Gatsby*

History holds undeniable power. As F. Scott Fitzgerald observed a century ago, its sheer weight often pulls us backward, even as we live our lives moving forward in time. Like the doomed Gatsby, history can trap us in the struggle to break the gravity of our own errors and those of our ancestors. But the practice of historical thinking can also be a resource that grants perspective on the present and allows us to imagine different futures. Thinking historically allows us to inhabit different eras, considering past events in the present and also through the lens of those who have created prior interpretations of those same events.

The Americans, both Northern and Southern, who fought in and lived through the US Civil War relied on history in this way. In particular, they used history to define and justify rebellion, to anticipate the course of civil conflicts, and to understand the relationships between military violence and social and political change. As these verbs—"define," "justify," "anticipate," and "understand"—indicate, history provided Civil War Americans a vocabulary for how to think about the conflict.

In this book, I use the tools of intellectual history to consider Civil War Americans' conceptions of the past and to explore how they used history to establish the meaning and significance of the conflict. I do so by examining a point of historical resonance that is surprising but unmistakable in the archive of the Civil War era: Time and again, Civil War Americans looked to the history of another civil conflict, the English Civil Wars of the seventeenth century, as they sought to navigate their crisis.

A short but telling example to start: In the waning days of the US Civil War, the Confederacy sent a group of "peace commissioners" to meet with Abraham Lincoln at Hampton Roads, Virginia. It was a hopeless effort; Lincoln would accept peace only with reunion of the seceded states and the end of slavery, while Confederates fought for independence and to preserve slavery. During the meeting, Robert Hunter, one of the Confederate commissioners, referred to the willingness of King Charles I to compromise with Oliver Cromwell's Parliamentary forces, who had seized control of England under force of arms in 1646. "Lincoln laughingly responded: 'I do not profess to be posted in history. On all such matters I will turn you over to [Secretary of State William] Seward. All I distinctly recollect about the case of Charles I, is, that he lost his head in the end.'"[1]

Lincoln's coy dismissal of Hunter's historical analogy revealed that he knew more than he claimed. Parliamentary forces executed Charles I in 1649. If he refused to act like a modern-day monarch, neither did Lincoln mean to act like Charles's antagonist, the inflexible Oliver Cromwell, as Confederates and Northern conservatives often claimed he did. Union victory was less than two months away, so Lincoln's demurral of Confederate offers proved strategically wise. Lincoln had little reason to compromise with victory at the doorstep. As it turned out, Lincoln lost his head too, though not in the official state-sanctioned way that doomed Charles I. His comment at Hampton Roads seems an eerie anticipation.

This diplomatic episode is well known among historians, but few have considered the use of historical thinking that framed the interaction. I was one of those historians who overlooked the reference for years. Then, in the course of research for another book exploring the ways Americans compared their own conflict with civil wars happening elsewhere at the same time (such as the 1857 Indian Rebellion, the Taiping Rebellion, and the 1863 Polish Uprising), I recognized how often Americans referenced seventeenth-century England.[2] Now I see clearly that both Union and Confederate negotiators, like their respective constituencies, came to Hampton Roads with keen interest in and knowledge of the seventeenth-century conflicts within the British Isles. In this critical moment and many others throughout the American conflict, they called on that knowledge to shape their thinking, their rhetoric, and the public meaning of what transpired.[3]

This book is the result of concentrating on such historical references in Civil War rhetoric, grounded in deep reading in a wide array of nineteenth-century newspapers and periodicals along with the speeches and letters of major figures in the war. As I read, I discovered the pervasiveness of seventeenth-century analogies. I also identified that the use of these analogies varied based on people's membership in one of four political communities— Northern radicals and Northern moderates (both members of the Republican Party), Northern conservatives (almost always members of the Democratic Party), and Confederates. Although the boundaries between these categories remained fluid throughout the war, political differences in the North shaped the course and consequences of the war. Most prewar abolitionists became radicals during it; they wanted to destroy slavery altogether, and many hoped to use the power of the state to reshape Southern society itself. Northern conservatives expressed little concern for enslaved people or about the role of slavery in American life; though usually committed to the Union, they guarded the constitutional protections threatened by civil war and pursued a generous peace. Northern moderates navigated between these poles, seeking the preservation of the Union and the destruction of slavery through careful and democratic means.

This book uses the discourse of history to expose the intellectual architecture of the conflict and shows how history itself shaped the course of the war. The narrative that follows reflects the braided relationship between past and present, quoting nineteenth-century Americans as they quoted seventeenth-century figures. I track how Civil War participants used history-as-war rhetoric across three chronological phases: the prewar and secession debates, wartime discourse, and struggles over the war's conclusion and its meaning. The ubiquity and variety of uses of the English past in the US Civil War enabled me to construct a narrative that covers the whole of the war, though the nature of the rhetoric and its political meanings change in each chapter.

After considering the competing historical perspectives these groups brought to the conflict, I offer three main arguments about the US Civil

War itself and the nature of historical memory more broadly. First, I argue that alongside the overwhelming importance of slavery to the war's causes, fighting, and outcomes, concerns about the fundamentals of constitutional governance played an important role in shaping Northerners' reactions to the conflict. Second, the debate among Northerners determined the course of the war in ways nearly as profound as the basic divide between Federals and Confederates. Third, Northerners' uses of the English past help us understand the reconciliationist conclusion of the war.

At the same time, the arguments among Civil War Americans remind us of the slipperiness of metaphorical, especially analogical, language. When people incorporate historical analogies into their thinking, the words attain a magnetic charge that makes them hard to separate.[4] The power of analogies can wed people to counterproductive, even self-defeating, patterns of behavior. Still, historical analogies are nearly impossible to resist; for creatures that make meaning out of the world, history provides one of the readiest sources.

Because this book is mostly intended to explain the American experience, readers may come to it unfamiliar with the English experience. What follows is a short summary of the seventeenth-century conflict, intended to provide background for the numerous claims that nineteenth-century Americans made about the war. Throughout the text itself, I ground those discussions in more detailed explanations.

Unlike the US Civil War, which divided along reasonably clear sectional lines, the English Civil Wars involved conflicts in Scotland and Ireland as well as internecine strife in England itself. Today's historians now typically refer to the "War of Three Nations," though out of loyalty to the primary sources I use the most common nineteenth-century title.[5] Trouble began in 1637 when King Charles I and Church of England archbishop William Laud tried to impose the Book of Common Prayer on a Church of Scotland that increasingly supported a presbyterian rather than episcopal structure. When Charles required funds for an army to quell the unhappy Scots, he was forced to call a parliament, which he had not done for nearly a decade (itself a source of serious concern for many people). Grievances accumulated within the "Long Parliament." Seeing opportunity, Catholic Ireland rose in revolt in 1641. Between 1642 and 1646, English factions fought, aligned with either the king or Parliament; the Royalist forces lost, and Parliamentarians took Charles under a form of house arrest.

Despite his confinement, Charles refused to make substantial concessions to the authority of Parliament. Meanwhile, tensions grew among Parliamentarians, who were increasingly divided between moderates sympathetic to the Crown and a radical faction of Protestants (some of them dubbed "Puritans" by their opponents) led by Oliver Cromwell, who had risen as a military and political figure during the 1642–46 fighting. By 1648, a second civil war erupted. Cromwell, commanding a force known as the New Model Army, emerged victorious. In 1649, Cromwell's forces executed Charles I, dissolved the monarchy, and declared the creation of the English Commonwealth. The Royalists rose once more, led by Charles II in league with Scottish supporters. But this effort failed as well, and by 1651, violence within England itself came to a close, with Charles II fleeing to exile in France.

Violence in Ireland had continued throughout the period and ended only after Cromwell's brutal campaign across the southern counties of the island in 1649–53. Despite the republican turn under Cromwell, he declared himself Lord Protector and ruled as a quasi monarch until his death in 1658. Cromwell's son, who succeeded him, could not manage the country, and a coalition of former Parliamentarians and Royalists brought Charles II back to assume the throne in 1660 ("the Restoration"). For two decades, then, England, Scotland, and Ireland experienced rapid and radical change but ultimately returned to the stability of the constitutional monarchy.[6]

Even as nineteenth-century Americans drew parallels between their world and the mid-seventeenth century, we need to recognize the significant contextual differences between the two eras. In the seventeenth century, the English regarded as natural the deep intermingling of religious practice and state power. The long bloody century preceding the English Civil Wars—from the start of the Protestant Reformation in 1519—witnessed violence across much of Europe and the British Isles, fundamentally organized around religion. Because Americans separated church and state, by 1860 social divisions around race, ethnicity, and class, rather than religion, structured most public violence and political conflict.[7] Moreover, the government of seventeenth-century England was organized in fundamentally different ways from the American system. In England, political power was divided between the monarchy and Parliament, with the latter dependent on the former.[8] In antebellum America, the presidency and Congress were coequal branches, and power was contested around political parties.[9] Finally, the seventeenth-century conflicts involved three discrete kingdoms (Scotland, Ireland, and England), each with their own partisans and goals. The English organized their world around order, stability, and obedience, while Americans organized theirs around (white, male) equality, autonomy, and ambition.

Despite all these differences, nineteenth-century Americans perceived similarities in how each place reacted to the mortal threat of civil war and availed themselves of seventeenth-century analogies throughout their own conflict.¹⁰ Americans invoked Puritans, Presbyterians, and Parliamentarians repeatedly, but they did not do so consistently. Partly, this owes to the blurry distinction between memory and history that prevailed in the mid-nineteenth century. Contemporary scholars distinguish these ways of knowing the past, but Civil War Americans did not. They lived before the rise of professional history and its expectation of documented sources of knowledge. Instead, Civil War Americans' culture was steeped in stories about the past and the widespread circulation of popular historical narratives.¹¹

Just like we do today, people interpreted the past differently and used their interpretations to justify their own conduct and malign that of their enemies, military or political. History emboldened participants on both sides and sharpened sectional and partisan disputes over the purpose and meaning of the conflict. Federals and Confederates disagreed, and Northerners disagreed among themselves. Northern radicals wanted to reanimate the republican tradition inaugurated by Cromwell. They marshaled the Puritan cause to argue for hard war, emancipation, and a punishing peace. Southern conservatives saw the same history as a tragedy that was being repeated, this time with themselves as the victims. They hoped to return the United States to the world of hierarchy and obedience present before the English Civil Wars. Northern moderates threaded between these contradictory readings of the past, identifying with the Parliamentarians' defense of popular rights but rejecting Cromwell's methods of conquest and reconstruction in Ireland. My concern here is not to assess the accuracy of these interpretations. Instead, I use the rhetorical conflict over history as a way to explore how Civil War participants conceptualized their conflict.

The slippage between historical reality and its representations in analogy and metaphor means that even as the Civil War's participants used history, history used them. Memories of the earlier conflicts shaped how people imagined and understood their world.¹² History created possibilities, empowering people to imagine what was feasible or likely in war based on what occurred in previous wars. Civil War radicals foresaw the possibility of constitutional change remaking the very nature of the republic. Inspired by the seventeenth-century Parliamentarians, they helped end 250 years of racial slavery and helped create an unbreakable American union, purging the compact theory of the Constitution from American political life. At the same time, putting themselves on the side of the English in the seventeenth century predisposed Northerners to using violence to maintain their sovereignty. Conservatives, both Northern and Southern, read the English past as a cautionary tale about the dangers of military despotism and the unpredictability created by war. Slaveholding elites, in particular, interpreted history in ways that reinforced their conservatism, encouraging skepticism about the very democracy that enabled them to claim popular support for the radical act of secession in the first place.

Analogies and metaphors, historical or otherwise, are tricky, even dangerous, forms of thinking, as participants in the Civil War often discovered to their surprise. Civil War Americans used history as intentional rhetoric, often in the form of weaponized analogies. But at the same time, historical thinking possesses an unconscious force. Analogies and metaphors steer people toward certain conclusions. For instance, during the Civil War, abolitionists endorsed hard war and Northern conservatives condemned military force, both positions that contradicted what members of these groups believed in the 1850s. By choosing specific historical moments to emphasize, participants absorbed the embedded suppositions and orientations of the earlier historical actors. That is, even as participants strategically deployed particular historical examples to further their interests, those examples shaped participants by affecting their patterns of thought and action.[13] This process is in some way analogous to Michael Pollan's brilliant explanation of the coevolution of people and apples, in which fruit uses human beings to perpetuate itself.[14] Metaphors possess no more cognition than apples and less of a reproductive drive, but they also persist and adapt over generations, shaping our behavior in subtle but important ways. Historical consciousness, and the literal and figurative language that carries it, provides us with the frameworks we use to situate ourselves in time and space. We should handle it cautiously.

My concern with the historical imagination of the Civil War's participants differs from how historians of memory have investigated the conflict in recent years in two important ways. Over the past two decades, historians have focused on the ways that Americans described the Civil War since it happened—as a tragedy or a triumph, as a rebellion, as a war of Northern aggression, or with the seemingly neutral but still political moniker of "civil war."[15] The study of American memories of the conflict speaks both to the ways that history informs political conflict and to the ways that political disputes alter the meaning of history. As a result, memory studies are as much histories of the eras they chronicle—the late nineteenth and early twentieth century in the most important studies—as they are of the 1860s.[16] Where these studies have read history forward from the Civil War to today, my project reads the connotations and denotations of Americans' wartime language backward.[17]

Making Poetry from the Past

Second, memory studies in recent decades have focused exclusively on the national character of memory, of the role it played in national politics and vice versa. Historians have overlooked another important strand of memory-making, which occurred when people drew stories outside their own national or cultural tradition into their pool of memories. There is no question that Americans built a distinctly national culture during the early republic—visible in schoolrooms with McGuffey readers, in parlors where David Ramsay's and Frederic Bancroft's histories of North America rested on shelves, and in the parades, festivals, and fairs organized to celebrate the nation.[18] At the same time, Americans retained English literary and historical traditions for many years after the Revolution. Americans did not adopt a "global" perspective in the modern meaning of that word. For instance, they could have identified the history of religious conflicts in sixteenth-century Europe as analogous to their own fratricidal struggle, but the rise of ethnically distinct nations appears to have narrowed the field of relevant examples. Instead, American history grew out of the British past, and by 1860, Americans made use of that material without much postcolonial anxiety. A history one step removed offered less emotional charge, but because of this it could be used more creatively. Americans made extensive use of the history of the English Civil Wars precisely because it was not their own. This behavior marks a change not in the creation but in the use of history. Unlike those studies that emphasize the importance of felt history, one for which the actors maintained a deep emotional connection, this one emphasizes the importance of known history, learned through books and distant from personal experience.

Recognizing that history itself drove Civil War participants to more extreme positions generates an unsettling conclusion. It contradicts historians' oft-repeated claims that studying the past enables us to see a fuller range of possibilities, to envision paths not taken, and to engage in chronological empathy with people different from ourselves. Instead, in this period of crisis, many people weaponized the past, using it to bolster preexisting arguments. At the same time, Americans' respect for history imbued it with autonomous power, shaping as well as reflecting the course of people's thinking about the conflict. This process, too, had deleterious consequences. Competing interpretations of the past widened a philosophical divide between Southerners and Northerners. The Civil War drove white Southerners toward fatalism, while Northerners grew more whiggish, confident of the world's perpetual improvement.[19] The consequences of these orientations played out in the decades following the war as Northerners devised America's only homegrown philosophical tradition (pragmatism) while white Southerners bunkered themselves inside a pessimistic and closed society.[20]

Karl Marx, writing a few years after the US Civil War, critiqued the tendency to analogize wars to past conflicts, which he saw as yet another feature of the disingenuous nature of nineteenth-century revolutions. In Marx's analysis, so-called revolutionaries tied themselves to the past in order to subvert truly radical possibilities; their method was "to keep their enthusiasm on the high plane of the great historical tragedy." Writing a few years after the American conflict, Marx offered the example of how "a century earlier, Cromwell and the English people had borrowed speech, passions, and illusions from the Old Testament for their bourgeois revolution. When the real aim had been achieved, when the bourgeois transformation of English society had been accomplished, Locke supplanted Habakkuk."[21] As American historians know well, John Locke assumed a place as a secular prophet, one upon whom Thomas Jefferson relied to lead British colonists to revolution in 1776. Marx looked forward to a future revolution that would "draw its poetry [not] from the past, but only from the future."[22]

The US Civil War was not that revolution. All its participants drew their inspiration from the past. White Southerners genuinely hoped to return to the days of their honored dead—an invented past of cavaliers and ordered hierarchy. Contradicting Marx's formulation, Northern radicals summoned the past in order to promote a more radical revolution. To do so, they celebrated a history—the glories of Cromwell's commonwealth—that they knew had ended in failure. Like conservatives, radicals did not achieve all that they wanted, though few of them experienced the true cost of their failure. The genuine historical tragedy of the Civil War's conclusion was borne by African Americans, who were left after emancipation without full equality.

Northern moderates, just like radicals and conservatives, found the language of the past politically useful. Lincoln, among many others, endorsed a whiggish view of history that interpreted the past as prologue to a better future. His famous speech at Gettysburg began by lauding the founders for having created this "new nation, conceived in Liberty," and identified the war as a trial over sustaining it. To contemporary ears, this perspective on the past may not sound especially "moderate," but in the nineteenth century it represented a middle ground. Conservatives hoped to re-create the past. Radicals hoped to break free from it. Northern moderates tethered themselves to it. These distinctions helped generate deep policy disagreements among Civil War Northerners. The labels I use in the text remain imprecise;

Making Poetry from the Past

the boundaries between radicals, moderates, and conservatives varied depending on the context, but recognizing the importance of those differences helps us better understand how the war unfolded.

Lincoln relied on history because the Civil War created for Northerners what J. G. A. Pocock called, in a different context, "a problem in historical self-understanding."[23] Several decades ago, Pocock explained the ways that fifteenth- and sixteenth-century Italian writers imagined a "republican" political tradition later adopted by English and then American thinkers. Part of that initial Italian creativity was spurred by a crisis over the place of their republic "in time," that is, the possibility of preserving political order in a secular age without reference to God's will or biblical time scales. Historians of the US Civil War have not typically treated the conflict as a problem in time, but Lincoln's anxiety over whether secession signaled the end of the American republic suggests that it was. In the end, secession failed, slavery ended, and the Union persisted. With their anxiety abated, moderates like Lincoln interpreted Northern success as the capstone of the grand tradition of human liberty that began with the English Civil Wars and continued through the Glorious and American Revolutions. History itself enabled Americans to traverse the deadly and uncertain present of the Civil War and to imagine themselves into a limitless future.

Historical Thinking in the Nineteenth Century

> The dark threads of history looping back and forth and catching her and people like her in their grip, like snares.
>
> EDNA O'BRIEN, *House of Splendid Isolation*

For many people during the American Civil War era, both Northern and Southern, the English Civil Wars proved a foundational moment for thinking about rebellion, freedom, internecine violence, loyalty, territorial sovereignty, and state power. While Americans were knowledgeable about other civil conflicts, both historical and more recent, the English Civil Wars were the most proximate. Stories of King Charles I and Lord Protector Oliver Cromwell, of Archbishop William Laud and poet John Milton, of Puritans and Cavaliers, served as a shorthand in intellectual debates of the day.[1] During the sectional crisis and the war itself, Americans used the English Civil Wars' history to conceptualize, reassure, demonize, and defend. In short, history served as a war language.

Nineteenth-century Americans learned this language because they swam in a sea of print. Newspapers, pamphlets, novels, poetry, plays, and histories saturated their world.[2] Immersed in this literature, people developed deeply held perspectives on the relationship between the past, present, and future. During the Civil War, these perspectives shaped how people assessed the possibilities and meanings of events.

How did they come to this knowledge? By the middle of the nineteenth century, some students in the United States would have been formally taught the classical history of England, from Alfred the Great through the Glorious Revolution and beyond. For students attending colleges and universities, most study focused on classical history; they read Livy, Tacitus, Xenophon, and other Latin and Greek scholars.[3] That said, students at the era's leading schools referenced the events of the English Civil Wars in personal correspondence and in journals. They usually absorbed this material from independent rather than classroom reading.[4]

Most Americans who encountered English history did not do so in a classroom but in the course of their adult lives, through personal reading.[5] This practice, of what we could call lifelong learning, emerged as part of the new democratic landscape of antebellum America. Active citizens were expected to know and engage with the past. Charles Sumner, the future abolitionist senator from Massachusetts, used to arise "before daybreak to read Hume and Gibbon" (the two most famous eighteenth-century English historians) while he was a student.[6] Admittedly, Sumner proved an unusually voracious reader, but the fact that he encountered history through his own reading was not exceptional. Histories of England proliferated in the 1850s, receiving reviews and advertisement in a wide range of American newspapers. People also learned history through performance and lecture. Lyceums and town halls featured speakers who offered biographies of leading figures and of pivotal moments. Theaters hosted history-based drama, most especially Shakespeare's plays, which introduced thousands of Americans to the English past.[7]

Historical fiction offered another avenue to the past for nineteenth-century readers. Walter Scott was one especially popular author who blended documented and imagined pasts. His 1826 novel *Woodstock, or The Cavalier* centered on events during and after the English Civil Wars. According to one scholar, "Scott decided [that Charles I] was legally right but morally wrong, and concludes 'the war must be justly imputed to a train of long-protracted quarrels, in which neither party could be termed wholly right, and still less entirely wrong, but which created so much jealousy on both sides as could scarcely terminate otherwise than in civil war.'"[8] Charlotte Brontë reached a similar conclusion a few years later. In her 1847 novel *Jane Eyre*, the eponymous protagonist bemoans that he "who wished to do right could act so unjustly and unwisely as Charles the First," while at the same time lamenting, "I pity him, poor murdered king."[9] Scott's and Brontë's international popularity contributed to the ubiquity of this history. But popular American writers also added perspective. In Harriet Beecher Stowe's 1854 travel account of Europe, she observed destruction still visible from the English wars, all blamed on Cromwell, yet concluded that the Puritan movement was "the most precious to us, [as] the linear descendants and heirs."[10]

Ordinary people—Northern and Southern, Black and white—took history seriously at the time and possessed what may seem, to modern readers, like unusual stamina for long-form nonfiction writing.[11] Authors and publishers produced volume after volume, and the ubiquity of historical references in people's conversations, letters, and journals gives evidence that they used the past to inform their decision-making.

In the first half of the nineteenth century, historical writing itself gained a new degree of public authority as a source of knowledge. According to scholars of the era's print culture, historical works accounted for roughly one-third of all best-selling books between 1800 and 1860.[12] In particular, histories of England circulated widely within the United States in the 1850s.[13] These included eighteenth-century classics such as David Hume's *The History of England*, Henry Hallam's *The Constitutional History of England* (both of which Lincoln read), and Samuel Gardiner's early work (his multivolume histories of the English Civil Wars were not published until later in the century).[14] At least two of the seventeenth-century chroniclers—John Temple and Edward Hyde, first Earl of Clarendon—retained their notoriety in the nineteenth century. Clarendon's *History of the Rebellion and Civil Wars in England* remained an oft-cited piece throughout the American conflict. Many Americans regarded Clarendon as the gold standard for historical re-creation, with several expressing some variation of the *National Intelligencer*'s expectation that the history of the US Civil War would only be written "when some future Clarendon shall sit in judgment on the character and motives of its authors."[15]

Two English historians merit special mention because they revised how popular American audiences understood the earlier conflict: Thomas Carlyle and Thomas Macaulay. At the beginning of the nineteenth century, Cromwell attracted few admirers, but Carlyle, one of the most well-known and highly regarded English writers of midcentury, changed this situation.[16] Carlyle edited a collection of Cromwell's speeches in 1845, which gave English-language readers a chance to know the man on his own terms.[17] Carlyle hoped British readers would come to appreciate their own "Cromwelliad," his term for the experience of the seventeenth century, which propelled England to its greatness.[18] Other historians took inspiration from Carlyle's generous reading to offer their own revisionist takes, with one 1863 account even imagining the possibility of a "liberal" and "constitutional" order under Cromwell.[19] In the United States, Carlyle inspired Joel T. Headley, one of the most successful popular historians of the day, to write a full biography of Cromwell.[20] Headley's status as a leading nativist opposed to Catholic immigration (he was elected New York's secretary of state on the American Party ticket in 1855) made Cromwell a natural figure to celebrate. Headley believed Americans should lead in revising the general view of Cromwell because "the great questions of constitutional and personal liberty, which he settled, have been the foundation of every revolution for the emancipation of man, which has since taken place."[21] Cromwell and the English Civil Wars belonged to America as much as to England.

Although Carlyle's traditionalism and his strong belief in racial hierarchy earned him many Southern admirers, his position on Cromwell did not. As historian David Hall observes, Carlyle sympathized with white Southerners' foils, the Puritans: "In [Carlyle's] hands, Cromwell and indirectly, Puritanism, became 'the last of all our Heroisms.'"[22] Heroism, as a concept, was another Carlylean specialty. In 1840, Carlyle delivered a series of lectures on the topic, which he published the following year in a widely reproduced book, *On Heroes, Hero-Worship, and the Heroic in History*.[23] This text offered the clearest road map to what we today call "great man history." "The history of what man has accomplished in this world," Carlyle wrote, "is at bottom of the History of the Great Men who have worked here."[24] The book examines various modes of hero-ship: divine, prophetic, and poetic, culminating in "the hero as king." Through this lens, Carlyle began the process of reinterpreting and celebrating Cromwell's greatness.[25]

Even more popular was the historian Thomas Babington Macaulay. His writings, essays, and books had truly global reach, and they circulated widely in the United States in the years before and during the US Civil War.[26] Macaulay possessed the ability, like playwrights of previous eras, to make history accessible to his readers.[27] Some commentators suggested that sales of Macaulay's works in America were surpassed only by those of the Bible.[28] Macaulay's most famous work was titled *The History of England from the Accession of James the Second*, the first 150 pages of which narrated and summarized the English Civil Wars through the Restoration. Macaulay's interpretation of that era influenced many American readers, including Abraham Lincoln. Macaulay's history is listed in the inventory of books from the Springfield law office that Lincoln shared with William Herndon; it also appears in records of Lincoln's borrowing from the Library of Congress while he served as president.[29] What he would have encountered was a thoroughly whiggish history, meaning a strongly teleological account of the rise of English liberty, one rooted in the seventeenth century.[30] Macaulay's introduction to the Long Parliament that was to rule England for twenty years is typical of his tendency to judge even those he viewed as mistaken within the longer trajectory of the rise of constitutional safeguards: "In November 1640 met that renowned Parliament which, in spite of many errors and disasters, is justly entitled to the reverence and gratitude of all who, in any part of the world, enjoy the blessings of constitutional government."[31]

Macaulay embodied the whig historical philosophy.[32] Part of this approach entailed rehabilitating Cromwell, in particular by positioning him within the nineteenth-century lineage of liberty. As one historian notes, "Cromwell was assigned a place beside Washington and Bolivar."[33] Like Washington, Macaulay was no narrow partisan. He opposed the extremes of both political parties in his own day and "saw history as the record of 'progress'—progress, in his view, not towards 'freedom' but, by means of freedom, to ever greater prosperity."[34] The result was that his writing appealed to Northerners and Southerners. During the conflict, Edmund Ruffin, the fire-eating Virginian who fired the war's first shot at Fort Sumter, returned to his *History of England* for a third rereading. "Was surprised to find how interesting it was to me still," he recorded in his diary.[35]

The US Civil War occurred during the heyday of a vision of universal and universalizing philosophical and historical speculation. Intellectuals believed they were articulating laws that applied across societies (or should apply once a society reached the same level of development as England).[36] The arrogance of this position has been thoroughly critiqued, but our modern rejection of such a posture does not lessen the influence these attitudes carried in the eras in which they proliferated. Macaulay's sense of English superiority did not diminish his popularity. To the contrary, Macaulay embodied and influenced a range of fellow thinkers and readers.[37] Americans found it easy to transfer Macaulay's celebration of Britain, which extolled England as a natural world leader because of its constitutional order, into their own national vernacular.

Radicals and reformers of the Civil War era diverged from Macaulay; they possessed a greater sense of urgency. As a result, although abolitionists relied on Macaulay at times, they idolized the bold thinkers of the seventeenth century itself, most especially John Milton. Americans both Northern and Southern (including Lincoln) read Milton's poetry for inspiration, which offered an imaginative and allusive entry into the past.[38] Although current readers may find *Paradise Lost* a difficult text, Milton's work possessed genuine popular appeal in the nineteenth century; references to his work appear in many contexts.[39] His prose writings held even greater fascination for Northerners who identified themselves with the reforming tradition in English life.[40] In those pamphlets and essayistic writings, Milton articulated a defense of freedom that retained its relevance in the nineteenth century. "How glorious it is to behold Milton," one Northern newspaper wrote, "emerging from the shadows of those dark ages, wherein the huge overshadowing clouds of despotism had well nigh blotted out all the stars out of the firmament of liberty."[41] During the English Civil Wars, Milton served as "secretary for foreign tongues," a combination secretary of state and universal translator. His front-row seat (indeed, active participation) in Cromwell's reign tarnished him irrevocably in Southern eyes and enhanced his luster for approving Northerners.

The literary scholar Tony Davies has explored the interactions of seventeenth-century texts with great insight. Describing Milton's political writings, Davies writes, "'The words of a dead man,' as Auden wrote of Yeats, 'are modified in the guts of the living': and the intensively active and transformative appropriation of the lives and writings of the seventeenth-century English republicans by the ideologues of the Atlantic Revolutions, the strong misreadings to which they subjected them, must now be admitted to constitute part of the meaning and significance of those writings."[42] Nineteenth-century Americans participated in this process by reading, borrowing, and creatively misunderstanding Milton and his contemporaries just as previous Americans had done before them.[43]

Davies borrowed the phrase "strong misreading" from Marx, who used it in his analysis of Napoléon's seizure of power in revolutionary France. Marx saw that "social and political revolutions, if they are to succeed, must also be cultural revolutions; that as much as institutions and formal ideologies they require imagery, memory and forms of identity; and that those things can only be derived from a relationship with the past that must always be deeply ambivalent, at once admiring and evasive."[44] White Southerners relied on seventeenth-century Royalists as a form of identity that anchored what they hoped would be a revolution back to the past. Northerners (even conservatives) maintained more distance from the era. They did not invoke the history in order to imitate or recreate it; instead, they used the imagery and memory of that previous conflict in order to promote their own vision for what they wanted the American Civil War to accomplish.

As a result of all this reading and misreading, Americans developed a sophisticated engagement with history. Understanding this engagement—how people thought about history at a particular point in time—requires a seemingly technical concept: historiography, the study of how historical interpretation changes over time. Historiography recognizes that historians' accounts of the past shift based on changes in the broader culture to which they belong and based on the discovery of new evidence. Nineteenth-century Americans responded to both these forces, and they did so as part of a broader Anglo-American intellectual world, as Carlyle's and Macaulay's popularity suggests. One key historiographical point is that the Civil War's participants did not make the neat division that we possess today between history and memory or between popular and academic strains of historical writing. According to most scholars, recognizably modern historical writing—an interpretive practice based on the close reading of primary sources—only began to emerge in the late nineteenth century.[45] Yet this interpretation misses the dynamism of historical thinking in the early nineteenth century. Indeed, self-proclaimed historians and writers of all sorts challenged the previous century's dominant approaches to the past.[46] This writing created a new generation of readers and thinkers who used history to interpret their world.[47] My effort in what follows is to describe what Michael Hattem, in a different context, calls "history culture," that is "all references to and uses of the past" at play in a given society.[48]

Noah Webster's *An American Dictionary*, in its third edition by 1847, revealed the in-between state of American thinking about the past. On the one hand, Webster defined history as "an account of facts," the narration and knowledge of those facts, and "description; an account of things that exist."[49] The last definition, in particular, conveys the emerging sense among "scientific" historians that they could generate an impartial if not objective account of the past.[50] At the same time, Webster allowed that nineteenth-century history differed from that of previous eras in "admit[ting] the observations of the writer" and identified "causes and effects" as one of these additions to the simple chronologies compiled by annalists. Disputes over causes and effects formed the basis for the modern version of history as an interpretive discipline. Before professional historians fully committed to that orientation, regular people seem to have grasped the method. Throughout the Civil War, readers consulted what they regarded as authoritative histories of the seventeenth century, heard speakers discuss the era, and assembled a historical vision. The result was not a folk or popular memory; neither was it a primary-source-driven academic analysis. It existed somewhere in between

Historical Thinking in the Nineteenth Century

these poles, rife with misunderstandings and deliberate misrepresentations, but nonetheless powerful in carrying the authority that nineteenth-century people gave to the past.[51]

How did all that reading shape the nature of nineteenth-century Americans' historical mind-set, beyond a more rigorous and formal pursuit of truth and objectivity? According to Hattem, three modes of interpretation dominated in early America: millennial, cyclical, and linear/progressive. The millennialists believed in a chronology shaped by God, not man. The cyclicalists posited shared laws for the rise and decay of republics. They only partially shared the fatalism of the millennialists, believing that by returning to first principles they could forestall a decline regarded as inevitable by classical thinkers. As Hattem observes, for cyclicalists, "learning about and heeding the lessons of the British past could, in a sense, delay the future."[52] A third group believed in progress; history, for them, entailed the working out of laws embedded in human society. Adherents to these various perspectives tolerated philosophical ambiguity, even outright contradictions. For instance, Frederic Bancroft, an early and influential national historian, today regarded as whiggish in his faith in American exceptionalism, believed that American history was a "realization" of God's plan for the world.[53] Nonetheless, the Civil War revealed that these perspectives on the past also carried sectional and ideological relevance. Throughout the war, Confederates expressed a nearly fatalistic millennialism; they begged God's favor and rejected any progressive faith in man's capacities. Northern conservatives endorsed the cyclicalist view that Americans must heed the cautionary tale of the seventeenth century in order to ensure America's stability in the nineteenth. Northern moderates and radicals both endorsed a whiggish progressivism, but they differed over the timing and mechanisms of change. Moderates did not possess the urgency of radicals, and they shared some of the conservatives' belief in the necessity of ordered and legal change.

Last, we need to understand the contours of the particular conversation about the English Civil Wars in the mid-nineteenth century.[54] By the 1840s, three "rival lines of interpretation" prevailed in England and found rough parallels in America. According to historian Michael Braddick, "A dominant Whig version saw the events of the 1640s as a battle for a balanced constitution, which was finally won in the revolution of 1689. The meaning and triumph of the crisis was the restraint of the Crown by Parliament." Lincoln and Northern moderates followed this line of thought. "An alternative Tory view did not so much defend Charles I, his policies, or the early Stuart constitution, as emphasize the dangers of disorder and the imperative need to maintain political order and religious decency. It favoured respect for the church, monarchy, and social hierarchy, and recoiled in horror at the excesses of the mid-century." Perhaps not surprising, white Southerners identified with this approach. "A third, less influential, strand of radical Whig interpretation emphasized the abstract principles enunciated in the course of these crises—religious toleration, civic rights, republican virtue, and the dangers of executive tyranny. But it also saw in England's revolution unfinished business, and a need to sustain these causes for the future."[55] Though not a perfect fit, abolitionists and Northern radicals expressed these values.

My argument in what follows rests not on the volume of references that nineteenth-century Americans made to seventeenth-century England (though the references were ubiquitous) but on the relationship between those references and the kinds of policies people pursued. The lessons people drew from the seventeenth century shaped how they acted in the nineteenth century. If the gap between these eras seems so wide as to render comparisons of little value, consider our current predicament, in which anxious editorializing about America's political polarization compels us to discussions of the US Civil War. We reach into the past instinctively, confident that a preceding episode of a violent political rupture contains lessons to help us navigate the present. This practice, of seeking illumination if not outright instruction from the past is itself an established political tradition, but our approach to the US Civil War remains so circumscribed by the physical and chronological boundaries of mid-nineteenth-century America that we often overlook what the participants themselves knew: they had intellectual resources on which to draw to understand their plight. The historical consciousness of mid-nineteenth-century Americans was elastic. Even as they learned from the past, they also interpreted the past, like we do, in ways that satisfied their political and ethical agendas. Historical actors such as Charles I and Cromwell served as more than mere markers; Americans' interpretations of the wars of the seventeenth century indicated whether and how they trusted the process of change within popular constitutional systems.

This study relies on broad reading in Civil War newspapers and journals combined with deeper analysis of a smaller number of historically minded individuals. Foremost among these on the Northern side were the Radical Republicans Charles Sumner and Wendell Phillips. Sumner, the abolitionist senator from Massachusetts and chairman of the Senate Foreign Relations Committee during the war, possessed a deep knowledge of global history and an indefatigable work ethic. His Senate speeches, which run to dozens of pages, often entailed primary-source research and carefully constructed arguments, many of them rooted in the European past. Phillips, a leading white abolitionist, wrote and spoke throughout the war. Even more than Sumner, he relied on English Civil War analogies in his arguments. "One thing is certain," Phillips explained during the frustrating slow days of early 1862. "Our fathers' history reads us a lesson."[56] Opposing them was Samuel S. Cox, an Ohio Democrat who was equally well versed in English history and nearly as loquacious. As Cox told his Senate colleagues, "The closest analogy to our condition is to be found in the English civil war beginning in 1640."[57] The *New York Herald*, a leading conservative voice—though pro-Union throughout the conflict—deployed seventeenth-century references continuously. The *Herald*'s peer in the South was the *Richmond Daily Dispatch*, which referred back to the English conflicts with some regularity. A wide range of newspapers and weeklies or monthlies reprinted articles from the *Dispatch* or the *Herald* or made their own comparisons. The rhetoric that analogized the conflicts appears across the full gamut of the Civil War's participants, from Lincoln and Jefferson Davis to common people.

The challenge for intellectual histories of war is to show that thought, and not just the material forces of war, matters. A cynic might note that the propulsive force of the Civil War demanded immediate reactions that precluded time for deliberation. I do not deny that the pressures of war accelerated and increased the demands on policymakers—emancipation policy, for instance, was clearly ad hoc—yet there is also evidence that people reflected on their actions and the world around them. Even in the midst of day-to-day fighting, newspapers and journals were filled with exegetical passages on the nature of war and its meaning. We can also see—again in the history of emancipation policy—the intentional change and adaptation that moved the United States from a position that protected slavery to one that abolished it. My argument—that we need to take seriously the ways that the Civil War's participants conceptualized, explained, and argued about the meaning of the war—stands alongside others that emphasize material rather than intellectual forces.[58] Sometimes, the war's participants acknowledged this intentionality directly, as in this passage from a leading weekly: "A civil war is not and never can be a mere question of fighting. Foreign wars, which involve merely questions of territory, or succession, or special insult or injury, may be waged exclusively by technical military means, by ships, armies, and guns. But a civil war, which involves a conflict of political principles or social systems, or the defense of natural rights, is not to be disposed of so readily. The contest in such cases is between the principles quite as much as the brute force."[59] Participants in the American conflict used history as one weapon in their fight over such principles.

The Cultural Origins of the Civil War

> Of crime made law we sing, how a powerful people
> turned on its own heart its conquering hand.
>
> LUCAN, *Civil War*

The question of what caused the Civil War has, rightly, consumed an enormous amount of historical attention over the last 160 years. Given the scale of death and destruction in the war and the consequences of reunion and emancipation, understanding why the war happened is self-evidently important. Historians today rightly emphasize the divide between Northerners and Southerners over the future of slavery within the United States. Few are willing to call the war inevitable, but neither does it seem surprising given sectional animosity and its role in the collapsing two-party system of the late 1850s. Participants in the war drew distinctions between the regions that made the differences seem insurmountable. In 1858, Abraham Lincoln lamented a "house divided," while William Henry Seward, a leading Republican and Lincoln's secretary of state, identified what he called an "irrepressible conflict" between the sections. Indeed, reading editorials and speeches from 1860–61 makes one wonder how the union stood for its first eighty years.[1] These divisions were cultural as well as political. Emphasizing unbridgeable cultural distinctions, as many white Southerners did, helpfully concealed the raw economic motives underlying the South's defense of slavery. Recourse to the language of history grounded Southern nationalist claims in a deeper bedrock than the sectional rhetoric of the 1850s. Southerners hoped that by presenting the regions as historically distinct places holding mutually exclusive values, they would naturalize the idea of separation.

The theory of cultural difference developed by white Southerners, in particular, demanded national autonomy. That theory identified a lineage connecting them to the Royalists who defended Charles I in the English Civil Wars. It anchored them in a world of hierarchy and order. As with most group identities, the theory drew as much strength from identifying what white Southerners were *not* as from what it claimed they *were*. In this case, looking to the conflicts of the seventeenth century, they were Cavaliers and not Puritans.

Northerners offered a more cautious embrace of the analogy, though some abolitionists, especially New Englanders, took pride in carrying on the original Puritan legacy in their efforts to build a new Jerusalem.[2] In the mid-nineteenth century, their prophetic vision centered on abolitionism. During the sectional crisis, latter-day Puritans opposed slavery but often did so while conveniently forgetting New England's own history of enslaving.[3] This historical distancing, and the physical distance from the Southern states, encouraged them to assume an absolutist position on slavery. The result, in both cases, was that each region's interpretation of history propelled them toward war.

CAVALIER REDUX

In response to abolitionist criticism, over the 1840s and '50s, white Southerners developed what historians now call the "proslavery defense," a synthesis of historical, philosophical, religious, economic, and political arguments for the necessity of Black slavery.[4] Slaveholders and their allies especially hoped to secure the support of white nonslaveholders, an essential bulwark in the increasingly democratic Southern states. The proslavery defense offered a comprehensive and direct route to this goal. At the same time, white Southerners also crafted a cultural interpretation that celebrated what they asserted as the unique and positive characteristics of the region, an "invented tradition" that selected from a range of historical events, creatively misread migration patterns and histories of ethnic identity, and buttressed claims of distinctiveness along with the justification for racial slavery. Southern apologists regularly supported their claims with reference to the English Civil Wars.[5]

Mark Twain famously blamed the Civil War on the author Walter Scott. Like most things Twain, his observation blended humor, irony, and insight. Looking back on the 1850s from the postwar era, Twain and other commentators identified how white Southerners' obsession with a culture of chivalry and Romantic ideals blinded them to the realities of nineteenth-century warfare and statehood under the federal government. Noble young men, reared on fantasies of cavalry charges and gentlemanly duels, found bloody and prolonged industrial-age warfare a surprise. It would be easy to lampoon this fatal misperception if the war's consequences were not so terribly tragic, often for people other than those who inaugurated it. The aristocratic past to which white Southerners aspired was found not in the fictive worlds of Scott's *Ivanhoe* or *Waverley* but in the actual world of Charles I and his supporters during the English Civil Wars.

According to Southern propagandists, these historical actors (known as Cavaliers), embodied a set of values that retained their utility into the mid-nineteenth century. Above all, soon-to-be Confederates valued Cavalier ideals of social order and stability. The *Southern Literary Messenger* summarized the English Civil Wars in language that highlighted such ties: "The monarchy was overthrown, the royalist and church party trampled in the dust, and the mad reign of fanaticism and intolerance established upon the ruins of everything like conservatism and established order."[6] Maintaining order, in this view, required that all members of a given community respect the hierarchy that gave it shape and structure.

By 1861, Confederate statesmen proclaimed their belief in social, especially racial, hierarchy as central to their new national project. Alexander Stephens, the Confederacy's new vice president, bemoaned the attitude of Thomas Jefferson and his peers at America's founding who believed that "the enslavement of the African was in violation of the laws of nature." "Those ideas," Stephens argued, "were fundamentally wrong. They rested upon the assumption of the equality of the races.... Our new government is founded upon exactly the opposite idea."[7] Inequality, in Stephens's view, defined the natural order, and government should conform to that reality. Confederate newspapers explained this faith in hierarchy and order as the Southern legacy of their Cavalier forebears, who were distinguished by the fact that "they honor authority, as authority from God. And, having thus the mind which knows how to obey, it knows how to command." In contrast with the Cavalier, the Puritan (analogized to Northerners and New England abolitionists in particular) "has contended for that idea of liberty which claims a perfect equality for each individual of the human species." Such an approach to governance was sure, as Stephens explained, to bring the whole nation to ruin.[8]

DeBow's Review, the leading commercial journal in the South, extolled the glories of the Cavalier in a series of articles during the 1850s and through the war itself.[9] The fullest expression of these ideas emerged in J. Quitman Moore's 1862 essay that identified a lineage from the eleventh-century Norman conquest through the seventeenth-century Cavaliers to nineteenth-century white Southerners. In the beginning was a faith in "aristocracy, based upon the feudal relation . . . a social condition, resting on the principle of subordination, and recognizing the family as the primary basis of social union." As Moore well knew, Southern propagandists had been extolling the household nature of plantation agriculture as the most durable and generous system of labor and social relations in human history. In contrast, Moore maligned the Puritans' system of "Democracy, founded upon the idea of an unlimited individualism, and without any reference to the conservative organism of institutions."[10] These two contrary systems warred in the seventeenth century, and they remained antagonists in the nineteenth. Moore articulated the values of the Cavalier: "The builder, the social architect, the institutionalist, the conservator—the advocate of rational liberty and the supporter of authority, as against the licentiousness and morbid impulse of unregulated passion and unenlightened sentiment."[11] In his reading, conservatives resisted the passions of revolution and held fast to institutions (in the earlier case, to the king rather than Parliament). "These were the parties . . . from which sprung the two nationalities that now divide the empire of the American continent." Today, he declared, the struggle is between "licentious liberty and an enlightened conservatism."[12]

As Alexander Stephens elaborated, enlightened conservatism protected a hierarchy less religious or rooted in the glorious legacies of feudal Europe but rather one that generated benefits for ordinary white men.[13] Slaveholding elites such as John C. Calhoun might have grumbled about democracy, but it expanded apace throughout the era, which made celebrating inequality a tough political sell. To address this paradox, Stephens and other Southern politicians, such as South Carolina's James Henry Hammond, focused on the ways that racial hierarchy and bondage enabled greater equality within the white community. Hammond's infamous "Mudsill" speech, delivered in the US Senate in 1858, offered the starkest framing of this perspective. Hammond demeaned the very practice of ordinary labor and celebrated the wisdom of the Southern system that consigned such work solely to Black men.[14] At the same time, Southern political leaders expressed real anxiety about the behavior of poor white men. In Stephens's correspondence with his brother Linton and with Howell Cobb (another Georgia politician), they shared concerns about the ability of the Republican Party to attract the support of Southern nonslaveholders.[15] In a healthy political system, Stephens would have strategized for how to retain or win back supporters; in 1861, he abandoned that system altogether.

Despite the political imperatives in a community where only 25 percent of Southern households owned slaves, would-be Confederates' use of Cavalier rhetoric drew them toward the language of class and revealed the hollowness of their claims of white solidarity.[16] This took the form of simple descriptions, such as identifying Cavaliers as "the most honorable and high-minded class of men in Great Britain."[17] It was Jefferson Davis who made the argument most explicitly. In a widely reprinted speech to the Mississippi state legislature in late 1862, Davis condemned Northerners as "a traditionless and a homeless race; from the time of Cromwell to the present moment they have been disturbers of the peace of the world." Most problematic, from the perspective of this nineteenth-century Cavalier, Northerners were "a people whose ancestors Cromwell had gathered from the bogs and fens of Ireland and Scotland."[18] The *Southern Literary Messenger* concurred, noting that "the Puritans, at home, constituted, as a class, the common people of England."[19] In a different article, the *Messenger* characterized how the two lineages even produced differing physiognomies: "There is, however, even yet, a frankness about the Norman-British yeoman—a squareness of build—an independence of gait—a loftiness of stature—a boldness of countenance—a darkness of complexion that you look for in vain with the namby-pamby, pigeon-breasted, dull-visaged, pale-faced, goslin-rounded, Anglo-Saxon of the day."[20] Coming at a time when the US president was elected partly on account of his rise from humble origins—Lincoln's log cabin and his early years as a "rail-splitter" played a central role in Republican Party campaign material in the 1860 election—the difference could not have been starker.

White Southerners developed an elaborate historical architecture to buttress their claim to the Cavalier image and promulgated it widely. Moore's genealogy offered the standard account: French-speaking Normans carried their civilized and enlightened ways to England in the eleventh century, the

Royalists of the seventeenth century ennobled the culture in their tragic defense of King Charles I, and then those same Royalists formed the majority of white emigrants to the Chesapeake Colony in the 1650s and '60s.[21] According to the *Richmond Daily Dispatch*, "The South was settled in great part, though not entirely, by men of Cavalier stock, the North, principally by English Puritans, many of whom were of the respectable middle classes, many 'lewd fellows of the baser sort,' and a small proportion of Cavalier descent."[22] A writer in the *Daily Richmond Whig* similarly proclaimed, "More than half of England was imbued with puritanism and sided with Cromwell against the crown. Virginia and Maryland, the Southern colonies, were conservative and sided with the crown."[23] Confederates invoked this imagined lineage throughout the war, ironically demonstrating not the exceptional South that its defenders so often celebrated but a region deeply implicated in the currents of global history.[24]

Just as important to Confederates as the Cavalier was their foil, the Puritan or Roundhead.[25] According to white Southerners, the historical figures, like their abolitionist descendants, were religiously obsessed and intemperate. Their most telling vice was fanaticism, which manifested in judgmental attitudes and a willingness to impose their views on others.[26] Puritans' self-professed virtue was mere hypocrisy, because their only real interest was money. One Southern critic identified the unfortunate genealogy that paralleled the virtuous one carrying Norman glories to the American South. In this case, the line of descent ran from the Reformation of Calvin and John Knox to the Puritans through Cotton Mather to Wendell Phillips and John Brown. "Everybody knows," the writer concluded, "that they have been the same arrogant, self-righteous, conceited race—each man thinking and acting on the belief of his own infallibility, and of other people's fallibility."[27]

Louis T. Wigfall, a Texas senator who served in both the US Congress and Confederate States Congress, explained the family tree and their character: "[Puritans] helped Cromwell to cut off their King's head. After that, better than even the Puritans, they were called Independents; then they were called fifth-monarchy men; and then Cromwell had to run them out of England ... and then they got on that ill-fated ship called the Mayflower, and landed on Plymouth Rock." In a clever sound bite, Wigfall combined the Puritans' love of money and shallow moralism: "After selling us our negroes for the love of gold, they began stealing them for the love of God."[28] Another Southern voice, recognizing some value in seventeenth-century Puritans, proclaimed, "The Yankee is a degenerate Puritan—the lineal descendant of the Mayflower Pilgrims, with all their trail of avarice, hypocrisy, and coming, intensified by transmission." In this telling, "the great talents of Cromwell, who usurped the power which he found them abusing, were not able to eradicate, or even to diminish, the intense hatred of the Puritan name. England has never tried them since. She got enough of them at a dose, and she cannot be tempted to a repetition. They will succeed no better here."[29]

Confronting the main issue in the American Civil War, Confederates attributed the failure of the Puritans in the 1650s to their focus on liberty. According to a critique issued in the *Richmond Daily Whig*, "The Puritan is the ultra liberty man of the world—both in religion and politics. He is not willing to be under authority, as authority, of God or man. His pride of individual right is so extreme, that he must have all rule, and authority, and power."[30] Another critic observed that "while loving liberty, they yet make the poorest republicans, and enjoy the least freedom." This was because, "having liberty which they do not appreciate, they run into anarchy."[31] The irony of this critique of absolute autonomy coming from slaveholders appears to have been lost on white Southerners at the time. Instead, Southern propagandists echoed the charge, proclaiming their opposition to the pursuit of liberty. "We now come to the Southern Revolution of 1861," a midwar editorial observed, "which we maintain was reactionary and conservative—a rolling back of the excesses of the Reformation—of Reformation run mad—a solemn protest against the doctrines of natural liberty, human equality, and the social contract, as taught by Locke and the American sages of 1776."[32]

Here, then, was the real Confederate hope—to reframe the sequence of thought and debate that led from the English Civil Wars to the 1860s. They promulgated a lineage that began with the earlier counterrevolution of 1660, the "Restoration," incorporated the American Revolution, and would lead to a bright future as slavery expanded across the continent.[33]

Just as Jefferson had learned from John Locke, Thomas Hobbes, a political theorist who matured during the English Civil Wars, offered conservatives their own anchor in the seventeenth century. Before he wrote *Leviathan* (itself inspired by the insecurity of the two-decade-long civil war era), Hobbes, in *Behemoth, or The Long Parliament*, blamed the conflict on universities and ministers for offering people the knowledge with which they challenged the king. As one scholar explains, for Hobbes, ideas themselves were, in effect, "an ideological arsenal."[34] "For once [people] 'read the books written by famous men of the ancient Grecian and Roman commonwealths,' in which 'popular government was extolled by the glorious name of liberty, and monarchy disgraced by the name of tyranny,' they quite simply fell 'in love with their forms of government.'"[35] The men who led the South into the

Confederacy complained of a similar shift in American political thought, as state governments liberalized over the 1830s and '40s.[36]

Confederates' hatred of all things Puritan meant that they had to ignore one of the most useful seventeenth-century sources for their own political effort: John Milton. Milton's ties to the Commonwealth established by Cromwell made him anathema for most white Southerners. This was a recent change. Milton's republicanism was precisely what inspired Thomas Jefferson to rely on Milton in his campaigns for religious freedom, divorce, and perhaps even parts of the Declaration of Independence.[37] But just as white Southerners left behind Jefferson and his inconvenient statements on equality, so they abandoned Milton.[38] Among Milton's many relevant political writings was *The Tenure of Kings and Magistrates*, a pamphlet published just after the execution of Charles I. Milton's arguments in *Tenure* about the sovereignty of the people could have offered useful intellectual support to fire-eaters. Milton believed that "men naturally were born free . . . born to command and not to obey." The result of this autonomy was an absolute right to choose one's leaders. "It being thus manifest that the power of Kings and Magistrates is nothing else, but what is only derivative, transferr'd and committed to them in trust from the People, to the Common good of them all, in whom the power yet remains fundamentally, and cannot be tak'n from them, without a violation of their natural birthright."[39] Further, Milton wrote, "since the King or Magistrate holds his authoritie of the people, both originally and naturally for their own good in the first place, and not his own, then may the people as oft as they shall judge it for the best, either choose him or reject him, retaine him or depose him though no Tyrant, meerly by the liberty and right of free born Men, to be govern'd as seems to them best."[40] What were white Southerners doing in secession other than rejecting the election of Lincoln as president?

Milton's arguments justified removing any officeholder who violated the public good. As one scholar notes, "These assertions of the right of self-determination are about as categorical as can be imagined."[41] Or, in another context, "Milton was proposing not a theory of resistance as much as a theory of revolution."[42] Confederate elites had certainly read Milton's political writings—and they continued to respect his poetry—but their refusal to acknowledge the relevance allows us to see the impossible contradictions in the Confederacy's position. The act of secession, based on hastily convened votes (and only ratified by popular vote in a handful of states) required the most radical philosophical posture, but they could not admit that position. This is partly the paradox of a slaveholder's rebellion and partly their actual conservatism, which used a democratic mechanism to pursue a new hierarchical political order. George Fitzhugh, an idiosyncratic Southern thinker, detested Milton and offered repeated criticisms, classifying Milton as "representative alike of the ultra-liberal doctrines of the Puritans, Independents, and Infidels, and of the vulgar despotism of Cromwell."[43] Ignoring Milton's arguments about political sovereignty, Fitzhugh scorned Milton's claims to advance liberty: "To say liberty is good is absurdly false and charlatanism."[44] Fitzhugh was often intellectually ahead of his peers, though his reading reflected the core Confederate position: "Liberty and anarchy are synonymous."[45]

We can see the potential energy of a pro-Confederate reading of Milton by reviewing an Ohio abolitionist's take on the subject. Published by a journal, the *Anti-Slavery Bugle*, known as "the most significant—and perhaps the only—voice of Garrisonian radicalism west of the Appalachian," the article nonetheless admitted to the right of states to secede.[46] Under the headline "A Northern Plea for the Right of Secession," the article quoted extensively from Milton's *Tenure of Kings and Magistrates* to argue that popular sovereignty was the most important virtue of a democratic system. Though the author did not sanction Southern actions in this case, his reading of Milton led inexorably to support Southerners' right to secede: "Supreme political power inheres in the people of any given territory, that they have the right to do politically whatever is not in its nature unjust. They may form, modify, or abolish their government as shall seem best to their own judgment." Quoting Milton again, the article identified the source of this right not in the Constitution but in God's plan for people. Anticipating the arguments that Northern conservatives and Confederates would make, he declared that "a government which is strong by the military power over its own citizens, is not a free-government, but a despotism."[47]

In the event, Confederates did not replicate the *Bugle* editor's argument. No paeans to John Milton appeared in Richmond. Perhaps this was wise. Even the *Bugle* took for granted the process of state democracy at midcentury. Nowhere in the long editorial did the writer question *who* made up "the people." The shapers of the Confederate state believed that white men alone should rule. But the pressures of war created cracks in such foundational assumptions.[48] White women, for example, claimed political agency on the basis of their position as loyal wives and mothers. They did not achieve full equality, to be sure, but the demands they made and the response from state and national governments in the South expanded the political collective. Enslaved people made similar demands, and in rare cases the Confederacy recognized that Black people possessed a political consciousness (as when slaves were tried by courts-martial).[49] This was a bridge too far, even for the war-pressed Confederacy. They had only to look north or to read Frederick Douglass's petitions for Black citizenship on the basis of military service to recognize the fragility of their position. Confederate leaders ignored calls to enlist Black men into the army until the final weeks of the war precisely because doing so would repudiate their system of race and, with it, government itself. "If slaves will make good soldiers, our whole theory of slavery is wrong," proclaimed Georgian Howell Cobb.[50] This was not the only instance in which Confederates ignored an opportunity to marshal history to their side, but the resonance of the *Bugle*'s arguments at a crucial moment in the secession winter compels us to recognize that endorsing Milton's framing would have connected them to a radical past and, Confederate leaders hoped, above all, to somehow affect a conservative revolution.

The whole intellectual apparatus constructed by white Southerners and later by Confederates urged people to interpret Northern and Southern society as fundamentally distinct.[51] It offered a nineteenth-century version of what we would call today a "clash of civilizations" argument. Such a framework, influenced by the Cold War and articulated starkly during the US "War on Terror" of this century, asserts that the differences between two value systems can be so pronounced that violent conflict is inevitable.[52] The passive construction of a sentence like that should be our first sign that this form adopts an antihistorical mode of argument; without people, it relies on sociological abstractions to move history.

Nonetheless, white Southerners insisted that Puritanism was the defining feature of the North and Cavalierism was the defining feature of the South, partly because it portrayed the Civil War as a cultural struggle disconnected from slavery. Indeed, one of Richmond's leading papers declared, "We have often observed that this contest is a revival of the old war between the Puritans and Cavalier[s]." Viewing the war as inevitable enabled Confederates to avoid admitting even the presence of a moral debate over slavery. "We have never supposed that the existence of slavery is the cause of the long and irritating strife which has resulted at last in an appeal to arms," the *Richmond Daily Dispatch* announced in 1861. "Slavery is the occasion, but only the occasion of that strife."[53] Louis Wigfall, speaking in the US Senate in early 1861 before resigning his seat, critiqued William Seward's higher law and the "Massachusetts school of politics" in language rooted in the English Civil Wars. "This doctrine of perfectability in the people of the free states is of New England origin. It began before your Revolution; long before that. It began when Charles lost his throne. Old John Knox started it, and then it got down into England." The crisis of secession forced fire-eaters such as Wigfall to frame their ideas in the most extreme fashion. By the end of the speech he flatly denounced the contention that "all men are created equal."[54]

White Southerners who absorbed this rhetoric of racial, even civilizational, difference between North and South concluded that the scale of dissimilarity compelled separation. Disregarding slavery, or any material motivations, made it difficult for them to explain why secession was necessary in 1861 when it had not been necessary in 1831. If the two sections were peopled by fundamentally incompatible communities, how had the union stood for eighty years? Nonetheless, as recourse to historical analogies increased during the conflict, Confederates' sense of the inevitability of separation hardened. "As surely as that people have been literally abolitionists, through all ages and in all demoralizing guises," the *Southern Literary Messenger* wrote, "so surely has the time come when, like the Java reptile which dies in its bloom by the excess of its own poison, they have reached the zenith of their power, and brought themselves to the eve of their own abolition."[55]

Confederates' reading of history gave them the confidence to adopt such sweeping and absolute characterizations, in part because as they interpreted the seventeenth century, the English Civil Wars concluded with the victory of conservatism and order. In 1660, the republic was dissolved and the monarchy reestablished; Charles II returned to England and assumed the throne. Twenty years of violence and turmoil had been brought to a close by a reassertion of hierarchy. Trusting to the analogies of history, Confederate apologists could foresee their eventual triumph. In this way, history did little to humble white Southerners or encourage them to appreciate contingency and paths not taken. Instead, it stiffened their resolve to persevere as their supposed Cavalier ancestors had done two centuries earlier.

THE NEW PURITANS

When it came to characterizing Northern abolitionists, Confederate propaganda may have proceeded from malice, but in some respects the Confederates were not entirely wrong. Generations of scholarship on the Puritans has revealed just how complex and deep the religious imprint of the seventeenth century proved to be on North America. In the mid-seventeenth century, conflicts within English life over religious expression—between Anglicans led by King Charles and Archbishop Laud and the people who became the Puritans—shaped political and social change at home as well as in colonies around the world. For the colonists arriving in New England, Puritanism was the animating force that governed private and public life.[56] As Edward Everett, one of New England's most famous apostles for the Union, explained, the New World "was the visible extension of the kingdom of Christ."[57] Another nineteenth-century historian, John Lothrop Motley, summarized the Puritan errand in similar terms: "It was not liberty of conscience which they came to establish, but the kingdom of the saints."[58] In the seventeenth century, that spirit also emboldened New Englanders' military posture. During King Philip's War in the 1670s, the new settlers pursued a brutal war of extermination against Indigenous peoples that ended with the enslavement or exile of the survivors.[59] It was not until 1964 that Malcolm X observed, "We didn't land on Plymouth Rock; the rock was landed on us"—but long before this a wide range of people felt the pressure of Puritanism.[60]

Puritans came by their reputation for zealotry honestly. They believed the Church of England had lost its way and only comprehensive changes could restore purity. They wanted new, plain church buildings, congregational control of ministers, and simpler forms of worship. Most modern historians depart from the Southern characterizations of Puritans as moralistic hypocrites. Critics they were, but Puritans directed that skepticism toward themselves as often as others. They believed it was incumbent on them to return to an original Christianity, one uncorrupted by centuries of (especially Catholic) accretions. Puritans wanted to eradicate what they regarded as "human inventions" within the church by re-creating the age of the apostles. In the seventeenth century, this reforming spirit stripped the iconography from Anglican churches, pared back spiritual practices, and reshaped politics to operate in the guise of the holy. This example inspired mid-nineteenth-century reformers to address with equal enthusiasm the most idolatrous institution in American life: slavery.

New England abolitionists summoned their Puritan forebears in the fight against slavery. Literary scholar Kenyon Gradert has done the math: "America's most radical antislavery newspaper, *The Liberator*, invoked the Puritans over a thousand times in the its weekly run from 1831 to 1865—every other issue, on average." These references were not easy clichés; Northern radicals marshaled this reference on behalf of abolition, female empowerment, and labor reform.[61] Just like white Southerners conjuring a Cavalier past to sanctify slaveholding, white Northerners invented a Puritanism that met their needs. Rather than reject abolitionists' understanding of Puritanism as historically wrong or morally repugnant, we need to explain it and its influence. In this case, as Gradert writes, "memory actively aided an ideological revolution."[62]

The revolutionaries of the 1850s could model themselves on the seventeenth century precisely because their forebears had acted with similar ambition. Michael Walzer's study of the origin of radical politics in the modern world identifies the Puritans (and Oliver Cromwell chief among them) as the progenitors of a new type of political actor, the "saint." Born from the changes that propelled medieval Europe into modernity, the saint became the model for future reformers who believed in the necessity of destroying an old order in order to build a truly Christian world.[63] Abolitionists' idealization of Cromwell and his band during the Civil War fit their self-perception as a minority voice in antebellum America and offered them a model for how to reform the world.

The major change between the seventeenth and nineteenth centuries in the English-speaking worlds—the rise of popular democracy—only furthered the anxiety of Southern slaveholders. The Northern population far outstripped the South; in 1860, 22 million Northerners faced 9 million Southerners (of whom 4 million were Black). Alongside the early republic's population growth was a concomitant expansion of the franchise among white men. In the mid-nineteenth century, antislavery forces built coalitions by combining reform efforts and directing the energy of the state. The tension between personal conscience and the state's authority lay at the heart of the great English conflicts. Seventeenth-century Puritans struggled to determine how to challenge their monarch when he seemed to be sustaining a corrupt church. Could they put loyalty to God above loyalty to Crown?[64] Dedicated abolitionists posed a similar question two centuries later and found themselves, like William Lloyd Garrison burning a copy of the Constitution, alienated from the state. But another part of the antislavery community found they could marshal electoral politics to orient the federal government against slavery.[65] It was this prospect—of new Puritans empowered with a new army—that drove white Southerners to secede.

Charles Sumner, the strident antislavery senator from Massachusetts, could trace his familial descent back to early seventeenth-century migrants. His abolitionist bona fides made him public enemy number one among most white Southerners. In a late-war speech, Sumner accepted with pride the connection between Northerners and their Puritan ancestors. Some people "say that the conflict in which we are engaged is a continuance of the old war between Cavalier and Roundhead. So far as it is intended to say that the war is part of the ever-recurring conflict between Slavery and Liberty, there is no objection to the illustration." What he objected to was the other side of the characterization. Unlike Confederate readers of history, Sumner identified some merit in the Puritans' age-old enemies. "If it be intended that the Rebels are cavaliers, or descendants of cavaliers, there is just ground of objection. . . . They are not so in character, as their barbarism attests, and they are as little so historically."[66] Sumner was not the only one to reject the lineage. In an early war piece, the *Knickerbocker Magazine* condemned the "nonsensical comparison between Norman gentlemen in the South, and Saxon churls in the North." Like Sumner, the *Knickerbocker* dug into English history texts to rebut Southern claims. Adopting a thoroughly modern appreciation for genetic mixing, it mocked "this effort to extract blood out of a thousand descents, modified by a thousand crosses, and from a heraldic turnip after all" as "somewhat delirious."[67]

Reflecting a similar knowledge of Gregor Mendel's contemporaneous work on genes, Sumner described a complex peopling of the early colonies by the English, Huguenots, Dutch, Swiss, Jews, and more in lieu of the Confederates' straight line of descent from Normans to Cavaliers to Confederates. Anticipating the tenets of modern historical scholarship, Sumner cleverly quoted Virginia historians who recorded the dissolute origins of the first settlers.[68] He hoped to expose "a vainglorious pretension, which has helped to give the Rebellion a character of respectability it does not deserve."[69] Another Northerner, W. H. Whitmore, repudiated the myth with even more force. In his 1863 article "The Cavalier Theory Refuted," published in the widely read *Continental Monthly*, Whitmore combined primary documents from England detailing the composition of America-bound migrants with his own statistical analysis.[70] He dismissed Southern claims to noble stock as "based upon false presentences, and supported only by unblushing effrontery."[71] For both Whitmore and Sumner, the corollary to their dismissal of Southerners' claims was a celebration of the common men of the North.[72] In this view, the war would produce the great leveling that American democracy demanded—Southern slaveholders, denied their immoral claim on perpetual labor, would at last be brought equal to the workingmen of the North. As one widely reprinted article summarized the seventeenth-century conflict, "The great civil war of England, known as 'The Great Rebellion,' was also a conflict between the oligarchs and the commons, called again the Cavaliers and the Roundheads."[73]

Many Northerners celebrated their Puritan legacy. *Harper's New Monthly Magazine* denounced fire-eaters who had "endeavored, for unholy purposes, to excite bitter sectional animosities by disparaging the Puritan character and exalting that of the Chivalry." Instead, they cited a widely respected American historian, Frederic Bancroft, on the virtues of Puritans as opposed to Cavaliers. "Chivalry delighted in outward show, favored pleasure, multiplied amusements, and degraded the human race by an exclusive respect for the privileged classes; Puritanism bridled the passions, commended the virtues of self-denial, and rescued the name of man from dishonor. The former valued country; the latter, justice." In this account, it was Puritans who deserved praise for "plant[ing] in their hearts the undying principles of democratic liberty."[74] For some Northerners, especially New England radicals, the Puritan legacy was precisely what Americans needed to steer themselves through the tumultuous changes of the antebellum era. One journalist noted in 1846, "Puritanism and nothing else can save this nation. . . . The Puritan element, which demands religious freedom, as the birth-right of Heaven, in matters spiritual, is the nourisher of that civil liberty which releases the body from secular despotism in matters temporal."[75]

The leading abolitionist Wendell Phillips developed his admiration for the Puritans and Cromwell early. While a student at Harvard University, he read deeply in contemporary European and British history.[76] Even before this, he had identified history as a guide to living. "Those who failed to 'gain experience from past misfortune' inevitably squandered the 'wisdom and prudence' that could be gained from 'lessons so dearly bought,'" he wrote in his Boston Latin School composition book.[77] The lessons that Phillips absorbed, and then recapitulated in his wartime speeches, were decidedly whiggish. Phillips's roster of heroes—"Burke, Pitt, Wellington, Cromwell"—were Englishmen who had created the model of "ordered liberty" that he aspired to reproduce in the United States.[78]

Northerners also challenged Jefferson Davis on his preferred ground of class war. According to an account in the *Continental Monthly*, "The true cause [of the Civil War] is beneath and behind all these, taking its rise from the very foundations of English society in the dark ages, from the establishment of classes and distinctions of rank. . . . This antagonism reached its height in the Cromwellian era." The heroes of that era, the journal concluded, had been the Puritans: "The men of those times stand forth upon the page of history as the exponents of the great principles of civic freedom."[79]

The use of Cromwell and the Puritans as models for Northern behavior put radicals in the position of endorsing an argument from millennialism and radical theology. The key personification of this posture in the midcentury United States was John Brown, the leader of the failed slave uprising in

Harpers Ferry, Virginia, and before that, an antislavery warrior in Kansas. Apropos of that formative era, the *Leavenworth Times* referred to Brown in 1859 as "the Cromwell of Kansas."[80] Horace Greeley's *New York Tribune* referred to Brown as "the stern old Puritan of Harper's Ferry."[81] Wendell Phillips called him simply the "Old Puritan."[82] Phillips, more than any other abolitionist, lauded Brown in ways that linked him back to the seventeenth century. Brown, Phillips explained, "is the impersonation of God's order and God's law, moulding a better future, and setting it for an example. . . . This is the lesson of Puritanism, as it is read to us today."[83]

The *Continental Monthly*, a normally moderate Northern journal, expressed great eagerness to publish the lyrics to "John Brown's Body," the Northern marching song probably written by a Massachusetts sergeant and revised by Julia Ward Howe into the more decorous (though no less bloody) "Battle Hymn of the Republic."[84] The journal termed the song "that grim Puritanical lyric." "There!" the editors proclaimed. "If the soldiers of Cromwell and of Ireton had any lyric to beat *that*, we should like to see it. . . . Verily old Father Puritan is *not* dead yet, neither does he sleep; and to judge from what we have heard of the effects of this song among the soldiers, we should say that grim Old John Brown himself, far from perishing, is even now terribly alive."[85] In this respect, Cromwell served as the gateway drug for abolitionists, the historical link that moved them from nonresistance to the violence of John Brown.[86] Brown himself recognized the connection—he kept a copy of Joel Headley's laudatory biography of Cromwell "on his shelf next to the Bible."[87]

Puritanism left a complex association of meanings, ones that scholars have been exploring for centuries. Within the four years of civil war, it is possible to see how radicals associated themselves with Puritanism even as the meaning of that designation changed. From the initially hesitant and often facile attachment to Puritan forebears, Northern radicals reinterpreted them as the first democrats and as proponents of a civic equality admittedly at odds with the real Puritan experience in seventeenth-century New England. The distance between historical Puritans and their nineteenth-century admirers can be marked most clearly by the loss of the humility that came from recognizing people's spiritual powerlessness in the face of God's wrath.[88] Radicals' successes in the Civil War, most importantly the eventual abolition of slavery, imbued them with a confidence their ancestors would have regarded as delusional.

In their ability and willingness to adapt the past, the new Puritans were no more inconsistent than any of the other participants in the Civil War's history wars. In both the abolitionist and fire-eater cases, people adopted rhetorically aggressive readings. In these cases, history acted as an accelerant toward war, not a retardant. Today, historians celebrate the ability to see alternatives and possible outcomes as one of the chief virtues of studying the past. Whether the subject is the rise of slavery in the Americas or the response to the Great Depression, historians today are keen to identify paths not taken. In the buildup to the Civil War, participants, for the most part, weaponized the past. Their interpretations foreclosed possibilities. History proved to be one of the ways that Americans talked themselves into civil war. The gulf between Northern abolitionists' and Southern fire-eaters' conceptions of the past and of America's future left little room for compromise. I am not endorsing the perspective that treated these communities as moral equivalents and as equally culpable for propelling the United States into war, but we should recognize that the cultural divergence between these groups spurred the polarizing politics that produced secession and war.

Legitimate and Illegitimate Rebellion

> The present is where we live, while the past is where we dream.
> Yet if it is a dream, it is substantial, and sustaining. The past buoys
> us up, a tethered and ever-expanding hot-air balloon.
>
> JOHN BANVILLE, *Time Pieces*

Just as the Civil War's origins derived partly from the emotional attachments that people in both sections made to the past, the war's course lay partly in the intellectual uses made of that history. The English Civil Wars, in their plurality, offered latter-day observers multiple episodes of military violence from which they could learn. The two with the most relevance for the US Civil War were the civil war in England proper (what historians came to call the English Revolution) and the Irish Rebellion. These examples proved particularly important to Northern people, though they represented a different relationship between the past and the present than that chronicled in the first two chapters, one that did not invent or oversimplify lineages but instead appreciated the paradoxes and inconsistencies generated by military conflicts.[1] The study of the English and Irish experiences opens up a third interpretive path through the English Civil Wars, distinct from those fashioned by Northern radicals or Southern fire-eaters. Northern moderates looked to the seventeenth century not as a cultural model or antimodel but as a way to sort through competing claims about the legitimacy and durability of political communities.

Nested within the English Civil Wars were several rebellions. The era's precipitating event in 1637 was a Scottish rebellion, driven by anger over royal efforts to enforce the use of the Book of Common Prayer and other rituals that Scottish Presbyterians considered too Catholic.[2] A second was what the English considered a domestic conflict: a civil war among Englishmen that culminated with the execution of King Charles I. The third was what Englishmen regarded as a bloody and unjustified uprising by the Irish against England's right to rule the neighboring island. These histories provided nineteenth-century Americans with useful models of just and unjust rebellion. Unlike the partisan uses of Cavaliers and Puritans, the stories of seventeenth-century England and Ireland enabled Northerners to interrogate the nature of rebellion itself. In particular, they needed to differentiate the virtuous defense of a people's rights from traitorous disorder. The goal was to navigate between supporting revolutions that advanced the cause of liberty and suppressing revolutions that undid those earlier gains. Seventeenth-century English history gave Northerners a moral language to honor their cause and condemn that of the South and provided a vital precedent for their military response to secession.

The question of what constituted legitimate rebellion lay at the core of the Civil War. Looking backward, Northerners celebrated English Parliamentary opposition to the arbitrary rule of King Charles I as virtuous resistance to tyranny, while Confederates denounced his killing as regicide, a radical lurch toward anarchy, not liberty. Study of the Irish Rebellion, however, revealed deep ironies in both the North and South. Even as Republicans supported nationalist independence movements in Europe (including hints that Ireland belonged among the community of nation-states), they condoned British imperial sovereignty. The military logic of this position was driven by a desire to discourage British recognition of the Confederacy. Alongside this mercenary posture sat another motive, one that regarded the outcome of the seventeenth-century conflict—the lawful suppression of rebellion—as an important precedent for their own effort to retain territorial sovereignty over the Southern states.

King Charles I served as a polarizing figure during the American Civil War. White Southerners viewed the Parliamentarian challenge to his rule as illegitimate, while most Northerners believed that such resistance steered England, and later America, toward a government based on consent and the will of the people. Charles I, frontispiece from Richard Cattermole, *Cattermole's Illustrated History of the Great Civil War, of the Times of Charles the 1st and Cromwell* (London: Rutter and Pitcairn, 1866). Courtesy of Louisiana State University Library.

Confederates generated their own paradoxes. As they built a new nation grounded in racial hierarchy, they borrowed the language of liberal self-determination. The ease with which Confederates made peace with French imperial ambitions in Mexico (in the form of their support of Maximilian's invasion in 1862) and their pursuit of patriarchal control at home indicated their commitment to hierarchy, but it contradicted their public rhetoric of nationalist liberation, at the time mostly associated with European social reformers.³

The great conflicts of the seventeenth century shaped how people of the nineteenth century reacted to their own crisis, especially the question of how to morally resist the state to which they belonged. Before Enlightenment thinkers advanced concepts such as the consent of the governed or limits to executive power, Englishmen (even the conservatives among them) asserted that the rule of law existed and that the king was subject to it. In short, people must guard their rights because God would not sanction a tyrant.⁴ Ever cautious, even Parliamentarians claimed to be acting defensively, on behalf of the true English constitution. Two centuries later, Northerners such as Abraham Lincoln had to thread a similarly narrow needle, explaining the nature of consent in government in a way that ruled out the Confederacy but respected both American history and the expanding nature of democratic governance in the nineteenth century.

While Confederates rallied men to enlist in their armies with calls to defend hearth and home, Northerners had to convince enlistees to go on the offensive against their countrymen. Only a handful of genuine abolitionists joined the US Army intending to destroy slavery; most Northerners regarded secession as a fatal threat to democratic self-government and enlisted to preserve the integrity of the Union.⁵ Northern spokesmen who connected the English Civil Wars and the American conflict rooted their motives in deeper soil still. They positioned the Union armies in a tradition of advancing liberty that stretched across centuries.

The English Civil Wars of the seventeenth century proved especially important to Northern self-conceptions. Nineteenth-century histories consistently framed King Charles I, upon whose watch the various rebellions and civil wars began, as incompetent at best, corrupt and tyrannical at worst. As a school primer of the era summarized, "It was not only that the people [of seventeenth-century England] were illegally deprived of their property, they were equally unhappy with respect to their personal liberties."⁶ Another condemned Charles's whole line: "The Stuarts were all haunted by an insane desire for absolute power."⁷ Even those histories that remained skeptical of the turbulence of the Commonwealth era often resorted to sarcasm to describe Charles's grasping for power. "Having . . . discovered that parliaments were not to be converted into passive instruments of his will," George Brodie wrote, "Charles determined to renounce the use of assemblies which he could not control, and, by assuming the whole powers of the legislature, to disregard all the forms, as well as the spirit, of the constitution."[8] Thomas Macaulay's conclusion captured the spirit of most of his fellow historians: "Many English kings had occasionally committed unconstitutional acts: but none had ever systematically attempted to make himself a despot, and to reduce the Parliament to a nullity. Such was the end which Charles distinctly proposed to himself."[9] Despite being the legitimate king, Charles abused his position, and this violation justified the people's resistance. For nineteenth-century American readers, these texts made a persuasive case for the necessity of resistance to lawfully constituted authority.

As a people founded on revolution and with rebels such as George Washington and John Adams as the brightest stars in the national pantheon, Northerners needed to differentiate legitimate from illegitimate rebellion. In the first place, rebellion could only be justified against true oppression. *Harper's Weekly* pithily clarified this perspective by juxtaposing virtuous rebels with Jefferson Davis, who "completes the trio of names infamous in our history—Arnold, Burr, Davis. . . . He is not infamous because he is a rebel; for Cromwell and Washington were rebels. But they rebelled against real oppression for which there was no hope of remedy but in arms."[10] Davis, like Benedict Arnold and Aaron Burr, pursued a narrow and partisan agenda in arms despite the absence of oppression. For a nation like America, founded in revolution but that aspired to order and calm, domesticating or civilizing rebellion was a key rhetorical accomplishment.[11] The most effective way to accomplish this, particularly if it also challenged English sympathy for the Confederacy, was with history. "When the Parliament took arms against *Charles First*, what was the justification?" *Harper's* asked. "That he had violated the Constitution of England."

Nineteenth-century analysts established what modern readers could call a "red line," an action which, if crossed even by lawfully established authority, violated fundamental rights in a way that demanded redress. The problem, in the seventeenth century, was that the king asserted the right to define the power of Parliament, which would have "put the liberties of every Englishman at his mercy." *Harper's* acknowledged that "'the English never admitted the right of revolution.' But whether they have or not, they have practiced it. What is the foundation of the present system in England but 'the glorious revolution' of 1688 which drove *James Second* from the throne? What was its justification? The wrongs of the English people, which had no present or prospective legal redress." In this reading, it was exactly the British who had offered this gift to America: "That is the only right of revolution ever asserted in America, and that came in direct descent from England."[12] In a brilliant hindsight rendering of the definition of rebellion, one Northern journal declared, "Rebellion is a revolt against constituted legal power; that nothing can justify it but injustice and oppression; that, if successful, it becomes glorious, and is called a revolution, but that rebellions as a general thing have failed, unless the people were worthy of the independence they sought."[13] Northerners believed that the English of the 1640s and the Americans of 1760s were worthy; the Confederates of 1861 were not.

If the English Rebellion of the 1640s provided to Northerners an example of legitimate resistance to oppression, the Irish Rebellion of the same era offered the opposite: an example of illegitimate resistance justifiably suppressed. The relative success of Scottish Covenanters against King Charles in 1637 spurred the Irish to open resistance in 1641. Although modern readers, familiar with the Irish Revolution of the 1920s or the late twentieth-century history of "the Troubles" in Northern Ireland, may presume that Anglo-Irish hostilities stretch back to time immemorial, they, too, have a history. The first organized English invasion of the island of Ireland came under the leadership of Henry II in the twelfth century. In its wake, many Anglo-Norman settlers adopted Catholicism and intermarried with leading Irish families. The violence and political conflict that define the modern phase of Anglo-Irish relations began in the early seventeenth century, so readers should understand that the 1641 rebellion was a reaction to a relatively recent change in the economic and political order.

Most nineteenth- and twenty-first-century histories emphasize the violence of the rebellion's first year. During the early months of the war, rebellion spread south from Ulster. As it did, Catholics committed atrocities against their Protestant neighbors, who responded in kind.[14] The scale of casualties in Ireland was comparable to those suffered by central Europeans during the awful destruction of the Thirty Years' War, which had only just concluded.[15] As the rebellion extended in time, communities within Ireland created coalitions, which shifted and realigned over time in slippery and surprising ways. Confusing for us, the new state organized by the Irish rebels was known as the Confederacy. Under this government, from 1642 to 1649, a unitary Irish state governed most of Ireland and contended with armies representing Royalists, Parliamentarians, and Scottish Covenanters.[16] Charles initially raised a Scottish army to suppress the Irish Rebellion, but that army effectively became Parliamentarian over time, culminating in an effort to impose Presbyterianism on Ulster (Ireland's northern province). The Irish rebels, organized under the Confederacy, then found common cause with Charles and pledged themselves (for the most part) to support him against Parliament.[17] Despite the obstacles this alliance presented, it remained an important part of the war's legacy, one that allowed the Irish to emphasize the reasonable, even conservative nature of their enterprise. As a letter writer from the radical haunts of western County Cork wrote to a Fenian newspaper in 1863, "It was a struggle between Catholicism and Puritanism—between loyalty and revolution."[18]

English writers identified 1641 as a foundational historical moment of rebellion denied. The nineteenth-century historian Robert Vaughan analogized the Irish Rebellion to a similar rebellion in India a few years earlier—one which the English suppressed vigorously: "The frightful rebellion which had broken out in Ireland, and which moved that generation much as the Indian mutiny moved our own."[19] Histories, mostly written by Englishmen (even those by writers sympathetic to the oppression suffered by the Irish over the ensuing two decades), conveyed a singular image of an unjustified uprising. Macaulay, typical again, wrote, "The Irish broke forth into acts of fearful violence. On a sudden, the aboriginal population rose on the colonists. . . . Every post brought to London exaggerated accounts of outrages, which, without any exaggeration, were sufficient to move pity and horrors."[20] Macaulay's quasi-anthropological language suggests the degree to which even mainstream historians had absorbed a sense of Irish difference. For many, this racial or ethnic otherness explained both the persistence of rebelliousness on the island and the violent character it assumed. In one nineteenth-century history of the empire, the phrase "Irish Rebellion" headed three separate chapters (in sections addressing Elizabeth, Charles I, and George III, respectively) notwithstanding additional sections on "Popish plots" and the like.[21] In defending what it regarded as Ireland's genuine suffering, a Kansas newspaper modeled the reaction of readers reared on English history: "That the endless warfare of Irishmen against the British government proceeds more from a restless and insubordinate nature than any real grievances."[22]

In the United States of the 1850s, Catholic Irish, especially recent émigrés seeking to escape severe famine, had been regarded by many people as unassimilable and foreign. Their military service during the Civil War helped ameliorate somewhat the xenophobia rampant in the early American republic, particularly among the nativist faction identified as Know Nothings.[23] That said, recent improvements in the public image of Irish Americans (and I do not want to overstate the change in this regard, which took decades to diminish) did not alter Americans' historical understanding of the Irish in Ireland, and it was this memory that shaped American attitudes toward rebellion.[24] The successful English effort to suppress what they regarded as a desperate and savagely conducted war in the 1640s provided a model for Northern efforts to preserve the Union in the 1860s.

Even the most sympathetic nineteenth-century histories of 1641 identified the conflict as one in which the Irish behaved unjustly. Writers described the Irish mode of warfare as "the direful work of slaughter, horror, desolation." George Brodie's 1824 *Constitutional History of the British Empire* embodies this curious tension. On the one hand, Brodie recognized that the Irish regarded English colonization as a process that "saw themselves despoiled of their country by conquering invaders, amongst whom were distributed those lands to which they conceived their claim undoubted, and which the loss of necessarily brought misery, if not a wretched death to thousands."[25] At the same time, Brodie endorsed the wildest exaggerations of wartime killing. "Hundreds were pricked forward with spears to rivers and drowned in the stream," he wrote. "Inventive cruelty was then put to the rack; many were burned in their houses; some were dragged by ropes through woods, bogs, and ditches, till they expired; some hung on tenter hooks; some slashed and cut, to inflict the utmost torture without proving immediately mortal. The helpless innocence of infants did not protect them. Women great with child were first tormented until their parted with the burthens of their wombs—which were given to dogs and swine—and then destroyed with an indecency equal to the inhumanity."[26] Repeated like a mantra was the figure of 40,000 Protestant settlers killed by vengeful Catholics, a figure generated by Sir John Temple.[27]

Because Americans read the same history as the English, and used that material to shape their own rhetoric, it is worth briefly addressing the evidentiary base that enabled British historians to draw these conclusions. Like in the US Civil War, participants in the English Civil Wars relied on firsthand reporting to write histories of the wars. For the English, accounts of atrocities enabled them to delegitimize Irish rebellion. History, for them, became a narrative of Protestant victimhood and suffering, a mix of real and invented stories that fueled a century of policies. This approach foreshadows how Northerners and Southerners talked about their own experiences during the US Civil War. The key historical text underlying British interpretations was Sir John Temple's *The Irish Rebellion, or An History of the Beginnings and First Progress of the General Rebellion Raised within the Kingdom of Ireland . . .*

Together with the Barbarous Cruelties and Bloody Massacres Which Ensued Thereupon.[28] Temple was an Irish Protestant who served in the English administration in Dublin in the 1640s. His account, published in 1646, asserted a massacre of Protestants planned by Irish Catholics and encouraged by the pope. Temple's book became the standard account and was republished throughout the eighteenth and nineteenth centuries.[29] As historian Nicholas Canny observes, "Protestant explanations of 1641 remained undisputed as far as a British political nation was concerned."[30] Temple's interpretive scheme and the evidence he offered served as an essential basis for nineteenth-century historical writing. Robert Ross's *Outlines of English History*, for instance, recapitulates his numbers. "The first attempt was to capture Dublin. . . . This scheme was betrayed, and 30,000 men, now rendered desperate by failure, commenced a savage massacre which spread all over the country, and ended in the slaughter of more than 40,000 Protestants."[31] The sense of righteousness that Temple's volume kindled in English readers had its own parallel in the literature produced during the US Civil War, particularly in sermons and religious publications.[32] As Robert Penn Warren observed in the context of the American Civil War, "The man of righteousness tends to be so sure of his own motives that he does not need to inspect consequences."[33]

Temple's evidentiary foundation for his assertions about Irish violence derived from a collection of depositions taken by English officials in 1641.[34] Solicited mostly from Protestant refugees driven from their homes by war, the depositions contain verifiable reporting and gross exaggeration, often about sexual violence perpetrated against Protestant settlers.[35] Eager London printers published these depositions during the rebellion itself. As historian Eamon Darcy observes, "The intelligence gathered by the lords justices in the early stages of the rebellion, and presented to the wider world, immediately presented the rebellion as a Catholic plot."[36] Modern historians have parsed the depositions much more carefully; like the Federal Writers' Project slave narratives recorded in the 1930s, the sources contain important evidence but need to be contextualized rather than read at face value. At the time, the depositions and the London pamphlet literature reprinting the accusations inflamed tensions and generated a much more violent conflict for everyone. "Accounts of rebel violence," Darcy notes, "justified the use of excessive force by English and Scottish armies in Ireland in 1642 and again in 1649. After the successful conquest of Ireland by Oliver Cromwell, histories of 1641 appeared to remind authorities of what Irish Protestants had suffered during the previous decade."[37]

The American Civil War did not generate as neat a set of documents as the depositions.[38] The partisan affiliation, regional loyalty, and market competition among daily newspapers and book and pamphlet publishers ensured a more diverse body of published records. Still, Northern and Southern printers produced markedly different readings of the conflict. In both regions, popular publications emphasized the victimization of innocents at the hands of an enemy without scruples.[39] Having absorbed the model of how to defend or defame rebellious conduct in the pages of English histories, Americans quickly moved to "frame the narrative," as we would say today. This rhetorical front in the US Civil War has received less scholarly attention than the battle- and home fronts, but it was a crucial dimension of the struggle, both in the efforts each side made to secure foreign support and in shaping the meaning of the conflict in the postwar era.

Northerners relied on their reading of the past to deny the legality or constitutionality of secession, in particular by articulating a theory of revolution that Confederates failed to meet.[40] The white Southerners who built the Confederacy did not face the "intolerable oppression" suffered by the English under Charles's tyrannical regime. Clarifying their comments about legitimate rebellion, *Harper's* argued, "The insurrection of the slaveholding faction in this country is not criminal because it is a rebellion, but because it is the effort of a faction to overthrow the government of the whole people."[41] The *Atlantic Monthly*, another high-circulation journal, amplified this critique of the Confederacy. "Rebellion smells no sweeter because it is called Secession," it lectured, "nor does Order lose its divine precedence in human affairs because a knave may nickname it Coercion. Secession means chaos, and Coercion the exercise of legitimate authority. You cannot dignify the one nor degrade the other by any verbal charlatanism."[42] The contest over language was not semantic. Cassius Clay, the antislavery Kentuckian who served as Lincoln's ambassador to Russia, took pains to explain the differences to the British in a widely reprinted letter: "The word 'secession' is used to cover up treason, and delude the nations. They stand to us in the relation of one 'people,' the idea of 'State sovereignty' is utterly delusive." In a telling phrase that foreshadowed Northerners' interpretation of the seventeenth century, Clay analogized Ireland to the South: "In a word, they can no more 'secede' from the Union than Scotland or Ireland can secede from England."[43] John Lothrop Motley, the American historian, agreed, asking in an early war commentary what would happen if "Scotland should secede, should seize all the national property, forts, arsenals, and public treasure on its soil, organize an army [and] send forth foreign ministers." He expected that Britain would strike "a blow or two... to defend the national honor and the national existence."[44]

Northerners understood the importance of framing the moral architecture of the American conflict. "It is plain that rebellion, as homicide, may be an atrocious crime, or justifiable, or commendable, according to circumstance," argued the *Princeton Review*. "Whereas moral offences are always, and under all circumstances, evil. A good thief, or a good murderer, is as much a solecism as good wickedness. But a good rebel is no such solecism." Making reference to the English Civil Wars, the article concluded, "Hampden was a rebel, so was Washington; they and thousands of other good men have risen in armed resistance to constituted authority, and such resistance had been justified by the verdict of the enlightened conscience of the world."[45] Charles Sumner, the Republican senator, possessed one of the sharpest pens in Congress and a deep historical knowledge that informed most of his speeches. Early on, he identified the US Civil War as a "war of ideas, like that between . . . the arbitrary crown of Charles the First and the Puritanism of Oliver Cromwell, and like that between our fathers and the mother country, when the Declaration of Independence was put in issue." Anticipating the *Princeton Review*'s posture, Sumner explained, "Ideas are sometimes good and sometimes bad; and there may be a war for evil as well as for good. Such was that earliest rebellion waged by fallen spirits against the Almighty Throne; and such is that now waged by fallen slave-masters of ours against the National Government. I adopt the language of Milton, in his masterly prose, when I call it 'a war fit for Cain to be the leader of, an abhorred, a cursed, a fraternal war.'"[46]

Harper's made a similar effort to educate its large readership early in the war. "*Rebellions* are not necessarily just or unjust. But hitherto, as they have generally been risings of the people against tyranny, they have inspired sympathy in all generous minds. The great rebellion in England was the protest of the English people against the despotic, irresponsible prerogative of the crown." The article carried readers into the nineteenth century by assessing recent conflicts in Europe, such as the process of Italian unification, which were also classified as rebellions "because they were movements against established governments; but they are justified by the heart of mankind, because they were struggles against intolerable oppressions, whose consequences were worse than the woes of war." In this respect, rebellion could serve as a model for the world of how the people could maintain an orderly republic. The English believed in the providential nature of that model and of their global leadership.[47] As one scholar of the civil war era has noted, "Cromwell [believed] that England was struggling on behalf of the whole world, and not just the English, for civilization and liberty; that all the peoples of the world had a right to this inheritance."⁴⁸ This perspective prefigured Lincoln's proclamation that the United States offered "the last best hope of earth," in terms of the future of democratic government. For both peoples, responding to injustice was perceived as not just strategically wise but morally imperative.

In addition to radical activists, policymakers and legislators also derived inspiration from the interpretations advanced in popular journals and historical writing. Orville Browning, an Illinois Republican, proposed the same historical framing as *Harper's*. Referencing Henry Hallam's popular *Constitutional History of England*, Browning took special notice of "a revolution which, more than two centuries ago, brought to the block a tyrant whose oppressions could not break the spirit of the English people."⁴⁹ For Sumner, the English episode was likewise the foundational reference point for understanding the nature of rebellion. Delivering a lecture in the Senate on the relationship between war and rebellion, Sumner referred to "the disturbances which convulsed England in the middle of the seventeenth century, [which] were occasioned by the resistance of Parliament to the arbitrary power of the Crown. This resistance, prolonged for years and maintained by force, triumphed at last in the execution of King Charles and the elevation of Oliver Cromwell."⁵⁰

The English experience offered Northerners a model, like their own beloved Revolution, of legitimate resistance to authority. At the same time, Northerners drew reassurance from their interpretation of the English suppression of the Irish Rebellion. The English believed that the method of fighting adopted by the Irish (using violence against women and children) not only undercut the justice of their case, but it demanded a hard war and a hard peace. An illegitimate rebellion put the enemy in a weak position to ask for charity. This posture found a ready reception among Northerners angry over secession and increasingly surprised at the hostile reception of US troops as they entered the South.⁵¹ "[Confederates] gave up their rights, their faith, their honor, when they became rebels," wrote a moderate Northern journal, "betrayed their country and took up arms to subvert its Government, and they have no right to complain if compelled to drink, and to drink even to the dregs, the bitter cup of humiliation."⁵² American Civil War historians have characterized the Union's slow adoption of "hard war" tactics as driven by multiple causes, most important the determined and effective military resistance of Confederate armies.⁵³ That shift in tactics was bolstered by their reading of history as well. If the fire-eaters' and abolitionists' readings of the seventeenth century help account for the war's origins, moderate Northerners' readings help explain its duration and intensity.

Committing to Civil War

> how hast thou disturb'd
> Heav'ns blessed peace, and into Nature brought
> Miserie, uncreated till the crime
> Of thy Rebellion?
>
> JOHN MILTON, *Paradise Lost*

A recognition of cultural difference or even a demand for national autonomy does not necessarily lead to war. Many people on both sides of America's sharpening regional divide in 1860–61 thought that physical conflict was unlikely. Northerners believed that white Southerners would temper their overreaction to Abraham Lincoln's election and accept the new political order, and white Southerners believed the North would allow secessionists to leave the union in peace.[1] One hundred sixty years later, secession can seem like the necessary prelude to Civil War, but people at the time lived through a long uncertain interval after Lincoln's election, even after the February 4, 1861, creation of the Confederacy. The choice to fight and what kind of fighting would occur demanded a separate calculation. As with the discussions over the nature of legitimate and illegitimate rebellion, these conversations were more intellectual than emotional, more clearly tied to Americans' reading of history than to their imaginative relationships to the past.

Confederates defended secession and military mobilization in a way that they hoped could both rally their own citizens and draw the support of foreign powers. The numerous contemporary histories of England and the British Empire continued to offer a useful parallel in the history of Ireland's struggle for autonomy. Although white Southerners rarely embraced the analogy with the vigor that they did the Cavalier legend, the evidence of the Irish experience neatly mirrored how Confederates imagined their position within the Union: as a distinct national community denied their rights to property and cultural autonomy within the polity to which they belonged.

In rejecting the Confederate argument, Lincoln pledged himself to preserve the Union because he regarded secession and democratic self-government as incompatible. Lincoln's political language during the Civil War remained consistent. It emphasized the Union's perpetuity and the ability of the Federal government, when empowered by a majority of the nation's voters, to curtail the spread of slavery by military as well as political means. At the same time, Lincoln maintained a view of victory that ended with bringing white Southerners back into membership in the American political community. To achieve this, he pursued moderate policies, ones that took account of the English experience in the seventeenth century in order to achieve a faster and more lasting peace.

IN DEFENSE OF PREEMPTIVE WAR

During the twentieth century, a series of political revolutions that generated social revolution—in Russia, China, and Cuba, among others—seemingly established an inevitable relationship between political and social change. This was not always the case. In the nineteenth century, political transformation did not necessitate property redistribution or broad social change. The Confederates embodied this curious position, pursuing what can only be termed a conservative revolution. Secession, by breaking up the existing United States, was regarded (even by many white Southerners) as a radical act. Future Confederate general Robert E. Lee explained to his son that "secession is nothing but revolution."[2] But the fire-eaters who led the Southern states out of the Union were anything but social revolutionaries. They seceded in order to preserve a hierarchical world.[3] A key intellectual challenge was how people who opposed rebellion reconciled themselves to the fact of being rebels.

Confederates assimilated themselves to the position of insurgents partly through a strategic reading of history. Southern nationalists had been building their arguments before actual conflict erupted, as when they objected to the emerging revisionist view of Oliver Cromwell. "Cromwell we consider great," *DeBow's Review* opined in 1860, "but only a great brute. . . . It has lately become the fashion, not only to speak in high terms of the military talents of Bonaparte and Cromwell, but to gloss over their treasons; and, worse than all, to commend and approve the military despotisms which they established and wielded."[4] Once the war began, Confederate readings of seventeenth-century history extended this interpretation by emphasizing the preservation of order and institutions. From this perspective, the "blood of their murdered king" stained the Puritans (and their descendants). "Their leaders, Hampden, Russell, Cromwell, and Vane, were not wanting in many of the higher qualities of statesmanship," another issue of *DeBow's Review* wrote, "but, being idealists in politics, and fanatics in religion, they became only grand architects of ruin, and left behind them nothing so imperishable as their crimes and folly."[5] Friends of the South, such as the notorious Fernando Wood of New York City (who as mayor proposed that the city declare itself independent in order to maintain trade with the South during the war), encouraged this view of the past, one that positioned Northern radicals (and their predecessors) as the true threat. From Congress, where he served during the second half of the conflict, Wood observed, "The like spirit of fanaticism now pervading this country had a duration of over a half century in England during its period of revolution. Ours is not the first instance in history in which the established order of things has had to yield to the destructive spirit of fanaticism and misrule."[6]

Unlike Northern conservatives, who appreciated the English Civil Wars because they formed part of the English tradition of liberty, Southern conservatives regarded the whole era as beyond redemption. Texan Louis Wigfall's description of Puritans helping "Cromwell to cut off their King's head" identified Confederates as the forces of rational conservatism.[7] What the Puritans claimed as just rebellion against tyranny was really mere anarchy. Having ruled out the Parliamentarian side in the seventeenth-century conflicts, prominent Confederate journals committed themselves to the Royalist side, condemning Cromwell as a despot and destroyer of the social order. It was a simple step for Confederates to replace Cavaliers and Puritans with noble Confederates and Black Republicans.

In contrast to Northerners' views on secession, Southerners built a theory of revolution that legitimized their actions. They did so despite the paradoxes in which such an effort entangled them, as Ann Tucker has recently shown in her comparative study of Confederate and European nationalism at midcentury. White Southerners found odd bedfellows when they pronounced their belief in national self-determination, which echoed the language of liberal reformers in Europe, with whom they otherwise had little in common.[8] As they tried to naturalize secession as part of the modern movement of nation-state-building, white Southerners reversed their earlier support for a powerful expansionary American state and condemned the United States as an empire of old. They must have thrilled to an early war article from the Dublin *Nation* reprinted in American papers. "If what is now passing in America took place in any of the old-world empires, it would be at least intelligible," the *Nation* wrote. The characterization of secession that followed—"unanimity never surpassed, and rarely equalled, declared, by free poll, in open day, by universal suffrage, that their interests and their feelings demanded the substitution of the Imperial Government by one of their own choice"—was even more generous than that offered by most Southerners themselves, who recognized the divided nature of their voting populace, to say nothing of the active opposition of enslaved people. Nonetheless, the Dublin *Nation*'s conclusion—"that [if] the imperial Government marched its armies to crush the demand in the blood of the 'rebels,' it would be nothing new amongst despotic systems"—echoed Southerners' new posture toward central authority.[9] Even as Confederates sought diplomatic support from Britain, they took succor from the Irish, who spoke with authority about imperial oppression.

Alongside their critique of the Union as overbearing, Confederates' rhetoric focused on the case for secession as a natural right possessed by all people. This effort, too, benefited from Irish parallels. John Lingard's summary of the mistreatment of Ireland in his 1860 *History of England* offered both a familiar history and a reassuring conclusion. "It was observed," Lingard wrote about pre-rebellion Ireland, "that new shackles had been forged for the national rights, new dangers prepared for the national faith; that the English parliament had advanced pretensions to legislate for Ireland." Lingard's conclusion explained the necessity of preemptive action given this intolerable trend line. "Why, then, should not Irishmen unite in their own defence?"[10]

Fire-eaters across the Lower and Upper South pressed this same question throughout the winter of 1860–61.[11]

The years 1641 and 1861 as the openings of failed rebellions became obvious only with hindsight. In both years, people subject to what they regarded as oppressive mistreatment launched preemptive actions to protect their rights. They did so at moments that came, in retrospect, to appear nearly inevitable. Nineteenth-century histories of Ireland made the moment appear destined: "With the forty preceding years' continuity of wholesale spoliation, galling oppression, terrorism, religious proscription, and national degradation still present to us . . . the reader will not be at a loss to account for the events which it now becomes our duty to relate."[12] In the American case, it was a decade and a half of bitter political debates over the future of slavery, the persistent local and occasionally broad-scale public resistance by enslaved people, an increasingly vocal abolition community, the rise of the political ideology of free labor, and the election of its new partisan advocate (the Republican Party) to the White House that propelled white Southerners out of the Union in the wake of Abraham Lincoln's election.[13] They viewed Lincoln's rise as capping an era of gross violations of their rights and a harbinger of worse to come. Nineteenth-century historians saw a similar posture among the seventeenth-century Irish: "In Ireland a rebellion, or more correctly a civil war, had commenced in 1641, provoked by intolerable oppression of the great majority of the people."[14]

The challenge for secessionists was to make a persuasive case for preemptive action. Their approach in this instance—using the example of the seventeenth century—required overlooking the habit of treating everything American as original. As historian Kariann Yokota has shown, the process of building a fully independent and culturally distinct United States in the decades after the Revolution embroiled Americans in deep contradictions. The markers of modernity that Americans needed to possess were nearly all European and more specifically British.[15] Michael O'Brien's magisterial intellectual history of the antebellum South offers a bold formulation: "In the early nineteenth century Southerners' intellectual traditions continued to be formed mostly by the older cultures of Europe."[16] As a result, acquiring cultural independence took longer than acquiring political independence. Americans trumpeted their scientific bona fides, with naturalists such as John and William Bartram chronicling new world discoveries (of plants, animals, and people).[17] What we would call today the social sciences required less self-promotion. Because scholars (American and British alike) assumed a uniformity of perception and behavior (at least among people of northwestern European descent), they could make comparisons to the English past without compromising their sense of national autonomy. As Michael Braddick writes about the seventeenth-century conflicts, "History offered fixity, therefore, but also the terrain over which the legitimacy of the cause was fought."[18]

The targets for such an argument resided both at home and abroad. Southern slaveholders represented one of the most socially and politically conservative populations in the United States; convincing elites with property to put themselves outside the regular systems of law demanded a compelling argument. Nonslaveholders likewise required convincing. Though they did not face the same immediate economic risk from the end of slavery as Southern elites, they formed the majority of would-be Confederate soldiers, and that sacrifice required an accurate and meaningful explanation. In 1861, as in 1641, some future rebels saw opportunity where others saw crisis. Most recent interpretations of the American South in the decade before the Civil War emphasize the power that slaveholders wielded over local, state, and national governments and their easy assimilation of modern technologies and economic strategies into a slaveholding society.[19] Emboldened by the power of King Cotton, slaveholding Southerners acted with an impunity that looked like simple arrogance after 1865. Despite the authority they wielded, they perceived themselves as besieged, blocked from expanding slavery and from recovering runaway slaves who escaped into Northern states. Pro-secession Southerners were deeply wedded to a future with slavery and came to believe that the future would be secure only outside the United States. In order to protect their power, they presented the new political arrangement as a natural right. That right was the neutral-sounding claim that all people were entitled to choose their own government. Obscuring the question of who counted as part of "the people," fire-eaters emphasized the growing antislavery attitudes in the North and their failure to ensure slavery's viability in the new Western territories. Over the 1850s, Southern nationalists cleverly framed each real or imagined threat to slavery as evidence of the subjugation of the white South.

The seventeenth-century Irish elites who led their rebellion expressed a similar dismay with the trajectory of English policies on the island.[20] Most histories (in the nineteenth century and today) of 1641 begin in the 1630s, with particular emphasis on the appointment of Thomas Wentworth (later Earl of Strafford) as Lord Deputy of Ireland. Wentworth sought to create religious uniformity along the lines imposed in Scotland with the Book of Common Prayer, though pursued with more vigor against the Catholic majority. He also upset the traditional land arrangements by displacing the Old English settlers (many of whose families had lived in Ireland for centuries) by offering plantation grants to New English landlords.[21] Robert Ross's 1860 *Outlines of English History* offered a remarkable catalog of maladministration: "His government generally partook too much of tyranny. He set up the authority of the executive government over that of the courts of law. He permitted no person to leave the island without his license. He established vast monopolies for his own private benefit. He imposed taxes arbitrarily. He levied them by military force." Wentworth also imposed egregious penal laws that disfranchised Catholics from the political process and most economic opportunities. Like historian John Lingard, Ross reached the conclusion that armed resistance was unavoidable. "It is not therefore surprising," he wrote, "that [the Irish] took advantage of the disturbed condition of England, and as both the English and Scotch had obtained concessions from the king, they resolved to unite for the same purpose."[22]

In truth, Wentworth only perfected the strategies that the English had been pursuing since Elizabeth's reign.[23] According to a leading modern scholar of the era, "There is also general agreement that the strife that is such a prominent feature of Ireland's sixteenth-century arose largely from English policies involving religious coercion, military conquest, and territorial colonization."[24] Nineteenth-century Irish historians were less subtle; in 1641, according to one, "Ireland was now prostrate under the iron heel of the tyrant Strafford."[25] In this reading, as in later Lost Cause histories of the Civil War, the initiators of rebellion cast themselves as the victims, forced into a difficult, even regrettable, decision by the callous actions of others. The long sad history of Ireland since the seventeenth century made clear the costs of inaction. A North Carolina newspaper chronicled the fate of Ireland "several centuries" after its subjugation: It was one of the "nations miserably cumbering the earth, which have been overrun and are now occupied and governed by another people."[26] Confederate readers understood that in order to avoid such a fate, vigorous action, even military violence, was necessary.

English offenses against seventeenth-century Ireland clustered under three broad categories: attacks on religion and Irish culture, dispossession of land, and the use of violence to control the population, all of which attained a similar new resonance in 1861 as the American nation fractured and open warfare began. In the 1630s, New English settlers carried a Reforming attitude of scorn for the Old English who had adopted Irish culture, often including conversion to Catholicism, and especially for the Catholic Gaelic Irish.[27] The English strategy of creating plantations created particularly acute grievances. "The generally accepted motive for plotting [in 1641]," one historian notes, "was that Wentworth's sustained attack on Catholic landholding, coinciding with an economic downturn, drove these especially 'bankrupt and discontented gentlemen' to desperate measures."[28] Desperation offers a common anchor for many preemptive actions. Histories portrayed the Irish of the 1630s in precisely these terms. "The Irish of Ulster," William Cooke Taylor observed, "were notoriously eager to engage in any enterprise which would afford a promise of redeeming their wrongs."[29] Like Southern slaveholders, Irish rebels regarded and presented their actions as self-defense.[30] Nineteenth-century histories, even ones written from England's perspective, sympathized with the island's Indigenous inhabitants during the difficult 1630s. "The Irish had many reasons for discontent," one explained, "the best lands were in the hands of the English, and the undertakers by whom they were managed treated the native Irish with much contempt."[31] Simple accounting made the same point: "The confiscation of the property of the inhabitants of about two-thirds of Ulster was a principal cause of the Rebellion of 1641."[32]

White Southerners would surely have seen many parallels between their condition and those of the seventeenth-century Irish. The question of land, as generations of scholars have shown, lay at the heart of the sectional conflict in 1850s America.[33] Southerners did not contend with the property seizures on the scale of those ordered by Wentworth, but the fate of Western territories generated a similar discontent. Slaveholders feared that an increasingly antislavery North would prohibit their migration with slave property into the West. Seventeenth-century Ireland and the nineteenth-century South shared more than the plantation. Both were agricultural societies; elites grounded their political and social authority in their ownership or control of land, which made challenges to that power (from Wentworth or Abraham Lincoln) an existential threat.

Last, a tradition of violence accelerated during the seventeenth century, a period that encompassed several major conflicts plus persistent violence between regional lords.[34] As one historian observes, "The near-constant spark and crackle of localised rebellion helped to bring Ireland to the brink of a major conflagration in October 1641."[35] During the US Civil War, some conservative observers, many sympathetic to the Southern slaveholding elite, likewise connected the long history of Irish resistance to grievous suffering. "All [Ireland's] rebellions were the reaction of suffering against rapine," claimed Congressman Samuel S. Cox, who quoted George Smythe's *Ireland, Historical and Statistical* to chronicle the land confiscations enacted by the

English.[36] The modern United States has earned a reputation as a naturally and persistently violent place in way that Ireland has not.[37] That said, Europe in the early modern era, especially the seventeenth century, was bloody and fraught ground. Ireland's history of violence was rooted, as historian David Edwards notes, in rebellions. Political rather than interpersonal violence predominated, both in the years before 1641 and in other eras of mass resistance.[38] In this, again, seventeenth-century Ireland and nineteenth-century America shared something. In the 1850s, Americans clashed over the settlement of the Kansas and Nebraska Territories, over slavery, and in street riots predicated on social and partisan divisions.[39] In both cases, even random, sporadic, and localized violence—when rhetorically mapped onto ideological or political divisions—provided fertile ground for large-scale conflict. White Southerners alert to all these structural similarities marshaled the evidence to encourage the fight against the hated Yankees. For instance, in South Carolina, Thomas Ryan argued that "Oliver Cromwell lives again in the person of Abraham Lincoln. Should they succeed in capturing Charleston the butcheries of Drogheda will be repeated in our streets."[40]

Like modern scholars investigating the US Civil War to identify the turning points of national dissolution, nineteenth-century historians believed they could learn by understanding the timing of the Irish Rebellion. According to William Cooke Taylor's 1831 *History of the Civil Wars of Ireland*, "Every insurrection which tyranny has provoked, broke out only when circumstances seemed favourable to the hopes of redress. The materials of a conflagration may be for years accumulating, but the presence of a torch is necessary to the bursting forth of the flame."[41] Taylor used the fiery metaphor to connect the relation between deep and proximate causes.[42] The necessary torch was the Scots, as Nicholas Canny notes, "Catholic leaders in all the provinces of Ireland were greatly impressed by the way in which the Scottish Covenanters had been able to dictate terms to the monarchy through the simple expedient of having resort to arms . . . [and] they would have calculated that the difficulties being experienced by the king in dealing with both his English and his Scottish subjects provided them with a unique opportunity to redress their own problems with a show of force."[43] It was thus England's strategic preoccupation with Scotland that encouraged the Irish to mobilize. Southern fire-eaters, the most eager advocates of Southern secession, showed they had absorbed history's lessons. They chose their moment carefully, seizing on Lincoln's election and his opposition to slavery's westward expansion to press secession while Congress was adjourned, James Buchanan a lame duck, and Lincoln not yet formally in office.

Despite all the parallels between the Southern and Irish cases, native-born Southerners only occasionally made explicit mention of 1641. Unlike their neighbors, Irish American Southerners identified the historical connections between Ireland and the contemporary South publicly and with great precision. They did so to demonstrate their own loyalty to the region and with the hope of nullifying the support Northern-bound immigrants gave to the Union. The first step in this complicated dance was to remind readers of the hostility of Northern nativists during the 1840s and '50s (though the South was hardly free of Know Nothings). As O. A. Lochrane explained to the Savannah-based *Daily News and Herald*, "The antipathy which disarmed and dishonored them, that has sneered at and jeered at the Irish name and nation, is forgiven and forgotten in the zeal of mob and enthusiasm which would subjugate us." In this telling, Northern immigrants' willingness to overlook nativism was a disavowal of an essentially Irish trait: "In volunteering for coercion, they establish a principle Ireland has resisted with all her genius and energy and manhood. The right of a people to select their own rulers—the right of a people to change their own government." Pledging himself to the South, Lochrane asserted, "We will stand by . . . the old Apostles of liberty, whose judgment and integrity we know stood far above the betrayal of a kiss." Echoing the histories of the era, Lochrane concluded that "no country has submitted to wrong without being enslaved. . . . Ireland, like a Cinderella, weeps and waits a glass slipper miracle. We must resent aggression when offered, or submit to indignities forever."[44]

Another Southern correspondent, this one signing as "Erionnach, The Dublin Irishman," penned a poem that identified the same core Irish values as shared with the white South.

> A nation rising its might
>   Its chains to break, its foes to ban—
> What patriot hopes a fairer sight?
>   What dearer to the Irishman?

Like many Confederate spokesmen, Erionnach ignored the obvious contradictions generated by claiming that a war to preserve slavery advanced freedom.

> Who sunders freedom wins us not;
>   Who weakens freedom injures all;
> Who lives not true to freedom's lot,
>   His pride has planned his certain fall.[45]

In an honest postwar assessment that captured the lingering bitterness over the supposed treachery of Northern Irish fighting for the Union, *DeBow's Review* explained, "We were always of opinion that the Irish immigrants who quitted their native country because of the oppression of England, should have strongly sympathized with the Southern States.... The Scotch and Irish rebellions [of the seventeenth century], so called, were both wars for secession; for regaining the separate sovereignty, and recognized representation of each of these States."[46]

THE NEW NEW MODEL ARMY

The seven states of the Deep South seceded after Lincoln's election but before his inauguration. Living in Springfield, Illinois, during this interlude, Lincoln remained quiet, deferring to President James Buchanan's lame-duck leadership, which put the United States in the passive position of opposing secession but doing nothing to stop it. Even after assuming office, Lincoln moved cautiously. This conservative approach to the war remained his default mode during the conflict. Throughout 1861, the Union military pursued what historians have called the "rosewater strategy," because it treated Confederate civilians and property with respect and gentleness.[47] Lincoln's faith in a limited war strategy reflected his own confidence that a majority of white Southerners remained loyal to the Union or were at least capable of being talked back into right relations to it. It also reflected an awareness of the extraordinary difficulty of managing civil conflicts without laying the seeds for future conflict. The history of the English Civil Wars offered the most valuable lessons in this regard, even with the important differences in size, geography, and nature of political organization.[48] Despite the chronological and geographical distance, the key issue in the English Civil Wars remained the same as the one in the American conflict: how states maintain legitimacy. Secession forced an American reckoning with the process of how people expressed their consent to participate within the American state and when and how they could withdraw that consent.[49]

For Northerners such as Lincoln, who hoped to preserve the Union and avoid war, the seventeenth century offered clear examples of what not to do. King Charles I, Archbishop William Laud, and Irish Lord Deputy Thomas Wentworth, arrogant in their complacency, blundered into a war that wrecked the stability they so valued.[50] Lincoln had long idolized Henry Clay, one of the "Great Triumvirate" of senators famous for their ability to craft compromises that temporarily bridged ideological divides (and whose legislative bargains also protected slavery).[51] Instead, by the late 1850s, the nation drifted under the direction of President Buchanan, a Northern Democrat who protected slavery with all the zeal of a convert. "We do not believe that any government—no, not the Rump Parliament [the one that sentenced Charles I to execution] on its last legs—ever showed such pitiful inadequacy as our own during the past two months," complained the *Atlantic Monthly* in early 1861.[52]

Buchanan's feckless response to secession left the nation dangerously exposed as Lincoln assumed office. Historians of the nineteenth century routinely deprecated the political abilities of Charles, Laud, and Wentworth, in essence blaming them for the conflicts of the 1640s. As listeners learned in an 1862 lecture given in Washington, DC, "the people hated the tyranny of Charles I, while they equally despised and loathed his ministers, Lord and Strafford."[53] One historian claims, "Had Charles entered into the negotiation [with the Scots] with sincerity, any future quarrel on this ground might have been prevented."[54] In particular, these men escalated pressure on their political opponents at inopportune moments, catalyzing opposition that culminated in violent resistance. For Lincoln and others, reading the history of this era would have strengthened their belief that firm, careful negotiation combined with reassurance (Lincoln's repeated pledge not to interfere with slavery where it currently existed) could deescalate the situation.

Of equal importance, once the war began, was what actions a state could take on behalf of its consenting citizens. A significant majority of Americans opposed secession and empowered the Lincoln administration to use force in response. For well-read Northerners, the English Civil Wars provided a wealth of examples of how to conduct military conflict. For instance, the Union's embarrassing loss along the banks of Bull Run in central Virginia in the war's first major battle in 1861 compelled Northerners to search out parallel examples to bolster public support and respond to English reporting that emphasized the Union's military unpreparedness. Published widely in Northern papers under the headline "Edgehill and Manassas," one article compared the inconclusive struggle between Parliamentary and Royalist forces at the battle of Edgehill with the recent encounter in Manassas, chronicled in embarrassing detail by the English journalist William Howard Russell: "We commend this scrap of English history to Mr. Russell and the *London Times*." Predicting what they hoped would be the path of the conflict in the United States, the article concluded, "It is proper to add, that the same men who fled so disgracefully from the first battle, afterwards, under a great leader, proved to be the most formidable soldiers which England ever produced."[55]

As the war continued, the accretion of power in Lincoln's hands worried even Unionists, but they, too, could find solace in the example of the seventeenth century. Worrying that "our present duty is to run the gauntlet between Anarchy and Despotism," the *Hancock Presbyterian* referred readers to the "most instructive" history of the English Civil Wars: "Whilst Charles sought to do what Cromwell subsequently did . . . Charles wished to gather all the powers of the government into his hands, that he might destroy them together." Instead, in a foreshadow of the sanction Republicans would offer to Lincoln's wartime authority, the journal explained, "Cromwell concentrated these rights that he might protect them from present danger, and restore them to the people when the storm had blown over."[56] Presbyterians recognized the danger—the president might feel compelled to hang traitors (even Democratic congressmen) or "set his foot on the Supreme Court"—but they trusted that Northern virtue and faith would hold fast and enable the country to defeat the rebellion and return to its peacetime norm. The paper's explanation of Cromwell's intention mirrored Lincoln's own explanation of his approach during the war. He recognized that suspending habeas corpus represented an unprecedented step but believed it was better to do so even if it contravened the Constitution. As he told Congress in July 1861, "Are all the laws, *but one*, to go unexecuted, and the government itself go to pieces, lest that one be violated?"[57]

The imagined relationship between the Parliamentarian and Union armies assumed a deeper and more potent meaning as Northerners came to appreciate that Confederates intended to fight a long war. In particular, the Parliamentary army, motivated by religious purity, served as a useful model for the North. "During the civil war in England between the Royalists and the Commonwealth," wrote one editorialist, "it was said by Ludlow to Cromwell: 'King Charles' soldiers are men of honor—we cannot beat them.' 'Then,' said the Protector, 'I will set men of religion against his men of honor.' The result is in history, and this history is to be reproduced in the mad war commenced by the Cotton States. They, too, assume the invincibility of 'men of honor'; but the Commonwealth they assail will set men of principle against these straw men of honor."[58] The question of motive was key here; Confederates claimed the mantle of chivalric Cavaliers, but Northern men drew upon what they regarded as still more noble convictions. "The courage of the tyrant hating Puritans was sustained and rendered invincible by their conviction of the righteousness of their cause," another editor wrote, "and an unwavering trust in the Almighty; and with such odds on their side, it is no wonder that they gave daredevilism its coup de grace, and established the Commonwealth. In all similar contests the result will be the same."[59]

The debate over Southern honor, and how Northern men interpreted that culture, has preoccupied many historians. In some accounts, the vigor with which white Southerners presented themselves as descendants of the old Cavaliers induced fear and quailing among Northern soldiers.[60] For those who quavered at the prospect of Southern armies, history offered an antidote—Northern soldiers could martial their own version of honor, taking comfort from the lessons of the English Civil Wars. They could emulate what Thomas Macaulay called "root and branch" men, who drove the Parliamentary army to success.[61] One Northern journal bragged that "our Roundhead type of character is very hard to deal with when once inflamed." This account emphasized not the zealotry of radicalism but rather a humble strength. "Our habitual industry becomes the channel of immense moral force in times of trial, and they who are accustomed to bear heavy burdens every day can bear up under loads that overwhelm prouder necks."[62]

A letter writer to the *Hartford Daily Courant* drew the lesson clearly: "We must imitate the conduct of Cromwell. The Parliament, in its controversy with King Charles, recruited its ranks at first with thousands of soldiers from the large cities. Four thousand Londoners enlisted in one day; but these levies were defeated again and again by the Cavaliers, till the stern and resolute Oliver rising in his seat demanded that they should go to the country and recruit from the God-fearing peasantry, who had been inured to the hardships of agricultural life." Then, the American analog: "Our cities have responded nobly; now let us go back to the plow-share and call for it to be turned into a sword, to be wielded by the stalwart arms of our rural population."[63] History offered both method and inspiration, though its eager call to turn plowshares into swords grimly presaged the all-consuming violence of the coming conflict.

The connection between Cromwell's army and the US Army was encouraged most explicitly when the American Tract Society published 50,000 copies of *The Soldier's Pocket Bible* and distributed them to Northern soldiers.[64] This was a reprint of a volume first published in 1643 and issued to Cromwell's army. The length of a short pamphlet (sixteen pages in one version), the *Pocket Bible* contained selected passages from the Old and New Testaments related to military service, organized under headings such as "A Soldier Must Put His Confidence in God's Wisdom and Strength," "A Soldier

Must Pray before He Goes to Fight," and "A Soldier Must Not Fear His Enemies." Some headings were proscriptive, for instance, "A Souldier Must Not Doe Wickedly." Although abolitionists regarded the *Pocket Bible* as evoking a Cromwellian devotion, its ubiquity and its use by Confederates suggests a wider, apolitical embrace. George Livermore, a Massachusetts lawyer, who owned an original copy, allowed the South Carolina Tract Society to reproduce the pamphlet for Confederate armies.[65] The American Tract Society itself was nondenominational; the hope here was that Christianity would ameliorate the worst aspects of military violence. The pamphlet proliferated in Northern army camps. In southwestern Pennsylvania, a local community embraced the Puritans' civil war legacy with even more eagerness. The 100th Pennsylvania Regiment carried the moniker "The Round Head Regiment." The region from which men were recruited was settled by "Round Heads of the English Revolution and by Scotch Irish Covenanters," explained the regimental historian, "men who had followed Cromwell, whose leading characteristics had been a devotion to the principles of liberty of person and of conscience."[66]

Other Northerners used the analogy to encourage a hard war after the evident failures of the rosewater strategy in 1861. Orville Browning, an Illinois Republican, exemplified the broad application of seventeenth-century history to the American conflict. From the floor of the US Senate, Browning encouraged a short, hard war: "If this is *war*, let it be war in earnest. Let it be quick, fierce, and terrible. It is both mercy and economy to make it so." To prove his point, Browning quoted from Henry Hallam's well-read *Constitutional History of England*. "Hallam's Constitutional History, takes occasion to comment upon a revolution which, more than two centuries ago, brought to the block a tyrant whose oppressions could not break the spirit of the English people," Browning declared, positioning himself strongly in support of the Parliamentary cause. The relevant passage from Hallam criticized the "half measures" of the first generation of Parliamentary leaders: "A resolute leader might have brought it to a close in a month. . . . If there be any truth established by the universal experience of nations, it is this: that to carry the spirit of peace into war is a weak and cruel policy. . . . By their moderation many lives and much property had been wasted." Browning carried Hallam's point into the American conflict: "Let us be admonished by the teachings of history, and learn wisdom from their lessons of past ages."[67] Macaulay, despite his evenhandedness on the English Civil Wars themselves, provided valuable support on this front as well. In frustration with the timidity of West Point generals, one periodical relied on "[Macaulay's] historical criticisms [which] strongly contrasts the failures of the Generals trained to arms during the English civil war, with the success of those who had emerged from civil life to lead armies." The paper's conclusion from this doctrine anticipated the vigorous war of Ulysses S. Grant and William T. Sherman to come in 1863, by quoting Macaulay's approval for the style of the Parliamentarians: "[Parliamentary Gen. John Hampden] *knew that the essence of war is violence, and that moderation in war is imbecility.*"[68]

In truth, Lincoln struggled to define and characterize the military struggle as an insurrection, a rebellion, or a revolution and, as a result, to fashion a consistent policy on how to treat the enemy. The issue was not semantic; identifying Confederates as "public enemies" (that is, legitimate soldiers in an enemy army) guaranteed them protections that classifying them as criminals or guerrillas would not. Lincoln never denied the right to revolution in principle—he regarded the American Revolution as the font of nationhood—but he regarded secession as destructive of that nation. Lincoln and Northern moderates such as Cassius Clay embraced a model from the English Civil Wars that focused on republicanism and the expansion of liberty within an institutional setting, an approach at odds with the bolder vision of social reform through war that abolitionists endorsed.[69] To do this, they had to interpret the earlier conflict with subtlety. Where Confederates saw only two sides—a noble king wrongfully killed and a destructive Puritanism—Northerners parsed the politics of the English Civil Wars era to reveal a third path, something akin to the whig interpretation described earlier by Michael Braddick. One of the key moments in the English conflict came with the creation of the New Model Army in 1645 and its increasingly prominent role in the country's politics. One of its leading historians concludes, "The rise of the New Model Army was the harbinger of the emergence of radical politics that transformed civil war into revolution."[70] As the next chapter will show, this was precisely what Northern conservatives most feared. Lincoln, too, zealously guarded the civil-military divide. The army, in American practice, is supposed to remain under civilian control and not shape politics. During the Civil War, the US Army never took on anything like the political role of the New Model Army, but there is no denying that Lincoln drew support from the army and that military necessity enabled a more radical agenda than conservatives wanted, if less radical than abolitionists hoped.[71]

One of the recent criticisms of Lincoln's way of waging war was the extraordinary latitude granted by the principle of "military necessity."[72] In 1863, the US Army published a set of rules governing the behavior of its army in the field. Known as the Lieber Code, after its primary author, political philosopher Francis Lieber, the code outlawed many categories of behavior by US soldiers.[73] It also included this circular loophole: "Military necessity, as understood by modern civilized nations, consists in the necessity of those measures which are indispensable for securing the ends of the war, and which are lawful according to the modern law and usages of war."[74] In short, actions necessary for victory were just, provided they did not explicitly violate the laws of war. For critics, then and now, the elasticity and self-referentiality of this phrasing seemed to license a wide range of unethical behavior. Lieber's phrasing reflected Lincoln's own beliefs, not necessarily about military action but politics. Despite what Northern conservatives said, Lincoln appreciated the extreme demands imposed on the state by civil war and sought to reconcile those within the American constitutional tradition.

Northern journals leaned into the connection between the Union and the original group of English reformers. In the first case, Lincoln had to be called to action against his natural preferences for peace and order. In the same way, explained a San Francisco paper, "the founders of the 'Commonwealth'—that one grand interruption of the long course of monarchical rule in England—were compelled by the popular voice to shed blood, and that the royal blood of the realm." Lincoln claimed not to control events but to have been controlled by them. Similarly, "Cromwell was urged to many a deed of rigor and cruelty by the stern necessities of the times, and those necessities were created by the overpowering will of the people, upon whose shoulders his government stood."[75] As the war advanced, Northern writers generalized and analogized with even greater vigor. In 1863, the *Western Reserve Chronicle* of Ohio lauded, "The cause of Cromwell was that of humanity, Christianity and freedom. He and his old covenanters fought for civil and religious liberty. The cavaliers fought to uphold a corrupt, cruel and despotic dynasty, who favored aristocracy and privileged classes, just as the southern slaveholding despots and aristocrats of our day do." Ignoring the historical changes in republicanism in the intervening century, the commonality of republican governments fighting for survival bound Americans backward in time. "This war now raging between the North and South is but another struggle in the world's history between the supporters of aristocracy and the friends of republicanism."[76]

White Southerners plunged the country into civil war acutely aware of the historical precedents for preemptive action. The sad fate of Ireland overrun and the Irish deprived of their land and freedom spurred would-be Confederates to action. So, too, it inspired Northerners, who saw in this history a precedent for the vigorous and violent suppression of a threat to the nation's sovereignty. For both sides in the war, history's lessons propelled them into bloody conflict.

The Language of War

> A battle was a distillation of time: many years of preparation and decades of innovation and change were squeezed into a clash of very short duration. And when it was over the impact radiated backwards and forwards through time, determining the future and even, in a sense, changing the past.
>
> AMITAV GHOSH, *Flood of Fire*

In the US Civil War, the North possessed advantages in finances, diplomacy, manpower, and matériel with which to fight. Confederates, like most insurgent powers, found themselves at a disadvantage in the rhetoric of war. Jefferson Davis needed to rally his people, so he and other Confederate leaders demonized the Yankees in ways that built on prewar sectionalist language.[1] Rhetoric-making was not restricted to official leaders. The press (especially in Richmond) did as much to fuel popular antagonism toward the North as anything happening in the Confederate White House. The *Richmond Daily Dispatch*'s relentless arguments for cultural difference provided no room for compromise, as clash-of-civilizations arguments never do. Rhetoric can encourage people to move ahead of their leaders—in the Confederate case, many white Southerners came to regard reunion as a fate worse than death and so committed themselves to a war that generated exceptional harm and suffering. On the rhetorical battlefront, Confederates reached first for the easiest analogy: Abraham Lincoln as the tyrant Oliver Cromwell. Like the rest of their language, this analogy left Confederates with little hope except for Lincoln's death.[2]

Northerners, although they often disagreed with one another, enjoyed a wider array of rhetorical options. Abolitionists took advantage of the unpredictable nature of warfare and of the legal elasticity generated by war to press Lincoln and the US Army to support emancipation and eventually the full abolition of slavery in the Thirteenth Amendment. Lincoln's initial goal when he called up the militia on April 15, 1861, was to restore the relationship between the seceding states and the federal government. Abolitionists, meanwhile, sought to compel his administration to recognize the centrality of slavery to secession and adopt emancipation as its policy. Abolitionists deployed every argument they could muster—ethical, religious, legal, diplomatic, political, and economic. They found the seventeenth century useful for reminding Lincoln of precedents for radicalization. Rather than shy away from the revolutionary changes of that earlier struggle, abolitionists hoped it could be a model for their conflict. They assumed perhaps the most surprising position of any political community in the Civil War. Many radicals identified as pacifists in the years before the Civil War.[3] In addition to opposing violence in principle, they perceived the US Army as friendly to slavery, most recently in the war against Mexico, which expanded US territory to the south. The advent of the sectional conflict and the possibility that the military conflict might enable emancipation changed that position.

Over the course of the Civil War, Northern radicals transformed into the chief proponents of a vigorous war.[4] Because emancipation would only happen with a prolonged conflict, they supported the escalation of Union military policy beyond Lincoln's narrow goal of reunion. In doing this, they marshaled the example of Cromwell, both as an effective military leader and as someone who used military power to reshape English society and politics. Much to the horror of Confederates, radicals explicitly endorsed the Parliamentary model to bring a hard war to the American South.

In both the Northern radicals' and Confederates' cases, Americans' uses of the past were less intellectual and more emotional than they had been as Northern moderates evaluated historical examples to understand the nature of civil war and state sovereignty. Both radicals and Confederates relied on written history, but they also read those histories selectively, crafting a memory of the past that suited their present purposes. We profit little from denouncing these people as disingenuous. They believed the analogies they promulgated from the history they read. Instead, their experiences should help us better appreciate the rhetorical power and meaning of even a dynamic and contested past. The vast differences in historical interpretation between Confederates and Northern radicals did not lead them to seek a common ground. To the contrary, their fight over the past fueled a stronger sense of just how alien these former countrymen seemed in the midst of war.

KING ABRAHAM I

When Northern newspapers compared the US Army to the New Model Army, it only inflamed Confederate fears. The original New Model Army was organized to purge the cautious politics that hamstrung the army in its confrontations with Charles's Royalist troops. In this effort, Cromwell successfully remade a nonideological institution into one galvanized by ideas. As a leading scholar notes, "In union with a radical minority in the Commons and the Lords, the army was the engine that powered the revolutionary momentum of 1648–9."[5] No American parallel existed in 1861. The officer corps of the regular army included no political radicals, and historically, the army favored slaveholders' interests.[6] Although Lincoln did not initiate changes in personnel or training, Radical Republicans did. In late 1861, they established the Joint Committee on the Conduct of the War to shape how the North prosecuted the conflict. Chaired by congressional Radicals, the joint committee stood outside the regular congressional committees, which allowed it wide latitude to investigate whatever its managers disliked.[7] In the case of its chairman, Ohio senator Benjamin Wade, this meant scrutiny of what Radicals' regarded as indecisive or incompetent military leaders. In particular, they wanted a more direct attack on slavery. Accomplishing this required the army to adopt emancipation as a war policy or, working from the ground up, to replace proslavery officers with abolitionist ones. Radicals pursued both tracks, with newspapers covering investigations, hearings, and congressional speeches in close detail.

Confederates, always eager readers of Northern papers, viewed the changes with rising concern and treated radicals' aspirations as established Northern practice. As in the war's opening moments, they sought recourse in seventeenth-century analogies to explain Union intent. The *Daily Richmond Whig* compared the administration's plans to "Cromwell's invasion of Ireland [which] was conducted on precisely the plans, and with identically the same purposes which actuate our foes. The reader will find the same treachery mark[s] every step of his progress." White Southerners feared most that Northerners might be planning to emulate Cromwell's postwar settlement. After military victory, the "whole kingdom [of Ireland] was surveyed, and the number of acres taken with the quality of them. . . . In this manner was the whole kingdom divided between the soldiers and the adventurers of money." Quoting from recent history texts, the *Whig* predicted a similar fate for the South: "The seizure of our country, schools, pulpits, with every State and local office by the most vicious and vindictive of our enemies, the lawless mixture of negroes, foreigners, and fanatics would so transform our once happy country that the doom of the poor Irish would be indeed an act of grace."[8] Abandoning the usual intracity newspaper competition, the *Richmond Daily Dispatch* agreed with the rival paper: "The most instructive lesson . . . is that quoted by the *Richmond Whig*, in reference to Cromwell's invasion of Ireland." The *Dispatch*, operating within the Cavalier-Puritan paradigm, identified a lineage of malfeasance: "The history of the whole Puritan race is one which gives no glimpse of hope that when the property of their neighbors is at their mercy justice or compassion will ever induce them to forego the opportunity of its appropriation."[9] According to the *Dispatch*, not even post-rebellion Ireland could predict the horrors that Yankees planned to impose.

It was not just land that the Union threatened. Despite its recent birth, Confederate propagandists already rued the nationalism that military defeat was sure to crush. If they were not vigilant, the Confederacy could join the ranks of other "oppressed nationalities." A North Carolina newspaper, drawing on floor debate in the Confederate Congress, observed, "As there are already certain nations miserably cumbering the earth, which have been overrun and are now occupied and governed by another people; and as the features of that unhappy sort of case are always, and in all ages and climates, almost the same, it is easy to survey it as a finished piece." The two most resonant examples for nineteenth-century Americans remained Poland and Ireland: "Several generations, in the one case, in the other several centuries, have passed by since those nations were said to be conquered." Returning to the 1650s, the article relied on the Earl of Clarendon, author of *The History of the Great Rebellion*, to anchor the discussion of the suppression of nationality.[10]

Union general William T. Sherman endorsed the same sentiment using the same analogy. "Many, many people," he explained, "with less pertinacity than the South, have been wiped out of national existence." Sherman, too, referred to the seventeenth century: "When the English army occupied Ireland, then in a state of revolt, the inhabitants were actually driven into foreign lands, and actually dispossessed of their property and a new population introduced." Sherman bragged that he "knows thousands and millions of good people who, at simple notice, would come to North Alabama and accept the elegant houses and plantations there."[11] Confederate papers reprinted Sherman's comments, hoping to generate outrage for what they regarded as his transgression. Yet another Richmond paper offered the historical parallel as proof of Northern perfidy: "It is a kind of transaction really unknown amongst civilized nations for many an age, and of which the last example in Europe was the ravage committed by Queen Elizabeth's generals in Ireland, and subsequent confiscation of the country in favour of English soldiers."[12]

While Union officers such as Sherman and abolitionists drew Confederate ire, Lincoln absorbed the majority of their historically informed wrath. Recalling the political philosophy given its modern shape by the English Civil Wars, a Confederate paper bemoaned, "The very name of Republican has been immolated by those who claim to be the only Republicans alive." The specific charge in this instance was that Lincoln greedily amassed power, using the draft as a tool of manpower control (an ironic charge given that the Confederacy had imposed its own draft nearly a year before the United States). For comparison, the paper positioned Lincoln alongside the most infamous tyrants in history: "The Yankee Congress has rendered him completely independent of all legislation whatever. It has, in other words, made him a Dictator . . . as complete as Cromwell was in England."[13] Confederate newspapers made frequent recourse to the analogy. During Christmas 1863, a Richmond journal lamented the sale of a biography of "that hideous Puritan, Oliver Cromwell," that appeared in bookstore windows. "We are surprised to see that this choice volume is not accompanied by the Life of Abraham Lincoln and the Life of the late lamented John Brown, whose soul is now marching on in the track of Cromwell." "Three kindred spirits," the paper concluded grimly.[14] Not so in the North, where newspapers gleefully reprinted reports of the seasonal sale of the new volume.

Confederates predicted that the Cromwellian Lincoln would surely wreak havoc on the South. Rejecting the whiggish vision of linear and progressive history, the *Richmond Daily Dispatch* "observed that there is nothing new in the moral world under the sun, because the changing theatre of human events exhibits, in different ages, under every different combination of human affairs, the certain operation of the same passions, desires and vices." As evidence, the newspaper considered the English Civil Wars: "When the English nation, in 1642, raised the standard of revolt against Charles I., their brains ran mad with visions of republican freedom. They as little anticipated the actual result as did the North in 1861. They did not expect that taxation was to be quadrupled, personal freedom destroyed, government carried on solely by the major generals of Cromwell, and themselves made the victims of the most crushing military oppression."[15]

As the *Dispatch*'s framing here reveals, Confederates and Unionists disagreed not just over their hopes for the future of the United States; they disagreed about the nature of history. Where Northerners, especially radicals, believed in the progressive, linear development of history, Confederates endorsed a vision of cyclical history.[16] They saw little chance for the progress so often lauded by Northern reformers and instead focused on man's unavoidable propensity for sin. Cyclical perspectives on the past contain a healthy dose of fatalism, which can be a dangerous thing for an underdog in war.

Left without a sturdier intellectual anchor, many white Southerners drifted. By the end of the war, the *Dispatch* expected only the worst. Nothing white Southerners had seen "afford[s] any reason to expect that the consequences of our failure would be less disastrous nor deplorable to individuals, to property and to society, than have been the consequences of defeat, without exception, to vanquished peoples." In fact, white Southerners anticipated worse. "We believe that the dispositions of England to Ireland and India, of Austria to Hungary, and of Russia to Poland, are benevolent and merciful compared to those of the Yankee Government to the Southern States." White Southerners had more to fear from Northerners because they were driven by "the fanaticism of Cromwell."[17]

AN AMERICAN CROMWELL

Abolitionists were a well-read group. Their public speeches and newspaper pieces frequently referred to European and world history. They knew the history of the English Civil Wars quite well. In particular, they saw the whole arc of the civil war era in England. The rebellions that created so much turmoil in the 1640s had mostly subsided by the early 1650s. Parliament institutionalized Cromwell's authority by appointing him Lord Protector, having previously abolished the monarchy. Charles II had moved abroad, though Royalist supporters hoped that he would return. When Cromwell died in 1658 he was succeeded by his son Richard, who lacked the skill to hold together the Commonwealth. Under new leadership, parliament invited Charles II back to England, and he assumed the throne in 1660. Although many of the policies enacted under Cromwell (particularly in regard to England's foreign policy) remained, the reimposition of monarchy and the end of the republic frustrated radical reformers. Notwithstanding the differences in the political structure of seventeenth-century England and nineteenth-century America, the lesson was clear: Social or political changes enacted during war must be permanently impressed into the structure of governance.

The most important manifestation of this process was the successful effort to amend the US Constitution to outlaw slavery—replacing Lincoln's wartime expedient of a proclamation of emancipation with the Thirteenth Amendment. Charles Sumner, always alert to historical echoes explained, "Ours is another Reformation and another Revolution. The attempted revolution for Slavery we meet by a counter revolution for Liberty."[18] Conservative critics understood the radicals' plans and condemned them in equally historical language: "The Roundhead of Cromwell's time talked of God's anger, and against the sin of Popery, just as his imitator now does of God's judgment upon the sin of slavery."[19] In the short term, radicals knew that they could not leave policy changes to chance.

There was nothing inevitable about the conflict moving in a progressive fashion, even with a Republican commander in chief.[20] To the contrary, wars often empower conservatism, strengthening the ability of governments to restrict speech, travel, and civil liberties. While wars are ongoing, however, it can be difficult to track the direction of political movement. The historian Charles Royster described the American Civil War as "anomalous" in the sense that Americans themselves could barely understand what they did. Convinced of their country's exceptionalism, the violence of the conflict dragged them back into history.[21] Still, their steadfast reluctance to acknowledge complicity in starting and escalating the war revealed how easy it was for war to become an autonomous force. Critics of the radicals read the same history and worried about how people could co-opt military violence for political gain. The *New York Herald* warned, "Past history should teach the important lesson to the people of the South that every step beyond the bounds of moderation must be disastrous to their own interests, and accomplish, by their own hands, the objects of their enemies."[22] Today, this passage reads as an uncannily accurate prediction of slavery's end.

Black abolitionists read English history carefully as well and drew a similar cautionary tale about the fate of radical change.[23] In one of the most devastating uses of this history, the abolitionist H. Ford Douglas denounced the Republican Party for its endorsement of white supremacy. He hurled the model of the English Civil Wars back at the Republicans, who congratulated themselves for imitating it. "Three hundred years ago, your English ancestors were opposed by the bloody Stuarts. You said the king had no right to violate your rights and trample on all law and justice. Charles the First replied that he would have his will, that the king could do no wrong. So you beheaded Charles the First." This tradition continued in the New World. "Afterward, your fathers came to New England, and again made battle upon the despotism of those same despotic kings of England. And you rose up against the power of George III and established the government of 1776." But whatever that cost, it did not produce any real freedom. "You have no true ideas of government or of law," Douglas thundered, "no conception, with all your boasts, of the true ideas of liberty."[24]

Radicals, more than other political communities in the North, anticipated what the dynamism of war allowed. With a moment of political possibility created by the conflict, Wendell Phillips and other leading abolitionists worked to create what Douglas termed "a true idea of liberty." First, doing so required opposing compromise. As Frederick Douglass, another Black abolitionist, worried in the war's opening moments, white Americans usually protected slavery when it was challenged. "Through many long and weary months," he wrote in May 1861, "the American people have been on the mountain with the wily tempter, and have been liable at any moment of weakness to grant a new lease of life to slavery." Douglass despaired that the North would grant what he called "demoralizing concessions to the insatiate Slave Power."[25] Abolitionists bemoaned this practice throughout the war. "Cromwell would have hung SLIDELL and MASON," one complained during the Trent affair, a naval dilemma between the United States and Britain, "but we, always compromising, consulted and yielded."[26]

Conservatives recast those concessions as necessary "compromises" that ensured the stability of American politics. With secession, white Southerners removed themselves from this conversation, but Northern Democrats (called "Doughfaces" by their political opponents for their willingness to be manipulated by the proslavery faction) participated on their behalf, obstructing Federal efforts to emancipate enslaved people, even when doing so offered the Union clear military advantage. Lincoln's awkward efforts to placate the North's diverse political communities drew radicals' ire throughout the war. As a result, abolitionists adopted an adversarial posture and advocated increasingly radical changes.

Their trajectory, they were no doubt pleased to see, was foreshadowed by the movement of their hero John Milton during the 1640s. Milton began the conflict as a Presbyterian but grew frustrated with early military failures and with Parliament's alliance with the Scots, which included an agreement to impose a Presbyterian Church on England, a feature that Milton objected to because it violated freedom of conscience. By 1649, "Milton was fiercely and openly anti-Presbyterian, and in *The Tenure of Kings and Magistrates* he denounced the Scots, the Presbyterians, and the Covenant—and made a bonfire of constitutionalism."[27] William Lloyd Garrison's days of making a literal bonfire of founding documents were over (Garrison had burned a copy of the Constitution at a rally in 1854), but American reformers sought a similarly radical revision of the country's fundamental charter. As historian Daniel Aaron has observed, "For any American who viewed secession as a 'foul conspiracy' against a God-ordained Union, Milton was the ideal War-laureate. His militancy, religious fervor, and rhetoric, and his Manichean imagery explained and illuminated the Secession War."[28] Milton's experience drove abolitionists to pursue deep change. "It takes time to abolish a system like slavery," Wendell Phillips argued. "It is no affair of a day. Great Britain attempted to abolish aristocracy in the days of Cromwell; and I think she gave it a death blow at the battle of Naseby, and on the scaffold of Charles the First; but it has been two hundred years dying." Turning back to America he concluded, "Whenever slavery is abolished, it will take a long time to do it. It has got so inwoven into the very heart of the institutions of the country as to make it hard to kill."[29]

Taking this step required the courage to cast off even law itself. Ralph Waldo Emerson, one of the forebears of the abolitionist civil war that Phillips championed, called for this decisive action against slavery in an 1851 jeremiad against the Fugitive Slave Act.[30] "To make good the cause of Freedom, you must draw off from all foolish trust in others, You must be citadels and warriors yourselves, declarations of Independence, the charter, the battle and the victory," Emerson wrote. Like radicals before and after him, Emerson grounded his appeal in the example of the original Puritans. "Cromwell said, 'We can only resist the superior training of the King's soldiers, by enlisting godly men.' And no man has a right to hope that the laws . . . will defend him from the contamination of slaves another day until he has made up his mind that he will not owe his protection to the laws . . . but to his own sense and spirit."[31]

In the English context, radicals came to see the necessity of extraconstitutional change. As one historian notes, "It began to seem that in opposing particular policies [seventeenth-century] activists were going beyond reform, and in fact were themselves bending the constitution, indulging in a dangerous populism and entertaining, for example, religious radicalism."[32] This process culminated in the execution of Charles I. Historian Ian Gentiles explains, "Killing the king had been an act of revolutionary justice, which means that it was a travesty of justice. The only thing that could be said in its defence was, as Cromwell later reminded people, that it was not 'done in a corner,' but in the full light of day."[33] There was no legal precedent for killing a king in English history—it happened outside existing law. This insecure legal foundation enabled a later Parliament to reverse course and invite a new king back home. Nineteenth-century Americans knew this awkward history. As Greg Downs notes, Civil War Republicans observed that "Jacobins and Cromwell's supporters had not found a safe place to terminate their revolutionary situations and thus had lost first control and then their republics."[34]

For his part, Lincoln clung to constitutional processes. He would have agreed with a wartime letter from an American to "an English friend," explaining why secession was unnecessary: "Indeed, violent changes of our political system are needless, and they must always be wrong, because this system contains in itself ample provision for changes being made peacefully, whenever the requisite number of the people desire them to be made."[35] Even as the war progressed, Lincoln pursued lawful change, which is why he promoted the Thirteenth Amendment with such vigor. Still, as Downs has observed, even this process occurred irregularly. "Republicans," Downs writes, "used military force to enact a constitutional revolution by coercing rebel states into ratifying new amendments that fundamentally transformed the Constitution."[36] This attention to the process of how the Constitution changed (not just the substance of that change) reveals an important continuity between the two conflicts. Unlike the radicals of the seventeenth century, who trusted to fate that their changes would last, nineteenth-century radicals embedded them within the nation's organic law.[37]

The radicalism of Northern abolitionists assumed a very particular face during the Civil War: that of Oliver Cromwell. Beginning in the 1840s, with Thomas Carlyle's popular edition of Cromwell's speeches and new biographies, and accelerating significantly once the war started, Cromwell became a model for decisive action.[38] *The Liberator* endorsed Cromwell's willingness to take action against the king as inspiration for the war against slavery. "When Charles I. was destroying England," the paper observed, "in such style as provoked resistance and led to civil war, the rescuers of the nation were greatly embarrassed and weakened by the influence of a superstitious reverence for his 'sacred majesty.' . . . There is prevalent in this country a similar feeling towards slavery, which for so many years has officiated as our sacred majesty." In response, the paper urged Northerners to emulate Cromwell, who "shocked timid people by declaring that he would not hesitate to kill the

Abolitionists embraced the radicalism of Oliver Cromwell's legacy, while conservatives regarded him as a symbol of excess.
Cromwell, frontispiece from Headley, *Life of Oliver Cromwell*.
Courtesy of Louisiana State University Library.

king in battle."[39] An English minister and friend of the abolitionists preached to similar effect, comparing "the evils which the friends of Abolition in these days had to contend with, to the difficulties which had to be overcome by the Parliamentary party in the days of Cromwell." The minister "reminded them how that great commander had rebuked the lukewarmness of his followers, and exhorted them to energy and action."[40] Cromwell himself offered guidance on how and when to push beyond the boundaries of domestic law and common practice. *The Liberator* approvingly quoted Cromwell on this question: "'If nothing should ever be done,' said he, 'but what is "according to law," the throat of the nation may be cut while we send for some to make a law! ... When matters of necessity come, then, without guilt extraordinary remedies may be applied.'"[41] Emancipation was exactly the "extraordinary remedy" that abolitionists encouraged Lincoln to adopt.

Unlike Northern moderates, bona fide abolitionists such as Wendell Phillips showed no hesitation about using Cromwell as their model for the war they hoped to see. These commentators saw in Cromwell's moralistic crusade to purify the church and state an exemplar for what the North could do in the Civil War. In a midwar speech at New York's Cooper Union, Phillips denounced the continued timidity of the Lincoln administration and celebrated Cromwell as an inspiration. For the North to win the war, "it is to be done as England did in 1640, by getting rid gradually, man by man, of those who don't believe in progress, but believe in the past." Phillips's main targets were West Point–trained generals such as Henry Halleck, because he believed this clique had cowed Lincoln. "Cromwell never succeeded," Phillips declared, "until the Long Parliament sloughed off every man that believed in the lords and left nothing but democrats behind. We shall never succeed until we slough off every thing that believes in the past, and bring to the front every thing that believes there is but one purpose—that is, to save the Union on the basis of liberty."[42] Phillips admired the characteristics that Joel Headley had used to define Cromwell in his 1848 biography—"his bold and decided action, his rapid movement, his rigid discipline, and boiling courage."[43] Phillips's zeal for emancipation sanctioned even an endorsement of Cromwell's antidemocratic practices with Parliament.[44] Phillips shared his message with more than just the community of abolitionists. In addition to tirelessly writing, he spoke across the country. Following a March 1862 White House visit with Lincoln, Phillips traveled to Cincinnati, Chicago, Milwaukee, Madison, Detroit, and Cleveland.[45] At each stop he spoke to large crowds with attendant press coverage.

In radicals' early war writings, they sometimes deployed the English Civil Wars as a kind of shield—aligning themselves with the tradition of English liberty and rights against Confederate usurpers. The *Pine and Palm*, a Black abolitionist newspaper, referred to secession as "this black rebellion of the oligarchy ... against the Government ... [and] against Government *in its principles*." Because Confederates had struck the first blow, abolitionists could claim to be defending law and order. "When Cromwell routed the forces of Charles I, and established the glorious Commonwealth of England ... justice sanctioned the deeds, and the world partook of the benefits."[46] Over the course of the US Civil War, abolitionists interpreted the Parliamentary cause in a more expansive way, identifying Cromwell not as someone operating within the English tradition but as someone remaking it. They hoped for the same in America.

Phillips referred to Cromwell constantly.[47] Bemoaning the slow pace of the North's Democratic generals in 1862, he recalled, "I believe that when Oliver Cromwell was asked, 'Would you shoot the king, if you got him?' and old Noll replied, 'Yes, quicker than anybody else,' he touched the nucleus of the difficulty in the English Commonwealth." This was a method Phillips could endorse. "Now, if you were to ask McClellan," he explained, "'Would you shoot slavery?' he would say, 'No; I am for settling this quarrel on the old basis.' On the contrary, if you asked Frank Sigel, or Hunter, or Saxon, or Frémont, the answer would be 'Yes, quicker than anything else, and thank God for the chance.'" Phillips believed that "it was only when our army comes under the command of such Generals, we shall have just such successes as the Parliamentary army had in England when it got under Cromwell and Ireton—men who understood the depth of the chasm that threatened to engulph the nation, and were willing to bridge it."[48]

Theodore Tilton, another prominent New Englander, thought the same. "We ought ... to leap into the van and issue a decree of emancipation. Oliver Cromwell, had he lived today, would have marched to Richmond, driven the rebel Congress from their Capital, and nailed a proclamation of emancipation upon the door of their legislative hall."[49] Conservatives identified the same parallel but regarded it as evidence of Phillips's corruption. A Democratic paper lamented that "in reading the sublime pages of Paradise Lost, we must forget its author, or we should hear, amid the seraphic harmonies of Paradise, that voice which was raised only in behalf of anarchy and crime." Americans had long admired Milton's poetry, but his support of Cromwell's regime invalidated all that. "We must ever regard as a monster to be forever execrated, a man of great genius, of refined and cultivated taste, who debased those fair gifts of Nature, by hooting on the ignorant and fickle mob, against the respectable part of society. And such a man was John Milton—without parallel, until modern times furnished a Wendell Phillips."[50]

Emancipation was part of the broader Northern war strategy adopted in late 1862. That approach abandoned the rosewater strategy, created by mostly Democratic generals in 1861. The Union's hard war strategy evolved in response to the Confederacy's successful resistance and targeted Confederate infrastructure and resources.[51] The strategy never involved directing lethal violence against noncombatants, but it authorized the US Army to consume or destroy foodstuffs, animals, and facilities such as mills, which created hardship for everyone in the South.[52] One dimension of the English Civil Wars included an infamous example of an even more violent hard war, when Cromwell invaded Ireland in 1649 and massacred surrendering soldiers (and noncombatants) at Drogheda and Wexford.[53]

The Irish Rebellion in 1641 remained foremost in English minds, and nineteenth-century historians justified Cromwell's conduct with reference to the nature of the Irish Rebellion, perceived through the lens of accounts like that of John Temple. George Brodie, in his *Constitutional History of the British Empire*, an otherwise whiggish account that criticized Charles's misconduct and justified Parliament's defense of the people's rights, nevertheless defended Cromwell's actions at Drogheda. The horrors of what Catholics had done in the conflict's opening moments (or, more accurately, the misrepresentations and exaggerations of those moments) meant that "the gates of mercy were barred against them in every breast."[54] Knowing this history (and approving of it) facilitated that process of hardening one's heart against the enemy in the American case. The Vermont-based *Manchester Journal* made the case for escalation in a fall 1862 editorial: "If the rebels cannot be conciliated they shall be conquered, and if they cannot be conquered they shall be subjugated, and if they cannot be subjugated they shall be rooted out from the land." The sequence advocated by the paper exceeded anything considered (or implemented) by Lincoln, but the editors felt empowered to offer it based on their reading of the past. "Our war to the South shall be what Cromwell's war was to Ireland—a war of extermination. It takes a Republic some time to raise the arm of its power, but when that arm falls, it crushes."[55]

When Wendell Phillips and other Northern radicals leaned on Cromwell's history to advocate for a hard war, they did not ignore his Irish campaigns. Although modern readers might imagine that Phillips's progressive politics would predispose him toward a dovish military policy, Phillips endorsed Cromwell's bloody campaigns in Ireland. "Such a war," he wrote, "[as the American one] finds no parallel nearer than that of Cromwell and the Irish, when victory meant extermination."[56] Nineteenth-century readers could, according to one paper, "call to mind . . . the atrocious butchery of Cromwell, at Drogheda, in Ireland, where, by his own confession, he treacherously put man, woman and child to the sword after the surrender of the town."[57] Another paper argued that "'extermination of Ireland' was the motto written upon his banner."[58] Before the war, most abolitionists professed nonviolence, but the opportunity to rebuild the South on Northern principles was too alluring to resist, even if it meant bloodshed. Federals could use war to remake Southern society, as Phillips believed Cromwell had accomplished in Ireland.

Seen in retrospect, the Puritan antipathy toward Catholics anticipated the abolitionist hatred of slavery. For Northern conservatives, this was their chief failing: "The grand keynote of the Puritan is, that 'slavery' was the cause of this war, and that as men and Christians, we should extirpate it."[59] Both seventeenth- and nineteenth-century Puritans drew strength from a sense of justice and righteousness—a crusading zeal that can blind people to their own extremism.[60] One Cromwell scholar observes that "what drove Cromwell and many other parliamentarians on in this crisis was a profound sense of righteous indignation against the Irish."[61] New England author Nathaniel Hawthorne, a critic of his home region, identified the same flaw in his neighbors. Hawthorne rejected "their self-righteousness, their fanaticism, and their scarcely concealed bloodlust."[62]

Abolitionists believed that Cromwell's willingness to use terror and murder to subjugate Ireland bolstered their arguments for a Northern campaign that would emancipate slaves and poor white Southerners alike, remaking the region in their image. According to a prominent commentator in *The Liberator*, such acts of imperialism were both common and beneficial. "All waves of civilization come from abroad to any people. Every nation under heaven has been conquered, over and over again. . . . Cromwell, too, another workman in that line, dealt in the same way with Ireland and Scotland, and for doing his work boldly and well, his name will live forever."[63] Slaveholders, another Northerner wrote, "see that the power of the U.S. Government is too mighty for them to resist; and that nothing but submission can restore to them peace, comfort, or prosperity. But they loathe the idea of submission; they are proud, and claim to be untameable." The solution was for the Union to adopt "the course which Cromwell, and afterwards William of Orange, pursued toward Ireland. Severity of the sternest kind brought that country to its senses; and similar severity would have similar effects upon the South."[64] As the US Civil War extended in time, the example of England's scourging of Ireland bolstered the decision of Ulysses S. Grant and Lincoln to bring a punishing logistical war to the South.

The violence inherent in these calls for rooting out Confederates demands some explanation. How could abolitionists and other Northern radicals propose such an apocalyptic style of warfare? Lingering nativism among abolitionists may have made it easier to perceive Cromwell's actions in Ireland as necessary for the South. Historians often segregate the story of antebellum nativism within its formal political contours. The American Party (the "Know Nothings" in common parlance) occupied what proved to be a temporary position within the rapidly shifting partisan landscape of the pre–Civil War years. Organized around the exclusion of immigrants, especially Catholic ones, from civic life, the American Party was eclipsed by the Republican Party within a few years. To their credit, most Republicans repudiated the noxious xenophobia that drove the Know Nothings, though splitting that party took years of careful planning and effort, and many people continued to distrust Catholics.[65] But the disappearance of a formal anti-immigrant political party did not erase the nativism that energized many white voters in the mid-1850s.

Most historians of abolitionism argue that reformers rejected nativism because it contradicted their core belief in individual liberty. As one of the movement's prominent historians explains, "Most abolitionists, like most evangelical Protestants, harbored deep suspicion of the international Catholic hierarchy, the religion's formalistic liturgy, and the solid anti-abolitionism of Irish immigrants. Yet they agreed with the Republican opponents of nativism that discrimination against Catholics or foreigners would constitute a fundamental violation of the free-labor individualism which lay at the heart of the party's ideology."[66]

Historians of Catholicism in the United States are not so sanguine. John T. McGreevy, one of the foremost chroniclers of Catholic life in modern America, concludes, "A powerful strain of anti-Catholicism shaped the antislavery movement."[67] Protestant reformers found structural similarities between the two systems that demanded their joint elimination. For instance, an Ohio abolitionist observed, "In this country, popery finds its appropriate ally in the institution of slavery. They are both kindred systems. One enslaves the mind, the other both mind and body. Both deny the Bible to those under their control—both discourage free inquiry."[68] The largest community of Catholics in the United States—the recent Irish immigrants—felt the sentiment lingered. Historian Angela Murphy concludes, "Irish Catholic suspicions of Protestant evangelism, out of which the antislavery movement in America grew, contributed to their refusal to join with the abolitionists."[69] A leading Irish politician, Daniel O'Connell, himself a dedicated antislavery person, believed "that there are amongst the Abolitionists many wicked and calumniating *enemies* of Catholicity and the Irish."[70]

Wendell Phillips, for his part, welcomed Irish Catholics into Boston in the 1840s, though his belief in the importance of not excluding residents did little to endear him to the newcomers. His biographer writes that Phillips's "glimpses of these immigrants certainly did not increase his respect for Irish culture.... Instead, Irish social behavior repelled him."[71] John Lothrop Motley, a boyhood friend of Phillips's, made his anti-Catholicism more public. Motley was a popular historian—author of the 1856 *The Rise of the Dutch Republic*—who served the Lincoln administration as an ambassador during the war. The *Dutch Republic* offered a whiggish interpretation of the Netherlands. It also included what a sympathetic reader referred to as "burning anti-Catholicism," directed mostly against the Spanish during the period of their rule in the Low Countries.[72] Irish immigrants to the United States were not blind to these attitudes. Tellingly, in an 1851 article, the *Boston Pilot* (an official diocesan publication) blamed the conflation of nativism and antislavery politics on "a recrudescence of Puritanism in its most extreme form."[73]

Those feelings did not dissipate during the Civil War. After 1861, Irish Americans and German Americans came under increased scrutiny by native-born Americans. German American units had the misfortune to experience several public military defeats, most infamous the collapse of the Army of the Potomac's Eleventh Corps during the battle of Chancellorsville. The result was a resurgence of the nativism directed at the "damn Dutch" so prominent in the 1840s and 1850s.[74] Irish Americans volunteered for military service in even higher numbers. They did not experience visible moments of public reckoning like the Eleventh Corps, but their political conservatism—and especially their hostility to emancipation and opposition to the draft—reinvigorated old suspicions about their loyalty.[75] As the war progressed, complaints from both inside the army and among civilians proliferated among Catholics. Many would have agreed with the Catholic Illinois private who complained that "the enemies of our race and religion are numerous everywhere."[76] Wartime nativism proved strongest in those places, such as Massachusetts and Pennsylvania, with old and distinguished traditions of abolition activity.[77]

Abolitionists did not adopt openly nativist language, but their opponents saw the same spirit at work. Democrats identified the continuities between seventeenth- and nineteenth-century anti-Catholicism. In 1864, the *New York News* criticized Radical Republican Horace Greeley's *New York Tribune* for attacking the Catholic Church as being in complicity with bar owners and other undesirables. "This assertion of the *Tribune* is put in a spirit of genuine Black Republican malignance.... The malice that thus wantonly attacks in such a manner a large and respectable class of men who confine themselves to their duties in private life, is the true emanation of the acridity of the

Praise-God-Barebones school of malignant self-righteousness." The Barebones Parliament was a Cromwellian institution, hauled out in this case as emblematic of Republicans' antidemocratic spirit. The *Tribune*, New York's leading radical paper, had alleged that Catholic clergy instructed people to vote for George McClellan in the presidential election. For another defender of the old faith, Civil War nativism assumed a modern form but harkened back to the Puritans of old: "The Cromwellian spirit of the days in which the Bishop of Drogheda was dragged from the altar to be murdered in his canonicals, has lost nothing of its savage intolerance in the bosom of the modern Roundhead."[78]

Whatever their lingering anti-Catholicism, abolitionists' true targets lay in the South, not the North. It is certainly true that Cromwell brought a religious zeal to war—historian John Morrill characterizes him as pursuing a "divine right revolution"—but his American admirers celebrated something more abstract: his ability to build a reforming army motivated by the spirit.[79] An 1862 discourse published by a Vermont minister identified this virtue in Cromwell: "He called out the moral force which lay in the hearts of men." This was precisely the attitude that Confederates and Northern conservatives had long feared about abolitionists. For some, the war created an opportunity to put that spirit into practice. "[Cromwell's] influence pervades our nation," the minister proclaimed, "and the clang of his sword resounds over this continent. We are placed in the vanguard of the struggles of the world."[80] Although Northern radicals typically opposed the more mercenary imperialism adopted by the United States throughout the 1840s and '50s, the language in this context reveals the global ambitions of committed reformers.[81]

In the American case, Northern radicals endorsed a religious crusade in their vision of the army that harkened back to this Cromwellian vigor. The *Christian Recorder* connected their unyielding political stance to spiritual certainty. "Compromises would be useless," the paper argued, "concession would be suicidal. If, in putting down the rebellion, war must come, let it come; if civil war, the worst of all wars, let it come." In their search for models, they grouped George Washington and Cromwell together, because both men put their faith in God. "But, above all, our trust for success *must be placed in God*. If he is with us and for us, all shall be well. Let us not trust in our wealth, in our numbers, in our rulers, in our army." The historical example clinched the case: "The soldiers of *Cromwell*'s army, were the invincible soldiers, because they were such men of faith, and men of prayer.... May our volunteers pattern after these examples. Guns and Bibles should go together. We want bayonets that can think not only, but bayonets that can believe and pray."[82]

Although Democrats and conservative Whigs dominated the officer ranks at the start of the war, and most early war recruits enlisted in order to preserve the Union, over time abolitionists helped build a more radical army. Some of this can be attributed to the changing sentiments of soldiers when they encountered the brutal realities of American slavery firsthand and saw the advantage to be gained from enlisting Black men into Union armies.[83] In other cases, the army changed because dedicated abolitionists accepted commissions and found their way to places where they could exercise leadership. One of the most important locations for this work early in the war was along the South Carolina coast. The Union navy captured the Sea Islands in November 1861, slaveholders escaped inland to Charleston or Columbia, and most of the 10,000 enslaved people from the area remained to welcome US troops.[84] The Union cycled through several commanders in the Department of the South over the coming years, but they were all dedicated to enlisting Black men into Union armies and using those troops to end slavery. The prospect of armed Black men attacking slavery terrified slaveholders and inspired Northern radicals with visions of remaking Southern society from the bottom up. Thomas Wentworth Higginson, the white commander of the First South Carolina Infantry, received orders in early 1863 to "carry the proclamation of freedom to the enslaved, to call all loyal men into the service of the United States."[85] This was the war that radicals had hoped the United States would fight.

The commander of the department in 1862, Gen. David Hunter, wrote a widely reprinted letter to Massachusetts governor John Andrew (an early proponent of Black enlistment) from Port Royal about his success in organizing Black regiments. Hunter blended racial condescension with a strong endorsement of the very characteristic—fanaticism—that white Southerners had been maligning as the miserable legacy of the original Puritans. "The regiments are hardy, generous, temperate, patient, strictly obedient, possessing great natural aptitude for our arms," Hunter wrote, "and deeply imbued with that religious sentiment—call it fanaticism, such as like—which made the soldiers of Cromwell invincible."[86] His subordinate Higginson concurred, writing that "it used to seem to me that never, since Cromwell's time, had there been soldiers in whom the religious element held such a place."[87] Higginson's men would have recognized the posture of New Model Army soldiers, as one historian summarizes them: "Putting their lives on the line in one campaign after another had radicalized them, while their victories had given them the confidence that the Lord had strengthened their arm, and that they were the humble instruments of some divine purpose for which

England had been singled out."[88] Certainly, Higginson and his soldiers would have agreed with the *Christian Recorder*'s assessment of where true spiritual power lay: "The Bible was not written, as many suppose, mostly by priests and preachers; but by hard-fisted working men, the Garibaldis, Cromwells, Washingtons and Lincolns of their day."[89]

The Dangers of Despotism

> News from the past is always current. Nothing wants to be, or can be, history.
>
> SEBASTIAN BARRY, *The Lives of the Saints*

One of the difficulties of writing Civil War history in a way that recaptures the unpredictability of the era is that we know the Union won and the Confederacy lost. Generations of historians wrote with this outcome as their guiding star.[1] As a result they generated precise diagnoses of the path the war followed. This approach had the unintended result of obscuring from view the paths not taken. Over the last generation, historians have worked harder to recapture the contingency of the conflict.[2] Political historians have an even more difficult task. Because the North preserved the integrity of the Union and abolished slavery, those end points feel inevitable. Even new histories of emancipation that reveal the army's hesitant and uneven support for freedom have not changed our certainty that slavery would end. From this perspective,

Republicans appear farsighted and bold, committing themselves and the country to ending slavery and persevering until they had accomplished their goal.[3] Democrats, on the other hand, appear mean-spirited and begrudging of even the modest concessions made on behalf of enslaved people and hostile toward the free people of color already living throughout the North. Their relentless criticism of Abraham Lincoln for his management of the war—on everything from military strategy and civil liberties to procurement and budgeting—strikes a dissonant note today. Like Southern slaveholders, they seem on the wrong side of history.

Historical consensus may recoil from wartime Democratic politics today, but we cannot ignore their actions. A significant number of Northerners supported the party throughout the war and carried their arguments about limits on federal power into the postwar era. My focus in this chapter is on the War Democrats—those mainstream conservatives who remained loyal to the Union but opposed many of the ways Lincoln fought the war, including, most important, emancipation. A wide range of political types counted themselves as Democrats before the war. That factionalism becomes more visible by comparing the ways that people used history. Where moderates such as Lincoln respected the whiggish trajectory of history as a story of progressive improvement, Northern conservatives adopted a more fatalistic reading of the past.

The outright racism and anti-emancipation posture of most Democrats—who often larded congressional floor speeches with casual and supportive references to a "white man's government"—does not look better in context. There is, however, an additional layer of their critique of Lincoln that merits attention: They read the history of the English Civil Wars as a lesson in the dangers presented by civil conflicts, a reasonable and common interpretation among historians at the time. They were not opposed to military intervention. To the contrary, Democrats championed the American invasion of Mexico in the 1840s. But sending American soldiers to conquer a people they regarded as inferior and in need of tutelage proved a very different thing than turning the power of that same army on people they considered fellow Americans. In addition to their critiques of Lincoln's war management, Democrats opposed the legal changes that his administration imposed, including the suspension of habeas corpus, confiscation of enemy property, and the arrest of political enemies (most famously, Congressman Clement Vallandigham). On all these topics, they read the English Civil Wars as strong cautionary examples. In short, the historical vision of Northern conservatives bolstered their animus toward Lincoln and gave them a more capacious language with which to attract Northern voters. Finally, because the Englishmen of the 1640s and '50s did not frame their era using the concept of race, it offered Democrats a purely political critique of Republicans.

In the 1860 election, Republicans won a majority of seats in both the House and Senate. Nonetheless, Democrats in Congress knew that they had a greater chance of shaping the course of the nation within its halls. Even as members of the minority party, Democrats had procedural options at their disposal and they had the pulpits of their respective chambers. Galvanized by a reading of history that saw the rise of despotism as a nearly inevitable result of civil conflict and by faith in the legislative power of Congress, Democrats hoped to prevent precisely the changes that Northern radicals sought. "To Congress also belongs the authority to determine when the resistance to the execution of the laws has ceased," Garrett Davis declared in the Senate, "when the insurrection has been suppressed, and when the invasion has been repelled. The President cannot take cognizance of either of those questions without the authority of a law of Congress."[4] In the event, Lincoln did not wait for Congress's approval and, relying on his authority as commander in chief, mobilized the US Army against Confederates. Nor did conservatives wait to deploy history as critique. In the war's opening moments, the *New York Herald* condemned Republican newspapers, because some seemed to prefer "to make way for a Cromwell, or a military dictator. As that can only be done by violence and anarchy, it seems a rather strange cure for disunion and disorder. The predecessor of Cromwell was superseded by the scaffold. Do our amiable contemporaries want to see the President of their choice superseded in that fashion?"[5]

The course of the English Civil Wars in the late 1640s gave people reason to approach the concentration of power cautiously. After the conclusion of hostilities in 1646 (a period usually designated "the first civil war"), different factions negotiated for authority. Charles I, still clinging to his royal prerogative, made secret alliances with Royalist Scots and they invaded England on his behalf. Although the Parliamentarian army defeated this group, Parliament itself continued to negotiate with Charles. This state of affairs produced a rupture between the army and Parliament in 1649. Led by Col. Thomas Pride, the New Model Army purged Parliament of members still inclined toward the king, setting up his trial and execution the following month. "Pride's Purge," as it became known, produced the "Rump Parliament," which tried the king for treason.

Worse still, from the perspective of strict constitutionalists in America, in 1653, Oliver Cromwell and the army then dissolved the Rump Parliament and replaced it with a group of hand-selected loyalists, who promptly appointed Cromwell Lord Protector, a post with powers akin to the king's but whose original power derived from his leadership of the army. To many nineteenth-century historians and to most Northern conservatives, this sequence demonstrated the ease with which popular political movements could veer into despotism. Complaining about the election of congressional representatives from a partially reconstructed Louisiana, one congressman warned, "If this thing could be permitted, how long might it be or might it not be before some Cromwell would send his Colonel Pride into these Halls to tell us begone; and, if we would not begone, to clear these benches as he did the benches of the House of Commons, at the point of the bayonet?" The danger he anticipated was the blurred line between civil and military authority.

> How long might it be before some great military genius or power
>   might bestride this House and our deliberations like a Colossus,
> "and we petty men
> Walk-under his huge legs, and press about
> To find ourselves dishonorable graves?"[6]

Northern Democrats anchored themselves to the Constitution the way Royalists of the seventeenth century had anchored themselves to the monarchy. In both instances, conservatives chose popular and enduring symbols of continuity. James Bayard, a Delaware senator who opposed any military response to secession (and was eventually expelled from the Senate for refusing to take the oath of allegiance), framed the issue in more apocalyptic terms. "Is the Constitution to be abrogated because you are at war? The doctrine is an exceedingly dangerous one.... If the great general principles that guard the individual liberty of the citizen against the aggressions of power are trampled down, even with a good motive, the time and the man will come who will take advantage of the precedent and usurp the power permanently and altogether. That is the course by which all despotisms succeed ultimately, and it always will be so." Bayard reflected the common understanding of the English conflict after 1653: "It was the course of things that followed in England after their revolution, until Cromwell finally dispersed the Long Parliament with the sword."[7]

Bayard returned to this example in the debate over indemnifying Lincoln for his suspension of habeas corpus. Rather than directly critique Lincoln, he emphasized what he regarded as the natural result of assuming that good intentions prevail. "When Cromwell entered into the civil wars of England as a soldier, do you suppose that he intended to overturn the liberties of England and make himself the despot of his country? Not at all, in my belief. His intentions were to put down the exactions and the abuses on the part of the Stuarts." Bayard's position reflected more nuance than Confederates ever adopted. His concern, he claimed, was "with the frailty that is necessarily incident to human nature, the power that was intrusted to [Cromwell] as the reward of victory spoiled the better elements of the man's character; and he ended by prostrating the very liberties for the purpose of vindicating and sustaining that which he entered the contest in the outset." Bayard concluded, "This is always the progress of human nature. It does not depend on the character of an existing President."[8] Bayard's position reflected an older conservatism that believed in the necessity of carefully monitoring executive power. Echoing this interpretation, another Democrat lauded the English Civil Wars era as the time when "arose those glorious efforts to fix the boundaries between the ruler and the citizen—to put restraint on the one, and give security to the other, which constitute the chief glory of England and the just pride of Englishmen."[9]

Concerns about civil-military relations were not confined to rank-and-file conservatives. The Philadelphia *North American*, ordinarily a booster for the Lincoln administration, emphasized the same history in a commentary on the Emancipation Proclamation. In their telling, Cromwell's essential moderation preserved the peace until his death, when the "free spirit of the English people . . . rose against the tyranny of mere military government, the government of soldiers."[10] Even John Milton expressed anxiety about the ways that the "republican moment" of 1649–53 gave way to the protectorate under Cromwell. Milton served the council of state under the protectorate, but he worried about the decline of virtue during the period. He believed that the country needed more civil and fewer military officeholders. Historian David Armitage argues that when Milton returned to writing poetry, "he produced in *Paradise Lost* an epic narrative which with hindsight could be seen as critical of the kind of policies pursued by the Protectorate in the later 1650s, the era of military rule."[11]

Even Republicans were aware that the demands of war encouraged an unprecedented growth in federal power. If the war had lasted only a few months, little might have changed. But four years of warfare, demanding the mobilization of over 2 million men (the prewar US Army contained 15,000 soldiers), and the accompanying economic mobilization to feed and supply those men required an active government.[12] Democrats critiqued nearly every change. The debate over three issues—habeas corpus, confiscation, and military arrests—illustrates the motives that drove Democrats to charge Lincoln as a despot. Historians of Civil War politics have described this constellation of issues in detail, though almost always within the confines of the American political tradition.[13] Further, in most tellings, Democrats' critiques on these issues are regarded as a smoke screen for their underlying opposition to emancipation. Instead, I am arguing that conservatives sought opportunities to broaden the appeal of their message and emphasizing historical claims to civil liberties rather than just anti-Blackness. Reading Democrats' critiques through the historical lens that many of them brought to bear on the Civil War suggests an intellectual foundation that accommodated, but was not reliant on, their racism.

Like Confederates, Northern conservatives identified Radical Republicans as a chief source of the country's woes. They did this by borrowing the language of abolitionists as modern-day Puritans. "The Puritanism of New England," Ohio congressman Samuel Cox complained, was "bred in the bone. It is the same now, that it was hundreds of years ago. Like begets like. Generation succeeds generation, with the same stamp of Puritan character; taking success for justice, egotism for greatness, cunning for wisdom, cupidity for enterprize, sedition for liberty, and cant for piety."[14]

In contrast to the radicals who celebrated Cromwell's vigor, Northern conservatives regarded him as a negative model of ideological excess that perverted a regrettably necessary war into a holy crusade. In particular, the measures that Cromwell took to suspend the regular patterns of governance contradicted civilian control of the military upon which the American system rested. "In our country at this moment," *Harper's Weekly* proudly announced, "if the President were disposed to abuse the enormous power confided to him, the army and the generals would be a restraint upon him. If the generals, or any one of them, were disposed to try the game of Napoleon or Cromwell, they would find themselves deserted by the army; which is not their tool, but in that case a body of fellow-citizens."[15] James Gordon Bennett's *New York Herald*, voicing the standard Democratic Party line through much of the war, made the English Civil Wars a persistent part of its efforts to curtail the radical elements of the American conflict.[16] His newspaper relied on English Civil Wars analogies and comparisons more than perhaps any other publication in the United States and mostly as a story of power run amok.[17] Despite being born in Scotland, Bennett expressed great contempt for Europe. His resort to this history represented a real fear that America was at risk for falling back into the worst of Old World habits.

Northern conservatives feared both Northern and Southern variants of radicalism. In early January 1861, before the Confederacy had even formed, the *Herald* cautioned against the "excesses [in England that] led to misrule and regicide; with the final establishment of the autocratic sway of Cromwell, who was succeeded by a more capricious tyrant than the father who died on a scaffold at Whitehall."[18] Instead, they counseled a middle path of cautious reform. Two months later, the paper complained that the efforts of Virginia's moderates to keep the state in the Union were being stymied by a rump group meeting in Richmond to compel secession. "It is feared that the result of the gathering will be a successful movement, *à la* Cromwell, to drive out and disperse the long Parliament, to wit:—the Union State Convention, which has been in session since the middle of February."[19] Conservatives could take solace from Thomas Macaulay's histories. His history of the civil war era warned of the dangers of a radicalized military, which in the English case then assumed control of the government. Like other mid-nineteenth-century writers, Macaulay lauded Cromwell's personal capacity and shielded him from responsibility for the worst excesses of his administration. Instead, he blamed the execution of King Charles I, the consolidation of power within Cromwell's hands, and property seizures of Royalist elites mostly on his soldiers, driven as they were by a Puritan zeal. "His troops," Macaulay wrote, "moved to victory with the precision of machines, while burning with the wildest fanaticism of Crusaders."[20] For Civil War Northerners, the warning could not have been clearer: They must resist the dangers of wartime radicalization. In particular, Northern conservatives challenged radicals from the war's opening moments, pursuing a deeply partisan politics even in wartime in order to limit the war's agenda.[21]

The *Herald* complained that even as the country was "in the midst of a revolution which threatens to shatter the government into atoms," abolitionists focused on ending slavery. In particular, it singled out James Watson Webb, a nationalistic Republican and publisher of a rival New York paper. "Henry Ward Beecher, in a lecture a few evenings ago, said he wished we had a Cromwell for President now. If Lincoln don't come up to the mark, by all means let Webb some fine morning stalk into the halls of Congress with the Wide Awakes at his back, armed with torches, disperse the assembly, then proceed to the White House and cut off the President's head, and proclaim himself 'Protector,' 'in the name of the Lord.'"[22]

Once the war began, the *Herald* turned its heavy guns against radicals, especially abolitionists, in the North. They equated abolitionists to "the

Puritans of England and the Jacobins in France [who] originated bloody civil wars in those countries which made them desolate." Their chief critique of the Roundheads, whose Protestant advocacy they respected, was that they "pushed matters to extremes . . . they began with the cry of 'Liberty of conscience,' in opposition to the religious supremacy of the King; but when they became victorious they insisted upon all other men swallowing their opinions on pain of death, and violated their own principle as it had never been violated before." The *Herald* wanted to defend the American system against the perils of extremism, right or left. "Republicanism so suffered from its identification with the Puritans that it fell with them, and though two hundred years have since elapsed it has never been able to rise again. Let the republican party, now in the ascendant in this country, beware lest they too bring the principles of republican government into disrepute."[23] The problem, as they saw it, derived from "the blood-thirsty abolitionists," who sought "a revival of the struggle which took place two centuries ago in England between the Puritan Roundheads and the rest of the nation. The vast majority of the people were against them, but by the military genius and iron will of Cromwell the fanatics were rendered successful for a time, after putting their king to death and deluging their native land with seas of blood." The newspaper explained that the cause died with Cromwell, because the people did not support it and they welcomed back Charles II with open arms. "That was the last of the Puritan faction in England. They have never revived. But their descendants here, the inheritors of their principles and their blood, now seek to inaugurate another civil war upon a question of morals, religion and social polity, in States over which they have not, and ought not to have, any control." The *Herald* hoped its conservative readers knew that, "like their ancestors in Great Britain, they are in a small minority, but by an accident and the divisions of the people they have contrived to get hold of the reins of government."[24]

On the question of habeas corpus in particular, many critics of the Lincoln administration harkened back to the Magna Carta and the deep foundations in English law for swift processing of the criminally accused. In the House of Representatives, Daniel Vorhees, an Indiana Democrat, quoted David Hume and Henry Hallam, offering an unusually forthright criticism of Charles I for arbitrary arrests. "But in the days of Charles I," he lectured, "our ancestors did not allow the subject to drop at the haughty bidding even of a king. They met the issue. Bold and fierce discussion followed, until the unwarranted arrest and imprisonment of five Englishmen gave rise to the famous Petition of Right, which was a clear and explicit affirmation of the principles of *Magna*

Charta, and an application of them to existing grievances." Vorhees charged Lincoln with resorting to similarly haughty bidding. Like many Northern conservatives, Vorhees critiqued Charles when he believed it was merited but proved no fan of his successor, Cromwell. "The struggle again commenced, and raged until Charles I fell beneath the ax of the executioner; and that mysterious and unexplained enigma of history, Oliver Cromwell, triumphed over him in the name of popular right and constitutional government. And though the practical fruits of this mighty revolution were for long years turned to dust and ashes upon the lips of England, yet the public mind of the world had learned a grand and overwhelming lesson." That lesson: "The English people taught mankind of every age and of every country that no sanctity of prerogative, no dignity of blood, no prescriptive customs, no pageantry of royal state, no bayonets surrounding the palace, can protect one man in plundering the multitude of their personal liberties." Importantly for the current situation, Vorhees believed that this history was widely known in the United States. "It is a lesson, sir, which the humblest American citizen knows by heart to-day and treasures up as an everlasting inheritance."[25]

The 1862 debate over the Confiscation Act likewise drew seventeenth-century analogies. This legislation served as a precursor to the Emancipation Proclamation. It authorized US forces to seize property from rebel civilians that was required for military purposes (a common right long established in the laws of war), and it also authorized the emancipation of enslaved people held by enemies of the United States.[26] During the debate on this bill, Edgar Cowan, a Republican, spoke out against confiscation in terms that Democrats cheered, noting that Lincoln exceeded even the worst English precedents: "Neither did the English conquerors of Ireland, in their long series of forfeitures and confiscations, from the time of Strongbow down to the rebellion of 1798 ever, at any time, venture upon such a sweeping measure as this."[27] Jacob Howard, a Lincoln ally, tried to defend the practice with reference to the same history: "I find it to be what it ever has been, an ordinary form of reprisals, a means of carrying on hostilities as ancient as the idea of property itself, receiving the practical sanction of all ages." Howard explained that "the history of the civil wars of England ever since the Conquest, has been marked by seizures and confiscations."[28] This defense spoke only to the legality of the policy, not its wisdom. Jacob Collamer, another Republican, read the same history as instructive of the gentlest possible wartime practices. He expected charitable treatment of white Southerners because "all rebellions that are unsuccessful, that are suppressed, among any civilized people, end in a bill of amnesty, from which some are reserved and exempted for punishment."[29]

If Republicans were able to alleviate War Democrats' concerns during the 1862 debate over confiscation, they had much less success when it came to military arrests. Although the vast majority of civilian arrests made by the Lincoln administration had little to do with politics, Democrats seized on the issue of civil liberties because it resonated with voters.[30] They received an unexpected gift in mid-1863, when Union general Ambrose Burnside arrested the Democratic gubernatorial candidate (and sitting US congressman) Clement Vallandigham.[31] Vallandigham was the most infamous Peace Democrat in the North. Nonetheless, his arrest gave all Democrats and many moderate Republicans a reason to condemn the administration's tyranny. New York governor Horatio Seymour proclaimed that the arrest "brought dishonor upon our country."[32] A Vermont paper that claimed to hold to the old Unionism of Daniel Webster and Henry Clay (relevant in 1850 but not as useful a decade later) conveyed a clear alarm about what it viewed as the drift toward despotism. "Past History, we may remark, teaches us but one lesson—and that lesson 3,000 years long, viz,—that when the *Military* becomes the Government,—the Lincoln's, the Chases, the Sewards, and the Stantons, are the very first to be swept away even by their own armies and that there ever spring up, from these armies, smart, adroit, unprincipled men, who seize the helm, and this too in spite of the civilians." The seventeenth century provided the clearest lesson: "Such is our English reading of the History, of Cromwell."[33] Democratic papers saw an obvious parallel. In a well-attended lecture on Cromwell in Iowa, the speaker offered a typical Northern conservative reading of the end of King Charles I that doubled as a critique of Republicans: "The growing aggressions of the King upon the rights of the people was the principal cause which ultimately led to the uprising of the latter and the dethronement of the former." The newspaper suggestively prodded its readers to see how it applied to Lincoln. "Though no parallel was drawn by the speaker between those times and our own; every reflecting person must have seen the analogy, and by a legitimate process of reasoning deduced the natural conclusion."[34]

Conservatives' frustration increased in direct proportion to radicals' success at making emancipation central to the Northern war effort. The *Herald*, like most conservative organs, objected both to the mode of change—the Federal government was taking action against slavery that Lincoln had expressly denied he possessed (though his comments pertained to peacetime, not war)—as well as the substance of that change, the emancipation of enslaved people. Although the policy changes came through the government, prowar papers like the *Herald* focused on abolitionists as the motive force.

Calling them the "secessionist abolitionists," the paper fumed, "Now they proclaim their determination to overturn the whole façade to its foundation, which was laid in compromise reconciling and harmonizing conflicting interests arising from diversity of soil, climate and population."[35] Democratic congressmen echoed this reading of the existential struggle within the North itself: "It is my deliberate and solemn conviction," explained one, "that either abolitionism or constitutional liberty must forever die. They cannot exist together."[36]

This clash over the value of compromise itself focused the ideological struggle in the North. "All compromise is an abomination to the intolerant Puritan spirit, which arrogates to itself the right to regulate the religious and political affairs of all mankind," the *Herald* complained. Instead, the paper encouraged a path modeled after their generous interpretation of Cromwell (one only a Northerner could make). "Oliver Cromwell . . . with all his faults and crimes, was a great statesman as well as a great general, and no fanatic as is generally believed." The paper quoted Armand Carrel's recently published *History of the Counter-Revolution in England*: "Cromwell was right against the royalists, because they were the enemies of the country; against the Presbyterians, because they were intolerant and did not understand the revolution; against the levellers because they demanded the impossible; finally against the fanatical republicans, because they did not comprehend public opinion." Making the American parallel clear, the paper asked, "Who does not see reflected in this mirror the factions which now distract the American republic? . . . 'The levellers,' whom Cromwell found it necessary to squelch, were but types of the agrarian crew led by Phillips and Greeley; and 'the fanatical republicans' have their character reproduced in the radical republicans of the present day."[37] In this telling, Lincoln could emerge as a wise Cromwell, resisting the radicalism of the abolitionists even as he suppressed secession.

In truth, Wendell Phillips offered conservatives plenty of ammunition.[38] In an 1863 address at the Cooper Union in New York, Phillips pushed ahead of Lincoln despite the recent enactment of the Emancipation Proclamation. "I do not believe in the Government at Washington," he asserted. "I believe in the nation; I believe in events; I believe in the inevitable tendency of these coming ten years toward liberty and Union."[39] Phillips's appeal to destiny rather than mundane politics reflected conservatives' long-standing fears. "In every revolutionary civil war there is a party which takes advantage of the general strife and confusion to gratify its insatiable lust for blood and crime," the *Herald* explained. "England had such a party during that series of civil wars which culminated in the execution of King Charles First. . . . Its peculiarities are a disregard of all principle, an irrepressible relish for slaughter, and a fiendish disposition to war upon the weak, defenceless, and womanly." Then, the contemporary parallel: "During our own civil war we call this party the abolitionists."[40]

Northern conservatives' interpretation of the English Civil Wars reveals an important dimension of their ideological position. Unlike Confederates, many of whom aspired to return to a world before Jacksonian democracy (indeed, centuries before), Northern conservatives accepted, even embraced, the rise of universal white manhood suffrage in the antebellum decades.[41] Democrats endorsed their own version of progressive change, one that entailed technological development and economic expansion directed for the benefit of white families as they spread across the continent. Democrats hoped to enable progress, in a Macaulay-ian framework, without radicalism. The most careful student of nineteenth-century American conservatism, Adam I. P. Smith, shows that in the mid-nineteenth century, "the advocates of a conservative course, or of conservative principles, also regarded themselves as advocates of progress."[42]

For the historian Macaulay, the chief danger of the English Civil Wars was the drift from absolute monarchy to military despotism.[43] Samuel S. Cox, one of the most careful readers (and quoters) of seventeenth-century history, knew his Macaulay. From 1860, he used the English Civil Wars as a cautionary tale, though in 1861 he offered a more positive reading, admitting that the era had generated value despite the excesses of Cromwell. Others in Congress concurred, regarding Cromwell as the embodiment of a historical confluence between power and the man. Still, they demanded institutional safeguards, a predictable position for political conservatives.

Conservatives promoted their vision of progress as the rightful inheritance of white Americans and protected it from those who threatened it. During the war, Democrats characterized abolitionists as the greatest danger. Fernando Wood, the New York Democrat, interpreted the English Reformation as a period when "men broke violently loose from the forms of religious ceremony, rushing with blind zeal to the opposite extreme; surging from a narrow bigotry to an ultraism far more dangerous to their salvation and involving certain destruction to their temporal welfare." This "fanaticism" led inexorably to the English Civil Wars, as Wood explained. "It created a power which swept before it the feeble effort made to resist it. It soon became irresistible. Constitutions, organic laws, and fundamental principles of law alike fell prostrate before its dreadful march. Charles I had neither the moral nor the physical power to maintain himself against it."[44] Wood, a member of the

Episcopalian Church, did not oppose the Protestant Reformation, nor did he defend King Charles against the accusations of misgovernment that led to his downfall.[45] Instead, Wood, like many Northern conservatives, put his faith in institutional oversight. Conservatives had long believed that American institutions—especially political ones such as the Constitution, political parties, and local government—provided a unique rigor to the American system.[46] Although Democrats such as Wood continued to preach the virtues of state governments, the rapid pace and inevitable centralizing demanded by war increased the importance of congressmen and the Federal courts as actors. Wood's concern was that radicals made it "a war of ideas, a thoroughly revolutionary war, an unholy breaking of the seals of the Constitution in order to accomplish the reorganization of southern society, in conformity to the plans of the socialist reformers of the school of pseudo-philanthropists."[47]

Despite their criticism of Lincoln, Northern radicals succeeded in pushing the administration to the left. The president issued the Emancipation Proclamation, the army enforced it, Black men enlisted in the army, and that mixed-race force imposed a hard, destructive war on the South. Northern conservatives saw only a string of policy defeats: the president suspended habeas corpus and Congress sanctioned him; the Confiscation Act authorized property seizure across the South; military commanders arrested and jailed civilians; and all their efforts to forestall emancipation and Black enlistment failed. Some turned bitter and even conspired against the United States.[48] Most maintained what they considered a loyal opposition, albeit one they believed was better attuned to ambivalence and the unpredictability of wartime. Given their failures, conservatives recognized their inability to control events.[49]

Still, there was one policy that remained central to Lincoln's war that conservatives had long favored: reunion. The growing importance of emancipation as a war strategy accompanied but never displaced Lincoln's belief in the perpetuity of the Union and the importance of bringing the seceded states back into right relations with the nation. Northern conservatives claimed that they, too, navigated by this star. This belief could be found, anchored in the English Civil Wars, most famously in Edward Everett's Gettysburg lecture. Preceding Lincoln on the podium that cold November day, Everett was an old-line Whig and antebellum friend of the South. Appalled by secession, Everett steadfastly supported the Union throughout the war, moving close enough to the Republicans to be brought onto the platform to commemorate the battle of Gettysburg. Although Lincoln's address at Gettysburg earned the greater share of lasting fame, Everett's speech (the main event of the day) was widely reprinted and discussed in Northern newspapers.[50] He "castigated this rebellion as a Satan-like apostasy from the Revolutionary Fathers," but Everett also called for a gentle end to the conflict by describing the course of the English conflict two centuries earlier.[51] "The great Rebellion in England of the seventeenth century," Everett declaimed, "after long and angry premonitions, may be said to have begun with the calling of the Long Parliament in 1640, and to have ended with the return of Charles II. in 1660,—twenty years of discord, conflict, and civil war . . . confiscation, plunder, havoc."

Like most Northern conservatives, Everett bemoaned the consequences of the war and the form of Cromwell's leadership—"a military despotism established on the ruins of a monarchy which had subsisted seven hundred years, and the legitimate sovereign brought to the block." But unlike many conservatives (and nearly all Confederates), he did not end the story there. "Such was the state of things for twenty years," Everett explained, "and yet, by no gentle transition, but suddenly, and 'when the restoration of affairs appeared most hopeless,' the son of the beheaded sovereign was brought back to his father's blood-stained throne." The lesson to Northern listeners was clear—gentleness and charity should guide the war's end. "By these remarkable steps did the merciful hand of God, in this short space of time, not only bind up and heal all those wounds, but even made the scar as undiscernible as, in respect of the deepness, was possible, which was a glorious addition to the deliverance."[52]

The gentle and forgiving conclusion to the war that Everett imagined remained distant in late 1863. Nonetheless, his vision, more or less, came to pass. His foresight and persistence, like that of Cox and other Northern conservatives, reveals the centrality of Northern politics to the outcome of the Civil War. The armies' accomplishments on the battlefield enabled but did not determine the war's consequences. Republican success on a range of issues—confiscation, wartime arrests, and most important, emancipation—has concealed the tenacity of Northern Democrats and their creative use of a variety of strategies, including the effective marshaling of history, to impose their vision on post–Civil War America. The history of Charles II's return inspired them to persist and reminded Americans to not assume the war's conclusion until it was reached.

Ending Civil Wars

> The historical sense involves a perception, not only of
> the pastness of the past, but of its presence.
>
> T. S. ELIOT, "Tradition and the Individual Talent"

Edward Everett's history lesson about how to end civil conflicts proved premature. The Civil War raged on for seventeen brutal months after his speech at Gettysburg. Despite this uncertainty, Northerners began debating the nature of the postwar world even as they continued the fight against Confederates in the field. From the radical perspective, the key challenge was how to move from a state of war to a state of peace with the gains of war intact. Conservatives hoped to ease that transition by returning to the "Union as it was." That prospect was never realistic, but conservatives mounted a variety of arguments to minimize the range and permanence of wartime changes. Northern radicals and conservatives argued along two lines, one legal and one ethical. The first line of dispute concerned the constitutional boundaries around what the federal government *could* demand of seceded states. The ethical dimension of the debate concerned what *should* be done. Radicals believed that traitors should be punished, and land confiscation offered a nonviolent and politically powerful way to accomplish this goal. Conservatives, drawing on the same history as the radicals, argued for the strategic wisdom of dealing generously with defeated foes. The fate of the freed people and the future of biracial democracy in the South depended on the outcome of the debate.

PROTECTING THE GAINS OF WAR

In 1660, just as King Charles II assumed the combined thrones of England, Scotland, and Ireland and ended the brief experiment in English republicanism, one of its chief spokespersons lamented the country's fate. John Milton wondered how "a nation should be so valorous and courageous to winn their liberty in the field, and when they have wonn it, should be so heartless and unwise in their counsels, as not to know how to use it, value it, or what to do with it or themselves." Instead, Milton lamented that "after ten or twelve years prosperous warr and contestation with tyrannie [the English had] basely and besottedly to run their necks again into the yoke which they have broken, and prostrate all the fruits of their victorie for naught at the feet of the vanquished."[1] This was surely a curious conclusion—that the victors in a war would bow themselves before the defeated. It was true that after Oliver Cromwell's death, a group of radicals made peace with some Royalists and brokered a new Parliament, which invited Charles II back to assume the throne. American radicals had been disappointed time and again with the concessions made to appease slaveholders. They knew, from Milton's observation and their own experience, that they had to press their temporary advantage to make wartime changes permanent. Theodore Tilton, a well-known abolitionist, wrote a poem inspired by Milton's friend and fellow poet Andrew Marvell's ode to Cromwell. Tilton's admonition to readers reminded them that "the Commonwealth of England, which by a successful war was placed upon a sure foundation of Freedom, was then, by an unsuccessful 'reconstruction,' slid back to its old corner-stone of monarchy. Let not the Republic of America, after a like war, suffer a like fate!"[2]

Massachusetts senator Charles Sumner had been thinking about this issue and preparing arguments since at least 1862.[3] In his telling, a rebellion generated the military power to suppress violence and the political power to ensure it did not recur. What the United States sought was "indemnity for the past, and security for the future."[4] In the context of the 1862 debate over the Confiscation Act, Sumner had responded to Democratic colleagues who insisted that the United States faced a war, not a rebellion, in order to ensure that Confederate soldiers would be taken prisoner and treated under the laws of war rather than executed for treason. Sumner would have none of it. "It would be an insult to the understanding," he lectured, "to say that at the present moment there is no Rebellion or that there is no War. . . . We are in the midst of *de facto* Rebellion and in the midst of *de facto* War. . . . You may call it Rebellion or War, as you please, or you may call it both. It is Rebellion swollen to all the proportions of war, and it is War deriving its life from rebellion."[5] Sumner turned to the English Civil Wars for precedent. "It would be needless to go further in order to show that we are in the midst of a rebellion and in the midst of a war. . . . A single illustration out of many in history will exhibit this double character in mistakable relief. The disturbances which convulsed England in the middle of the seventeenth century were occasioned by the resistance of Parliament to the arbitrary power of the Crown. This resistance, prolonged for years and maintained by force, triumphed at last in the execution of King Charles and the elevation of Oliver Cromwell."[6]

Like many Civil War Americans, Sumner relied on the Earl of Clarendon to frame the nature of the event. "The historian whose classical work was for a long time the chief authority relative to this event styles it 'The Rebellion,' and under this name it passed into the memory of men. But it was none the less war, with all the incidents of war. The fields of Naseby, Marston Moor, Dunbar, and Worcester, where Cavaliers and Puritans met in bloody shock, attest that it was war." For further proof, Sumner called upon "a greater than Clarendon—John Milton—[who] called it War, when, in unsurpassed verses, after commemorating the victories of Cromwell, he uses words so often quoted without knowing their original application:—'Yet much remains/To conquer still: Peace hath her victories/No less renowned than War.'"[7] It was victory in peace that radicals sought.

Sumner carefully defined the dual nature of the American conflict so that the Union could properly calibrate its policy—a military one to defeat the Confederacy and a political one to punish and discourage rebellion. The implications of such a stance were severe. According to Sumner, "The persons arrayed for the overthrow of the Government of the United States are unquestionably *criminals*, subject to all the penalties of rebellion, which is of course treason under the Constitution of the United States. . . . The same persons . . . are unquestionably *enemies*, exposed to all the incidents of war, with its penalties, seizures, confiscations, captures, and prizes."[8] This perspective required Sumner to overlook his valorization of Cromwell the rebel and highlights the ability of Civil War Americans to transcend the historically grounded logic of their understanding of the past. Sumner's position held obvious utility in the midst of the debate over the Confiscation Act.[9] On this important but narrow question, the Democrats' opposition had little historical or legal support. Sumner's examples of the legitimacy of confiscation spanned the globe, though he returned again to the English cases, citing the contemporary English historian Henry Hallam. "By the law of England, [confiscation] was the inseparable incident of treason, flourishing always in Ireland, where rebellion was chronic, and showing itself in Great Britain whenever rebellion occurred."[10]

In an 1863 speech, published in the *Atlantic Monthly*, which offered his ideas wide exposure, Sumner defended Abraham Lincoln's appointment of military governors in Confederate states retaken by the US Army. He hoped these men would reorganize political and economic power within the South to ensure a real and productive peace. Although Sumner wanted a larger role for Congress in appointing administrators, he bolstered Lincoln's practice by relying on his interpretation of the English Civil Wars. "There is nothing new under the sun, and the military governors we are beginning to appoint find a prototype in the Protectorate of Oliver Cromwell."[11] Attentive as always to the legal dimensions of military policy, Sumner sought to square military power with civil authority. Drawing on English historians again, Sumner quoted Thomas Carlyle on the criticism that Cromwell had received in his day. "'It is an arbitrary government,' murmur many. Yes, arbitrary but beneficial. *These are powers unknown to the English constitution, I believe; but they are very necessary for the Puritan English nation at this time.*" Then, Sumner cinched this precedent to Lincoln's actions: "Perhaps no better words could be found in explanation of the Cromwellian policy adopted by our President."[12] Though Lincoln probably grimaced at Sumner's characterization of his approach as "Cromwellian," he, too, emphasized the importance of necessity as a governing policy in setting war measures. Sumner, like Lincoln, recognized that the state of wartime increased the elasticity of the laws.

Sumner, of all people, knew that he could not cite the examples of the English Civil Wars as actual legal precedent. The American Revolution had created a new nation, and even as Americans carried over most of the British common law, they fashioned a new constitution. "International law" at the time consisted of philosophical precepts but nothing binding. As historian John Witt has shown, the Lieber Code (written by Sumner's friend and confidant Francis Lieber in 1863 for the US Army) formed the basis for the first coherent set of the laws of war, ones that European countries adopted after the American conflict.[13] The absence of enforceable international law made recourse to the wisdom of past policy all the more important.

Charles Sedgwick, a New York Republican, echoed Sumner's emphasis on necessity and his conclusions about confiscation in 1863. Speaking on the House floor, Sedgwick knew that good men, whom he called "Puritans, if you will; Roundheads, if you will; whose ancestors were the soldiers and companions of Cromwell," would rally to the support of the government. In addition to enlisting in the armies, such men would support the policies necessary to restore permanent order, which included land seizures. "I hope to see the estates of rebels distributed, under our homestead law, to emigrants; to see them divided in bounties to our soldiers; to see a well-considered system of land laws, in which all sales of the public domain in the rebel States shall be upon the invariable *condition* that freedom shall be impressed upon the soil. . . . These are some of the bitter but wholesome and necessary fruits of this rebellion. They put an end to the vilest aristocracy upon which the sun has ever shone."[14] This posture was particularly pronounced among political progressives such as Wendell Phillips and other radicals from the evangelical movement whose skepticism about Catholicism may have made them more likely to favorably recall the English hope of civilizing Ireland as they planned to remake the South.

Sedgwick's proposal called up memories of the seventeenth century. Unlike the comparatively amicable resolution reached within England between former Royalists and Puritans after the Restoration, the English punished Ireland for rebellion and for the perceived savagery of the conflict. At the conclusion of hostilities with the Irish Confederacy, the British Parliament adopted retribution as its "basic principle" of justice with respect to Ireland. The Parliament seized land to sell in order to pay off its debts, but the punishment was moral as well as financial. As a recent history observes, "Henry Jones, the Church of Ireland clergyman who had coordinated the depositions taken in Dublin after the 1641 Rising, carried an abstract of these with him to headquarters in 1652, and that did its persuasive work. The commissioners fully endorsed Jones's sweeping anatomy of guiltiness."[15] For the purposes of British history and memory, the Irish component of the English Civil Wars took its essential shape during 1641. In this view, the Irish showed themselves to be rebellious rather than loyal, prone to atrocity and murder rather than regular war. This selective memory justified postwar land confiscation and political repressions by the English. In the postwar writing on the conflict, the English considered it the best example of how a people forfeit their autonomy. Historian Eamon Darcy identifies "the 1641 rebellion [as] a real turning-point in Irish history. Memories of the alleged massacres were evoked to label Irish Catholics as barbaric, perfidious, or unfit for government."[16] The English confiscated land and imposed penal laws in order to rule Ireland as a dependency. The Earl of Clarendon's *History of the Rebellion and Civil Wars in England* made the lesson clear for nineteenth-century readers. Clarendon recognized that the Irish were "under as severe a captivity and complete misery as the worst of their actions had deserved" but believed "the Irish deserved dreadful punishment for their 'unnatural rebellions.'"[17]

Beginning in the wake of the war, extending through the post-1690 Penal Laws, and through the 1800 Act of Union, the English adopted a paternalistic posture that foreshadowed Northern (especially abolitionist) condescension toward the white South. The Protestant English regarded the Catholic Irish as both politically and religiously inferior. The punishment meted out to the Irish chastised their disloyalty and might correct their misplaced faith. Even admitting that Cromwell organized a terrible "despotism," nineteenth-century histories lauded the results. According to one, "Among the Irish [the British Empire] had better effects than [in North America]. It crushed the tyranny of their native rulers, and made property rise in value."[18] In the postwar settlement, English confidence in their own superiority led them to "advance plantation as the sovereign salve for Ireland's ills."[19] Memories of this injustice shaped Irish attitudes well into the nineteenth century. John McDonnell, a nineteenth-century Irish historian, observed, "The war lasted eleven years, and ended in the complete victory of the Puritans and subjugation of Ireland under the Cromwellian settlement—the most cruel wrong ever inflicted on this most miserable country."[20] Today's historians still endorse this interpretation. "It was a measure of the change in the English state wrought by Cromwell and his colleagues that, whereas the Tudors had taken decades to subdue Ireland, Cromwell did the job in three years," observes M. Perceval-Maxwell. "The result for Ireland was devastating. The land was destroyed, much of the ancient aristocracy was lost, estates were confiscated on a scale that perhaps not even Parsons imagined was possible, and by the end of the century the Catholic majority was excluded from the political process."[21] The thoroughness of Irish dispossession established a historical benchmark that empowered the rights of victors over unjust rebellions.

Nothing about postwar settlements is accidental or inevitable. Cromwell's administration and subsequent English officials worked diligently to drive out the last of the Gaelic Irish landholders. As one nineteenth-century history explained, the "subjugation of Ireland was [Cromwell's] next task," and "everywhere the Romanists fled before their terrible foe."²² Commonwealthmen and Restoration officials understood that the economic and social authority wielded by landlords in an agricultural society was the route to political control. Historian R. F. Foster explains, "What must be grasped from the early seventeenth century is the importance of the plantation idea, with its emphasis on segregation and on native unreliability."²³ The initial justification for the plantation project envisioned the space as either a site of civilization (the slow acculturation of the Gaelic) or of colonization (the forced planting of English norms). The war convinced most English of the impossibility of the former. Instead, first under Cromwell and then (with remarkable continuity) under Charles II and later, English administrators implemented a massive redistribution of property from Catholics to Protestant New English settlers. The war itself generated an additional motive for imperial action. As one scholar has noted, "English rulers legitimized the use of excessive force in English colonies. A key element in early modern colonial policy is revenge. English colonisers called for vengeance and re-colonisation when natives rebelled against their overlords."²⁴ Here, the Irish experience resembled what the English found in the New World, especially in their memories of the 1622 conflict with the Powhatan Confederacy and other episodes of colonial violence in the era. The English regarded uncivilized people as both needing English education and as legitimate subjects of state violence when they disobeyed.²⁵ Importantly, the history that Americans consumed taught them that, despite all the injustices Ireland suffered, English administration was for the best. Joel Headley's widely read 1848 biography of Cromwell acknowledged the massacres at Drogheda and Wexford and the confiscation of land, but it concluded, "Still, Ireland flourished under this yoke of iron, as it had never done before—public order was restored—the laws were respected—industry revived" and the plantations built.²⁶

Nineteenth-century historians viewed English policy through their own historical lens and, in some cases, also through biblical analogies. "The distribution of the greater part of Ireland thus made by the Cromwellians," historian William Cooke Taylor wrote, "was nearly as complete as that of Canaan by the Israelites; the example by which the Puritans declared that they were directed, and believed that they were justified."²⁷ Of equal importance to redistributing land was reallocating power from Catholics to Protestants. Thomas Macaulay observed that Cromwell "gave free rein to the fierce enthusiasm of his followers, waged war resembling that which Israel waged on the Canaanites, smote the idolaters with the edge of the sword, so that great cities were left without inhabitants, drove many thousands to the Continent, shipped off many thousands to the West Indies, and supplied the void thus made by pouring in numerous colonists of Saxon blood, and of Calvinistic faith."[28] The result held important consequences for the Irish and Indigenous peoples in North America and, more distant in time, for the defeated South. As J. G. A. Pocock observed of the 1640s context, "Leviathan was a figure born of civil war."[29]

The same has been said of North America in the 1860s.[30] Among the strongest proponents of Leviathan were those Radical Republicans who identified the postwar period as a liminal moment (constitutionally speaking) when they could build a more egalitarian South. In this sense, the English remaking of Ireland served as a model. In the view of Radical Republicans, white Southerners had alienated themselves from the national government and only a thoroughgoing reconstruction of the socioeconomic foundations of the region could ensure political stability in the future. This is what Thaddeus Stevens and other Northern radicals wanted to do after the war. In 1863 and beyond, Northern congressmen sparred over the question of whether the seceded states were in or out of the Union. This seemingly arcane and legalistic question was a preamble to determining what authority Congress would have to remake them. In short, Northern confidence in free labor and the triumph of Union victory emboldened a sense of America's destiny. This position anticipated what Robert Penn Warren later called the "Treasury of Virtue," in which Northerners who ended slavery and saved the Union felt "redeemed by history, automatically redeemed... not by a papal indulgence peddled by some wandering pardoner of the Middle Ages, but an indulgence, a plenary indulgence, for all sins past, present, and future, given freely by the hand of history."[31]

Northern conservatives recoiled at the idea of a deliberately Cromwellian policy, yet even some of them found common cause with Sumner's interpretation. Orestes Brownson, a Catholic convert who possessed a "thoroughly conservative and authoritarian view of society," supported the Northern war effort on behalf of the nation rather than individual liberation.[32] In the pages of his journal, *Brownson's Quarterly Review*, Brownson advocated whatever form of peace provided security. Mirroring the British attitude toward the Irish, he expressed no need to worry about rebels for their own fate. "[Confederates] gave up their rights, their faith, their honor, when they became rebels," Brownson wrote, "betrayed their country and took up arms to subvert its Government, and they have no right to complain if compelled to drink, and to drink even to the dregs, the bitter cup of humiliation."[33] Brownson condemned the Romantic liberalism of abolitionists—he supported emancipation solely as a war measure—and he allowed that the "Government may find it expedient, or even necessary, as a means of extinguishing the Rebellion, to adopt a liberal policy towards the seceded States, and to permit them on every easy and liberal terms, to resume their former *status* in the Union; but, if so, it will be for its own sake, not for theirs."[34]

Sumner endorsed Federal control over seceded states because he did not believe that white Southerners could be trusted to end slavery and create a genuinely equal society. More to the point, the radical vision of the Civil War extended to remaking the South. Wendell Phillips, at the war's conclusion, explained the fundamental irreconcilability of the two sections, "the history of two civilizations constantly struggling, and always at odds, *except when one side or the other rules.*" Given the Union's victory, it possessed the power to set the rules for Reconstruction. During the war, following the urgings of radicals like Phillips and the logic of Sumner, US forces confiscated land, Lincoln's military governors controlled the process of restoring the political agency of seceded states, and abolitionists lobbied for the government to redistribute seized land to freed people and Northern white migrants. Phillips hoped, as he said, to carry "Massachusetts to Carolina" by replacing the racial hierarchy of the old South with "a class of independent yeomen and artisan ... free laborers whose productive efforts supported common schools, free churches, and democratic institutions of all sorts. 'We must take up the South and organize it anew,' Phillips urged, 'to absorb six millions of ignorant, embittered, bedeviled Southerners [Black and white] and transmute them into honest, decent, educated Christian mechanics, worthy to be brothers of New England Yankees.'"[35] This proposal rekindled Edward Everett's characterization of the Cromwellian settlement of Ireland: "After the conquest of Ireland, in order to secure the obedience of that country, to hasten its advancement in civilization, and facilitate the administration of government, the Protector wished to introduce and establish there a sound and orderly population of the English stock, on which he could rely."[36]

THE STRANGE CAREER OF 1649

Where some radicals promoted the English conquest and appropriation of Ireland as a model for the ways the North should approach the defeated South, conservatives marshaled the same history as a lesson in what not to do. Rival senators took the evidence Sumner claimed as precedent to impose military rule on seceded states but treated it as a model to avoid. Lazarus Powell, a Kentucky Democrat, complained in particular about the use of military commanders in loyal states (like his own) to manage the registration of voters. "Sir, the elections, if conducted in that way, would be as much a mockery as they were in England in the time of Cromwell, when he laid off that country into twelve districts, and placed twelve major generals over them, clothed with absolute power."[37] Where Sumner lauded the "prototype" of military governors, Powell recalled the history differently: "How was it with Oliver Cromwell? The Protector appointed twelve major generals to take charge of the twelve districts into which he divided the British empires and they went forth armed with all power; they decimated the people; they taxed them at their discretion, and exacted enormous tribute from them, and in that way the people were held in subservience to the military authority."[38]

The dispute over reconstructing the governments of seceded states took concrete policy form with the congressional debate over the 1863 Wade-Davis Bill. Championed by two Radical Republicans, the bill created a high bar for the readmission of seceded states. It required 50 percent of a state's voters in the 1860 presidential election to take a loyalty oath to the United States and swear that they had never supported the Confederacy. Few white Southerners would have met this standard, and Lincoln subjected the legislation to a pocket veto. In its place, Lincoln's plan required only 10 percent of 1860 voters to take the loyalty oath. It enabled the quick reconstruction of Louisiana and presaged a smooth path for reentry by other Southern states. In trying to explain what seemed to many at the time (both Northern and Southern) as a strange shift in policy—from a hard war to a soft peace—historians have emphasized white supremacy and a deep conservatism on the question of property redistribution.

History, as Northern conservatives understood it, also argued for restraint. Ohio congressman Samuel Cox recalled the English Civil Wars to argue for the futility of wide-scale confiscation. "It ignores the first lesson of history, what has been truly called 'the principal observation of the best historians.'... Instead of disarming the rebel, it arms him, when nearly exhausted, with the weapons of revenge and despair."[39] Cox drew a clear conclusion about the negative consequences of England's oppressive postwar regime. "If I should wish to present a case where all the horrors of subjugation, penury, devastation, and confiscation have been felt, I would go to Ireland. Crushed by the cruelty of a system similar to that now and here sought to be inaugurated, Ireland points with skeleton finger continually in all her sad history her warning to our rulers."[40] In another speech several months later, as radicals and conservatives continued to sharpen their competing visions for the postwar era, Cox made the point even more explicitly: "We are powerful in proportion as we are national. If we should follow the advice of passion and treat the southern States now in civil war as England treated Ireland, we become weak and denationalized."[41]

Cox did not have to look far for a living embodiment of a rebel armed "with the weapons of revenge and despair." John Mitchel, an Irish nationalist banished to Tasmania who later made his way to America, became a leading voice in the Fenian liberation movements of the mid-nineteenth century (always from abroad—he could not return to Ireland itself). Mitchel also believed in racial hierarchy and offered a strident defense of slavery. During the Civil War, he lived in the Confederacy and worked as an editor at the *Richmond Examiner*. From that post, Mitchel cautioned his readers about what to expect from a reunification that would be little better than colonial dependency. As one historian notes, "Mitchel would keep at the forefront the idea of the parallels between Ireland and the Confederacy."[42]

At this late stage of the war, the foremost parallel was the possibility that the Union would confiscate and redistribute the property of the South's leading slaveholders. The political consequences of land confiscation drew Northerners' attention in the war's closing months, often viewed through the lens of the English Civil Wars. A Midwestern paper lamented that "[confiscation] must consolidate and intensify the South, and it must strengthen and arm rebel leaders there. . . . What Cromwell and the Kings of England attempted and achieved upon Ireland, is now, here, to be re-attempted. The very moment that fanaticism wins one victory, as that now over slavery, it devises other issues, thus now, of seizing and plundering all the land from the Potomac to the Rio Grande."[43] Another paper referred to the same history in a complaint about Union general Benjamin Butler: "Cromwell was cruel and vindictive, as is well established by his wholesale confiscation of estates in Ireland, as well as by his remorseless persecution of those of her sons, who, with courageous but mistaken zeal, clung to the fallen fortunes of the House of Stuart, and therein he was the prototype of Butler, who, on a small scale, has faithfully imitated his example, both in Louisiana and Virginia."[44] A third paper drew the ominous conclusion about the effect of these seizures for the political order in the British Empire: "During all these centuries the political system of the Government was built upon the principle of these dispossessions, *and this false principle became the fruitful parent of disorder, distrust, violence and rebellion.*"[45] Conservatives believed that a vindictive settlement would sour the chance for real postwar peace.

"The idea of expelling the rebellious population from the country, and of dividing up their lands among the soldiers, white or black, is a monstrous barbarism, the offspring of cupidity, and has as little affinity with patriotism as it has with the spirit of Christian philanthropy," editorialized the Democratic *National Intelligencer*. It, too, drew its example from English history. "It was the original sin of England, after her conquest of Ireland under Henry II., to adopt the policy of dividing the lands of the vanquished among the victors." In particular, the newspaper noted how this policy accelerated after Cromwell's victories, singling out the 8 million acres given to Cromwell's soldiers. "*It is the great extent of this cruel and unjust measure which has been the original cause of the disasters in Ireland, by nourishing profound feelings of hatred in the descendants of the dispossessed proprietors.*"[46] The *Princeton Review* echoed this advice, "All unnecessary punishments are positive evils. They exasperate instead of subduing; they exalt criminals into martyrs. The sympathy felt for the victim is transferred to the cause for which they suffer. Unnecessary punishment degrades justice into vengeance; all history proves its impolicy. Ireland, Poland, and Venetia, stand as examples and warnings."[47] It proved easy for Democrats, even War Democrats, to advocate a generous peace. Few had any concern for the Black Southerners who would be at the mercy of quickly reconstructed states (led, in many cases, by the men who had advocated secession and fought a war to preserve slavery). Instead, they looked forward to rebuilding the Democratic Party's cross-sectional basis.

Republicans championed the political rights of former enslaved people in the South but did not support land redistribution. Republican support for military reconstruction in Congress meant, in South Carolina and Louisiana and to a lesser extent elsewhere, that Black people could determine the course of Southern politics. But because in the American system material power so often determines political power, over the long term, Black political power in the South waned. Republicans did not, on a significant scale, appropriate or redistribute land in the wake of the war.[48] Black Southerners, already toughened by a wartime US Army that often treated them as disposable, were perhaps not surprised but certainly disappointed as the federal government abandoned the tentative steps it had taken during the war to reallocate land to Black families. Historians since at least the 1930s have debated the reasons for this outcome.[49] The standard explanations emphasize two elements: white Americans' racist assumptions about Black people's aptitude and work ethic (akin to English perceptions of the Irish in terms of productivity and initiative) and Republicans' steadfast commitment to property rights.[50] Both of these forces limited the possibilities for the bold reforms articulated by Radical Republicans such as Thaddeus Stevens. Racial solidarity undoubtedly played a central role in discouraging a robust Reconstruction. So, too, did reading the history of the Irish Rebellion.

As nineteenth-century historians explained, the English seized control of Irish land but this only exacerbated the Irish sense of grievance. "As a rule," Robert Vaughan argued, "revolutions, to be safe and permanent, must be based on moderation, and on a manifest sense of right and humanity." Emancipation represented just such a "revolution" in American social and political life, one that required delicate management to succeed. "To necessitate such extreme forms of change," Vaughan believed, "is to necessitate a long continuance of bitter disaffection, and almost to ensure the kind of reaction which seems for a while to undo all that has been done."[51] The Irish nationalist uprisings of 1848 and 1867 occurred while the histories of the seventeenth century upon which Americans relied were being written. Though neither of these moments posed a serious challenge to British rule, they demonstrated that no matter what prosperity the British claimed to bring to the island, political stability remained elusive. Cox made the same point from Congress: "From the time when the Puritans overran Ireland to exterminate and destroy . . . down to the 1st of January, sixty-two years ago, when the imperial standard floating from Dublin Castle announced to Ireland the depth of her degradation . . . there has been no union, no peace, no justice, no content for Ireland. That union, thus misbegotten of force and fraud, was weakness to England and ruin to Ireland."[52]

Instead, Cox and others referred to the charitable example of Charles II at the time of the Restoration in 1660. "The closest analogy to our condition is to be found in the English civil war," he explained. "The English people are our ancestors. They had what we have—a similar code of personal freedom, great municipal independence and a popular Parliament." Demonstrating the depth of his knowledge of the English experience, Cox here focused on the war's conclusion. "At Cromwell's death, eleven military governments, under Major Generals like Monk, held almost absolute sway. The three nations were represented in one Parliament, which, on Cromwell's death, had been dissolved for indocility. Conspirators had been punished with death. Confiscations were common." Nonetheless, according to Cox, in the face of such turmoil, wisdom and generosity prevailed. "Party vengeance was rampant then as now, but the people's representatives considered that they had to decide between a new civil war and a restoration. The latter was represented as clement, unexacting, prudent, and determined to adapt itself to the manners and wants of the time." Then came Charles II's amnesty declaration. "It removed all hesitation, and the restoration began. The king in that paper declared that he desired to compose the distraction and confusion of his kingdom, to assume his ancient rights, and accord to them their ancient liberties, without further 'blood-letting.' He therefore granted an amnesty to all who would return to their obedience.... He *conjured* them to a PERFECT UNION for the resettlement of all rights, under a free Parliament." In case his listeners did not follow Cox's callout to "union," he made the appeal directly: "Nor would the same sort of declaration from Abraham Lincoln be less powerful to restore the sovereign States to their old allegiance, especially if followed by a national convention and the restoration of a party not unfriendly to the entire union of all States, with their 'just rights.'"[53] Cox prayed for that which Frederick Douglass feared when the latter observed that "republics have proverbially short memories."[54]

For Northerners tired of war and eager for reunion with their Southern brethren, Cox's argument may have seemed both wise and humane. Who could argue with his litany of vengeful wars or his New Testament–style military policy? "Let the pitiless destruction of the Moors of Andalusia by Philip II, the merciless slaughter of the French in La Vendée, Claverhouse's bloody hunts after the Scottish Covenanters, the stained and cadaverous cheek of Ireland ... teach us by their history that powder cannot cement nor bombs bear messages of love."[55] Taking aim at Republican arguments that seceded states needed federal guidance before being readmitted to the Union, Cox argued, "If war blots out the States insurgent by virtue of its territorial and belligerent character, then war does by its violence what secession would do by its ordinances."[56] Underneath the legal debate, Cox articulated a vision of nationalism remarkable for whom it excluded. Cox quoted an English contemporary, the philosopher John Stuart Mill, on the nature of nationality:

> We mean a principle of sympathy, not of hostility; of union, not of separation. We mean a feeling of common interest among those who live under the same Government, and are contained within the same natural or historical boundaries. We mean that one part of the community shall not consider themselves as foreigners with regard to another part; that *they shall cherish the tie which holds them together; shall feel that they are one people; that their lot is cast together; that evil to any of their fellow-countrymen is evil to themselves; and that they cannot selfishly free themselves from their share of any common, inconvenience by severing the connection.*[57]

This inspiring definition of cultural nationalism served Cox's purposes only if listeners ignored the problem of race in American life, which Northern

Democrats were inclined to do. Virtually the whole Democratic Party agenda denied or obstructed a "common interest" and "cherished ties" with Black Americans. In light of this fact, Cox's repeated use of English Civil Wars analogies to describe the American Civil War proved convenient. It enabled him, and conservatives generally, to keep the public debate focused on the abstract issues of loyalty, nationhood, rebellion, and war that united the two conflicts. In the seventeenth century, the English regarded the Irish as uncivilized because of their Catholicism and because of their supposedly tribal communal structure, but the language of race had not yet developed. By returning time and again to that era, Cox obscured the significant contextual differences between the two conflicts. Cromwell had famously sent several thousand Irish prisoners into servitude in Barbados, but the sprawling conflicts of the 1640s and '50s did not turn on racial slavery, emancipation, or constitutional abolition. Parallels abounded, but as with every act of translation, the devil lay in the question of who constructed the comparisons and for what purpose.

WITH CHARITY FOR ALL

Despite the absence of race as a social category or analytical concept, the conflicts shared a causal similarity. In both the seventeenth- and nineteenth-century cases, ideas of civilization and progress were enmeshed in questions about how to accord cultural and social minorities a political position within a larger national community. Although the outcome of the English Civil Wars seemed to sanction, or even encourage, a heavy hand in the South, Republicans chose not to pursue the same conclusion as the English had two centuries earlier. In fact, they rejected the language on which the English grounded their civilizing project—the necessity of subjugation. "It is not subjugation, but the deliverance of the seceding states themselves from the domination of a tyrannical minority," argued the *Princeton Review*. "When the Independents under Cromwell overthrew the British monarchy, the mass of the people were quiescent, and submitted to the authority of the Protector. The English people were not subjugated when the appearance of General Monk's army emboldened them to throw off the bonds of the new government, and to return to their allegiance to the house of Stuart." Then, back to the present: "Neither will the South be subjugated, when the advance of the Federal armies enables the people to emancipate themselves from the dominion of the slaveholders, and to resume their wonted place in the American Union."[58] In this way, Lincoln followed the path of the whig historian Macaulay who, as his biographer notes, "carried Reform in order to avoid revolution."[59]

As the US Civil War drew to a close, moderates gained the upper hand in devising policies for the postwar world. Most important, they conducted no mass killings. After the Restoration, in line with Charles's amnesty proclamation, very few people suffered, but even then, nine of Cromwell's chief lieutenants—the "regicides"—were executed. In other mid-nineteenth-century conflicts—the Indian Rebellion in 1850s India and the 1871 Paris Commune most famously—victorious armies killed thousands of rebels. Not so in the United States, despite the obvious means for doing so—treason is the one crime specified in the US Constitution and almost always carries a death penalty. But owing to a host of factors, including calls for amnesty by leading Northern churchmen (such as Henry Ward Beecher), the United States executed only a handful of notorious guerrillas and the commandant of the Confederacy's worst prison, Andersonville.[60] Instead, debates among Northerners over appropriate punishments for rebellion occurred within a narrow set of nonlethal and nonviolent options.

Even still, Democrats objected to most of these, as Cox's vigorous critique of land redistribution demonstrated. Their political interests were plain to see—property occupied a central place in the American legal and political system and Democrats wanted the political advantage of bringing ex-Confederates back into the Union as loyal conservative voters. Still, that commitment to property rights united Democrats with many Republicans, including Abraham Lincoln. The result was that, tragically, freed people received little land in the war's aftermath, despite laboring on it for generations. Democrats such as Cox challenged the prospect of land redistribution as though abolitionists intended to transfer land belonging to white Southerners to Black Southerners. In fact, many white Northerners coveted the "abandoned lands" for themselves. In the war's closing moments, Northerners with capital often bought what little land was intended to be conveyed for recently emancipated people, who often lived on it.[61] In March 1865, Lincoln halted land sales altogether, terminating the efforts of some genuinely sympathetic Northerners who hoped to buy land and transfer the title to local Black Southerners. As historian Amy Taylor notes, "Lincoln was thinking about reunion—about the war coming to an end, and about the urgency of doing nothing to damage the prospects of stitching the Union back together."[62]

At war's end, Republicans—a political party with no Southern base—also worried about enabling a Democratic electoral advantage in the postwar world. Nonetheless, even as he appointed military governors and sought to accommodate seceded states to the reality of emancipation, Lincoln foresaw the futility of perpetual military rule. His position reflected

Edmund Burke's on the use of armed force to hold a community together: "The use of force alone is but *temporary*. It may subdue for a moment; but it does not remove the necessity of subduing again: and a nation is not governed, which is perpetually to be conquered." Burke wrote about the rebellious American colonies, but the applicability in the context of a civil conflict would have been apparent to Lincoln (a reader of Burke). "My next objection is its *uncertainty*. Terror is not always the effect of force; and an armament is not a victory. If you do not succeed, you are without resource; for, conciliation failing, force remains; but, force failing, no further hope of reconciliation is left." Having led the country through civil war and the end of slavery—confirmed by the January 1865 passage of the Thirteenth Amendment—Lincoln knew that he would need the cooperation of white Southerners. "Power and authority are sometimes bought by kindness," Burke wrote, "but they can never be begged as alms, by an impoverished and defeated violence. A further objection to force is that you *impair the object* by your very endeavours to preserve it. The thing you fought for, is not the thing which you recover; but depreciated, sunk, wasted, and consumed in the contest."[63] What Lincoln hoped to avoid was a depreciated union, one wasted, perhaps fatally, by war.

The overwhelming profusion of primary sources from the US Civil War enable today's historians to adopt a rigorously contemporary view of events. Loath to let the war's outcome shade our accounts, we move day by day encountering the conflict as participants did in all its complexity. It is good to be wary of the hallucinatory effects of hindsight, a mind-altering drug that must be taken in small doses. And while it is true that Lincoln could not anticipate the war's end, by reading histories of previous conflicts he knew that someday it would. The irony here is quite palpable: Lincoln, like us, looked to the past to see into the future. By consulting accounts of past conflicts, especially those of long tangled events such as the English Civil Wars, he knew that America's civil conflict would eventually conclude. On this point, Macaulay offered clear advice: War must be ended in a way that respects both sides and enables genuine reconciliation. In describing the uncertainty that arose after Oliver Cromwell's death and his son's ascension to rule, Macaulay celebrated the wisdom of restraint and generosity. "Our ancestors . . . forgot old injuries, waved petty scruples . . . and stood together, Cavaliers and Roundheads, Episcopalians and Presbyterians, in firm union, for the old law of the land against military despotism."[64] This rosy view of the Restoration reflected a settlement 200 years old. That chronological distance was part of what enabled the rosiness. Important, too, was the strong sense of English nationalism expressed in the historical actors that Macaulay identified and those he excluded from the union: the Scots and the Irish.

If it was Lincoln himself who checked Macaulay's book out from the Library of Congress during the war (rather than one of his secretaries, who also used his borrowing privileges), perhaps he used it to help consider the postwar world. The easiest route to sectional reconciliation would have been to appease white Southerners at the expense of the freed people by contracting or repealing altogether the Emancipation Proclamation. Lincoln refused to budge on this question, but in his second inaugural address he offered an olive branch—"with malice toward none, charity for all"—to his opponents. In this, he echoed not just Macaulay but another nineteenth-century English historian, Robert Vaughan, who offered a similar moral from his reading of the English Civil Wars. "As a rule," Vaughan wrote, "revolutions, to be safe and permanent, must be based on moderation, and on a manifest sense of right and humanity."[65] This was a difficult trick to conjure—as a committed whig, Vaughan professed that "what we want in the history of nations is growth; and growth is silent and gradual," even as he narrated two decades of tumultuous war.

Like Lincoln, *Harper's Weekly* contemplated how to reach the uneasy balance between subjugation and reconciliation at the war's end. Reflecting on a meeting of Virginians in postwar Richmond, the paper worried that "we can not expect that the ideas of Virginians or of the citizens of any other Southern State are to be reversed by their defeat on the battle-field." Instead, the Union must be vigilant in its peace. "We have settled conclusively the question whether the union of States shall be maintained. But there remains much yet to be settled in regard to the prerogatives of the several States as related to the General Government." The periodical drew, once again, on the 1650s for guidance. "The English Revolution was not consummated by the victories of Cromwell and the decapitation of Charles the First, but in the peaceful victory of the English people forty years later, when William of Orange succeeded James the Second. Fortunately for us the Slave Power can have no restoration: with the removal of the cause of our troubles our future is ultimately secure."[66]

Northerners demanded that emancipation stand, and it did. They also hoped to find peace with the South, which Lincoln did not live to see. Nonetheless, the eulogies for Lincoln after his assassination revealed an appreciation for what might be termed his un-Cromwellian generosity. As one newspaper assessed his last address to Congress, it believed he demonstrated a "grasp of principle, a dignity of manner, and a solemnity of purpose which would have been unworthy neither of Hampden nor of Cromwell, while his gentleness and generosity of feeling toward his foes are almost greater than we should expect from either of them."[67] It was the particular balance that Lincoln strove to reach between protecting the abolition of slavery and welcoming back the Southern states that garnered attention. Another paper noted about his second inaugural address that "the feeling for the bondmen and the sense of the great wrong done to them, with its inevitable punishment, seemed to rest with such solemn earnestness on his soul, that to the surprise of all and the derision of the flippant, an official speech became clothed in the language of the Bible." The result was that English and French critics "pronounced it a Cromwellian speech; but it had one peculiarity, which Cromwell's speeches never possessed—a tone of perfect kindness and good-will to all, whether enemies or political opponents."[68]

The Meaning of the Civil War

> Strange how things in the offing, once they're sensed,
> Convert to things foreknown;
> And how what's come upon is manifest
>
> Only in light of what has been gone through.
> Seventh heaven may be
> The whole truth of a sixth sense come to pass.
>
> SEAMUS HEANEY, "Squarings, xlviii"

Do rebellions occur because of a fatal flaw in a state? Can that flaw be remedied by a war? These were the questions that lingered behind much of the intellectual work Americans performed to explain their conflict. Abraham Lincoln provided one answer in his second inaugural address when he proffered that if "slavery is one of those offenses" that God willed to remove, then Americans "both North and South" suffered "this terrible war as the woe due to those by whom the offense came."[1] Lincoln's framing offered Americans a balanced account—the crime of slavery paid with the blood of dead soldiers—and avoided sectional blame. For Northerners less inclined to a beneficent providentialism, history could also answer these questions.[2]

Participants in the US Civil War knew they were living through a grand historical drama. The scale of mobilization, of death, and of social and political change all signaled they were making the world anew. But into what? The shifts in military fortunes during the course of the conflict, the changes in policy, and the unpredictability of war's effects made imagining that new world a tricky business. Nonetheless, people started shaping the meaning of the Civil War while it was happening. They did this in accord with their interests: Confederates contested Federals, conservatives battled radicals, women confronted men, Republicans opposed Democrats, Black people challenged white people. Some of this intellectual work looked rational, honorable, or prescient when the conflict ended; other aspects looked shortsighted, uncharitable, or cruel.[3] All of it depended on how participants organized their chronologies. Choosing a starting point created a perspective that led them to their various conclusions.[4]

As people made sense of the experience of war, they created the building material for later memory regimes. White Southerners began constructing what would later be called the Lost Cause—an interpretation of the Civil War that emphasized the Christian virtue of white Southerners, the base and mercenary motives of Yankees, and the gullibility of enslaved people.[5] This telling asserted the benevolence of slavery and viewed the war as a tragedy for both white and Black Southerners. African Americans and their abolitionist allies rejected this argument wholesale, believing emancipation and the abolition of slavery to be the war's most important legacy.[6] Northern conservatives emphasized reunion and the repudiation of secession, but as previously shown, they opposed emancipation and property seizures in the South.[7] My emphasis here is less on these now familiar interpretations, which derived their shape in large measure from their postwar political contexts, and more on the broad public efforts to satisfy people that the war merited the sacrifices they had made.[8]

Northern moderates such as Lincoln lauded the Northern army, celebrating both the defeat of the Confederacy and the end of slavery. At the same time, they explained the war in a more abstract but still satisfying way. Drawing on the connections between the English Civil Wars and the American one, they naturalized how violent civil conflict reshaped nations.[9] If radicals won the argument over emancipation, and conservatives won the argument over reunion, moderates crafted a durable, seemingly anodyne interpretation of the war, one that gained hold in the United States and around the world.

The significance they ascribed to the Civil War hewed to neither narrowly partisan nor strictly sectional purposes (though it served those ends as well) but to a nationalist vision that blurred the particular accomplishments of the conflict in favor of a general celebration of the *fact* of union.[10] The interpretation that Northern proponents developed, built on the memory of the seventeenth century, emphasized the nation-state. Proponents of this idea interpreted the US Civil War, like others in Western history, as evidence of the inevitability of national conflict within modern nation-states. Rejecting the argument that America represented an exception in world history, this approach emphasized its typicality, the predictability of rival communities fighting to determine their country's future and accepting war's pain to emerge more cohesive and powerful. Northerners believed this had been the English experience in the seventeenth century, and they hoped it would be the American one in the nineteenth.

A second, related strand of Northern meaning-making identified an even tighter connection between the English and American Civil Wars. It celebrated and made permanent the obvious outcomes (reunion and emancipation), and it accepted military violence and racial inequality as necessary for national harmony.[11] The latter were central features of Britain and its empire; they defined the American experience for the remainder of the nineteenth century and beyond. This perspective imagined twinned fates, of America extending Britain's whiggish pursuit of ordered liberty, and relied on a secular faith in political destiny. The lessons that Northern moderates drew from the US Civil War remain with us today; they govern how Americans and other people around the world react to civil wars and to public violence within national boundaries. This aspect of Civil War memory may not carry the emotional charge that accompanies our current debates about race and sectionalism, but it shapes our lives just as profoundly. These interpretations faded with time; today, Americans tend to emphasize emancipation as most nobly embodying the war's meaning. Even if we acknowledge that a war's legacy will change over time, understanding how its participants assessed this question remains valuable.

NATURALIZING CIVIL WAR

Many Northerners believed that the lesson of seventeenth-century history was that national development required revolutions and civil wars. Rather than regard these conflicts as unnatural or destructive, some Americans affirmed the productive role that war played in British and American development. Foreign wars featured prominently in liberal Britons' explanations of the century, principally as a means for bringing civilization to benighted peoples. Americans' interpretation of the English Civil Wars shifted the focus to the domestic realm. Northerners adopted a "lingua Britannica" that spoke of war and conquest as admirable tools of state-building.

In the first place, British history proved that all nations, even those committed to the constitutional protection of liberty, experienced serious challenges to their stability. At the start of the American conflict, *Harper's Weekly* offered a quick history of civil conflict in England to reassure its readers. "The history of England has been an endless succession of civil wars," it explained. "Over one quarter of the fifteenth century was consumed in the war of the Roses; yet the people quietly acquiesced in the Government of Henry VII." Then it turned to the more familiar seventeenth century. "At least half the kingdom supported Charles the First against the Commonwealth, and fought for him bravely; but when he was fairly overthrown and executed, they submitted, and were loyal to Cromwell. Half a dozen times, after the abdication of James the Second, the people of various parts of the kingdom rose in arms to restore 'the Pretender'; at many times during the reign of William the people of Great Britain must have been equally divided between the rival kings."[12] *Harper's*, like other Northern voices, used history to disrupt the American arrogance that regarded the country as outside the normal course of world experience.

Both Northern and Southern propagandists in the months before Fort Sumter may have induced Americans into a false sense of security, but English history disabused such beliefs. According to another early war commentator, "Wars, commotions, and revolutions, we thought were for other and less favored lands, but for us an uninterrupted future of peaceful growth."[13] The London *Morning Herald* agreed, observing that "reckless ambition, impatience of governmental control, treason and rebellion against the State, constitute a species of wickedness that will crop out occasionally in all countries and under every form of government."[14] The shock that America might share experiences with "less favored lands" compelled a reckoning. The *New Englander* reminded its Connecticut readers, "It is fit that we remember that all the nations that have ever achieved anything worthy . . . have passed through their seasons of national adversity." English history taught this lesson. "What would England have been without her wars of the Roses, and without the troubles and terrible conflicts of her great Revolution? Without these the English nation, English character, English freedom could never have been."[15]

Beyond the raw fact of conflict, Britain provided a sustaining example of the justness and value of a central state suppressing rebellion. In an extended response to a commentary in a British journal, a Northerner asked, rhetorically, whether "a Scotch or Irish Parliament [can] legally secede from the Kingdom of Great Britain and Ireland? And if they attempt such secession are they not rebels and traitors?"[16] This was precisely the experience of the English Civil Wars, which began with Scotland's rebellion in 1637 and was followed by Ireland's in 1641. As Americans knew well, England treated those actions as treason. A significant part of the English Civil Wars consisted of reasserting English rule over Scotland and Ireland. The Lincoln administration derived its authority to suppress insurrection from the Constitution, but the history of revolutions reassured Northerners that their denial of secession drew on global practice. In the sort of tautological reasoning that favored established powers, John Lord (later known as the historian Lord Acton) told a New York audience, "Rebellion is a revolt against constituted legal power; that nothing can justify it but injustice and oppression; that, if successful, it becomes glorious, and is called a revolution, but that rebellions as a general thing have failed, unless the people were worthy of the independence they sought."[17] The Scottish and Irish failures, like the Confederates, proved they were not worthy. England and America, the dominant and successful states in both conflicts, could claim true virtue.

That historical similarity made Britain's position of neutrality during the US conflict all the more frustrating to their supposed American friends. Northerners expected the British to support them just as Americans had supported the empire when the Indian Rebellion exploded in the late 1850s. "During the terrible rebellion in India, prayer ascended from every American church and every family altar in behalf of our brethren in the faith," one journal noted.[18] In a more pointed letter that turned the question inward, toward domestic stability, one American commentator hoped that "people [that is, the English] whose ancestors have always been engaged in civil war might easily see that a civil war here, of itself, neither proved nor disproved anything." He noted,

> You ask, why we don't give it up? For the same reason that England didn't give it up in any of her civil wars—the necessity of national unity. You ask, why we don't let the rebels go? For the same reason that you would not let London go, or Wales, or the County of Kent, even if a majority of those parts of England should seriously wish to go. For the same reason, nationally, that would prevent you, individually, from suffering your body to be cut into two, or three, or thirty-four pieces.[19]

Liberal Britons, to say nothing of conservatives, concurred. John Bright, one of the leading reformers, rallied the Union cause in an important speech in Rochdale in 1861. "Do you suppose," he asked, "that if Lancashire and Yorkshire thought that they would break off from the United Kingdom that those newspapers who are now preaching every kind of moderation to the Government of Washington would advise the Government in London to allow these two counties to set up a special Government for themselves?" More pointedly, given relations with the neighboring island, he probed, "When the people of Ireland asked that they should secede, was it proposed in London that they should be allowed to secede peaceably? Nothing of the kind."[20] Goldwin Smith, a stalwart British friend of the Union, made a similar point: "Suppose Ireland were in rebellion, what effect would the recognition of the insurgent government by a foreign power, say France, produce on the temper of the English nation? Would it make us more willing to yield the victory to the insurgents, and to acquiesce in the disruption of our empire?"[21] The pamphlet containing Smith's thoughts drew the attention of Francis Lieber, who urged Charles Sumner to share it with President Lincoln.[22]

By the mid-nineteenth century, national self-determination came to be regarded as an essential feature of the international order, especially in the Americas.[23] The *Times* of London published a letter from an American living there who defended the New World tradition of people revolting if they experienced oppression but also calculated the high cost of secession. "The process of disintegration," the author explained, "brings back the community to barbarism."[24] Secession unraveled the civic fabric that sustained peace and enabled progress in America. By the 1830s, a defining thread of that fabric was cultural nationalism, fostered through public ceremonies.[25] As the *Atlantic Monthly* explained on the eve of war, "The United States are not a German Confederation, but a unitary and indivisible nation, with a national life to protect, a national power to maintain, and national rights to defend against any and every assailant, at all hazards. Our national existence is all that gives value to American citizenship."[26] Cassius Clay, the antislavery Kentuckian who represented Lincoln's government as ambassador to Russia, reiterated this defense in a widely reprinted letter to the London *Times*: "We the people of the United States of America . . . are fighting to maintain our *nationality* and the *principles of liberty* upon which it was founded."[27]

Northern observers used the history of the English Civil Wars to interpret civil conflict as a natural part of national growth. Responding to critics, especially foreigners, who presumed that a civil war would destroy the United States, *Harper's* encouraged "these gentlemen [to] read history, and take heart. Civil war, we beg to assure them, is not an invention of the nineteenth century. It has occurred before, once or twice, in most countries, and, surprising as it may seem to the critics we address, it has hardly ever ended in a final separation of the belligerents."[28] Despite the editors' somewhat desperate tone—they promised that "after the lapse of a few years, the sometime enemies have been better friends than ever"—they made a valid point. The weekly *Frank Leslie's Illustrated Newspaper* agreed that even when destructive, modern nations could accommodate civil wars. "The publicists of England and France, the wish being father to the thought, have looked upon civil war in the United States as certain to result in political dismemberment." And yet, this conclusion stood "in disregard of the fact that the English civil war produced no permanent alienation of the parties engaged in it.... The hatreds and animosities of civil war are seldom perpetuated beyond the generation in which they have arisen."[29] This optimism, too, had its parallel in historical writing. About the English conflict, nineteenth-century historian John Forster proclaimed, "While the conflict continued, no servile passions inflamed or disgraced it; and when all was over, the vanquished sat down with the victors in their common country."[30]

This historical vision of the naturalness of civil conflict could be reinforced by a religious sensibility. "'To suffer is the lot of man,'" proclaimed a Northern minister. "Nations, too, like individuals, are bettered by the discipline of adversity. Storms free the atmosphere from corruption. Civil revolutions seem necessary at times to cure political distempers generated by long continued peace and prosperity." Referring to slavery as "distemper" reflected a white moderate's view of the problem, but the minister's conclusions supported the war's radical turn. "When revolutions come, the nations that battle for right principles are usually purified by the discipline of war. They give rise to new life." Provided that one believed emancipation was a "right principle," this line of thinking reified Northern purpose. And it did so just as England had experienced. "The 'Great Rebellion' in England seemed to engulf that nation in ruin, but actually resuscitated and saved it."[31] In this vision, history and war proved central to shaping the nature of freedom in the modern world.[32]

Despite the seeming radicalism of the language—which celebrated war as purification—the minister's vision conveyed the Northern moderates' argument: War cleansed and improved the existing government rather than weakening it. The same vision of war generating "new life" could be heard in Lincoln's speeches as well. In the Gettysburg Address, Lincoln famously celebrated "a new birth of freedom," though modern readers often forget that the closing lines remained subordinate to his opening ones that affirmed the purpose of the Civil War as ensuring that the original American nation "endured." Lincoln never lost his faith in the Union or his belief that it was perpetual. He did not choose war, but having come, he believed that war strengthened America by ridding it of slavery. The American house had ceased to be divided.

Commentators on both sides of the Atlantic made use of the 1640s to reveal the ways that wars could be productive as well as destructive. In one of his essays, the historian Thomas Macaulay imagined a conversation between Abraham Crowley (a poet and committed Royalist) and John Milton. Macaulay gave Milton more narrative time, reflecting his own leanings. His Milton proclaims, "That a deluge hath passed over this our nation, I deny not. But I hold it not to be such a deluge as that of which you speak; but rather a blessed flood, like those of the Nile, which in its overflow doth indeed wash away ancient landmarks, and confound boundaries, and sweep away dwellings, yea, doth give birth to many foul and dangerous reptiles. Yet hence is the fulness of the granary, the beauty of the garden, the nurture of all living things."[33] Similarly, an American, writing in a Boston paper, reminded readers that "dwelling upon the evils of war, entirely forgets the good which may result from wars waged in behalf of human rights; for I believe some wars have been so waged, and have entailed incalculable benefits upon the human race." His elaboration of this thesis drew on Milton's conflict: "War is beneficial, if it serves to loosen the shackles of tyranny and king-craft. The execution of King Charles I. was one of the best lessons ever taught the English people. When tyrants govern too much, their subjects are apt to question their right to govern at all. War then is justifiable on the part of a people, if to secure their rights against a tyrannical sovereign they can find no other alternative. When the battles of Newbury and Marston Moor were fought, England took a stride onward."[34]

George Cattermole's 1846 history of the English Civil Wars drew a related conclusion, one its American readers would have remembered as their own conflict drew to a close: "War, even in its most deplorable form, as it now raged through our country, is not an unmixed evil. Independently of those great results which a war of principle may ultimately secure, the horrors of a great contest—of a civil contest, perhaps, more than any other—are in some degree mitigated in the view of humanity, by the opportunities its progress may open for the development of personal as well as national energies."[35] Even Ralph Waldo Emerson, the peaceful sage of transcendentalism, offered a similarly unvarnished appreciation for the transformative power of war. "The first lesson of history is the good of evil," Emerson wrote, before turning to a series of examples from English history in which the oppressions of bad kings (William the Conqueror, John, Edward I) compelled the people to claim new rights. Emerson centered Cromwell in his list of great men whose actions, though often cruel, drove history progressively toward a better future. "Wars, fires, plagues, break up immovable routine, clear the ground of rotten races and dens of distemper, and open a fair field to new men." For transcendentalists like Emerson, who were also active abolitionists, it would be hard to imagine a more rotten den of distemper than the slaveholding South. "The war or revolution or bankruptcy that shatters a rotten system," he concluded, "allows things to take a new and natural order."[36]

Part of the intellectual effort to naturalize the idea of civil war involved neutralizing the language of revolution. As discussed earlier, Northerners identified strongly with the legacy of their own revolution and took pains to link it to the parts of the English Civil Wars that seemed genuinely progressive. But in the context of the 1860s, "rebellion" designated a type of civil conflict, one that did not always rise to the level of true revolution. Frederick Douglass worried about this issue during the war. Like other students of history, Douglass recognized that "rebellion is no new thing under the sun. The best governments in the world are liable to these terrible social disorders. All countries have experienced them."[37] Like other Northern participants in the Civil War, Douglass accepted, in this case even welcomed, military conflict if it could be bent in the direction of justice. The problem, as Douglass saw it, was that while most rebellions in history had pursued progressive ends by challenging despotism, the Confederates did the opposite. The slaveholders' rebellion degraded even the category of rebellion itself. "REBEL and TRAITOR are epithets too good for such monsters of perfidy and ingratitude," Douglass said in another context. "Washington, Jefferson, John Jay, John Adams, Benjamin Franklin, Alexander Hamilton, and many other brave and good men, have worn these appellations, and I hate to see them now worn by wretches who, instead of being rebels against slavery, are actually rebelling against the principles of human liberty and progress."[38]

Northern moderates remained consistent in preserving space for legitimate rebellion. A column written by the American historian John Lothrop Motley in the London *Times* proclaimed, "No man, on either side of the Atlantic, with Anglo-Saxon blood in his veins, will dispute the right of a people or any portion of a people to rise against oppression, to demand redress of grievances, and in case of denial of justice to take up arms to vindicate the sacred principle of liberty." Motley may have written this piece for a British audience, but he knew his words would find favor back in the United States.

"Few Englishmen or Americans will deny that the source of government is the consent of the governed, or that every nation has the right to govern itself according to its will.... The right of revolution is indisputable. It is written on the whole record of our race." Motley's column foreshadowed the eventual Northern position: "British and American history is made up of rebellion and revolution. Many of the crowned Kings were rebels or usurpers; Hampden, Pym, and Oliver Cromwell; Washington, Adams, and Jefferson, all were rebels."[39] Once again, the English heroes of the 1640s prefigured later American ones.

Recognizing a right to revolution was not the same as sympathizing with Confederates. Abusing that natural right—as white Southerners did— represented just as serious an error as denying it. This was why naming the conflict was so important. Historian Gaines Foster has offered the most sophisticated explanation of the postwar argument over the naming of the American conflict.[40] The US government's official collection of wartime documents, published in the 1880s and '90s, used *The War of the Rebellion* as its title. As Foster shows, the later shift among Northerners to the language of "civil war" represented a concession to Confederates. This language conferred a degree of legitimacy that the wartime generation had been unwilling to grant. By contextualizing the timing of this linguistic shift, Foster exposes the highly politicized nature of how we refer to wars after their conclusion. Nonetheless, during the conflict, Northerners used the language of "civil war" ubiquitously in their private and unofficial correspondence. They adopted this language not to appease white Southerners but because it offered a clinical terminology that put the United States in the mainstream of historical experience. Americans' uses of "civil war" to describe the violent suppression of domestic dissent joined them to an older tradition and reinforced the naturalness of civil war within modern nation-state development.

Some Northerners intentionally avoided defining the conflict even as they endorsed the view that domestic trauma was a natural part of national development. A Pennsylvania state senator, George Landon, offered a useful disquisition on the subject in 1862. "The careful student of history has learned this lesson, that every nation and every government sooner or later has its crisis, its ordeal, and I may say its test hour. It is called upon to pass through its political straits where its strength is proved or its weakness developed, where its dignity is illustrated, its folly exhibited, where begin its rise and progress or decline and fall." Landon referred listeners to the seventeenth century: "England had her ordeal when the head of Charles I. was brought to the block, and Cromwell, a common ploughman, siding with the people and with right, took his crown and his throne." Importantly, Landon's characterization of the English Civil Wars and of the American conflict avoided the definitional debate altogether—he lumped "insurrections, revolutions, and rebellions" together—even as he endorsed the positive value they brought. "These ordeals must come. They do no harm, they are rather beneficial; provided the people of the day are adequate to the emergency thereof. . . . This struggle of ours will do our country no harm if we are but true to ourselves, true to our history, true to the teachings of philanthropy and patriotism."[41]

Landon defined "harm" quite loosely. He was speaking solely about the integrity of national institutions, which he believed would come through the war intact, if not strengthened. This framing ignored the actual harm that the war produced. It reveals the ways that moderate Northerners' emphasis on the integrity of the state obscured the violence that was necessary to its preservation.[42] That same attitude was also visible in histories of England itself. François Guizot's 1851 history of the "origins of representative government in Europe" telescoped the middle decades of the seventeenth century within a teleological paradigm. He concluded that a "great revolution in the state of society broke out in the reign of Charles I., and determined that political revolution, which, after fifty years of conflict, finally established representative government in England."[43] "Fifty years of conflict" concealed quite a bit of actual suffering. Priya Satia documents a similar willed blindness among nineteenth-century Britons, when a liberal vision of historical change justified bloody military actions in India and the Middle East.[44] The US Civil War produced a demonstrably more progressive outcome—emancipation—than the British wars in Afghanistan (1838) or India (1857). But the moral triumph of emancipation, which white Northerners claimed as their own, led Americans to regard the war's outcome as unambiguously good.[45]

There is a strand of Civil War historiography in which historians skeptical about the limited degree of freedom granted to Black people with the end of slavery critique the war's outcomes. Usually designated as "revisionist," such histories question the value of the war, given how little seemingly changed.[46] My concern in this instance is not revisionist. Instead, I am drawing attention to the fact that the (mostly successful) efforts of Northerners to naturalize the Civil War as part of national development obscured the role of coercion in maintaining the American state. Northern victory in the war should remind us of the necessity of physical violence as a component of statehood, but contemporary Americans usually avoid this fact in public discussions. Studies of cultural nationalism and public memory insist, rightly, on the importance of emotional and cultural bonds that tie people to their nation. David Potter, among other commentators, alerted us to the persistent importance of a state protecting people's material interests.[47] Alongside these bonds stands force.

As most modern scholars are quick to point out, the very definition of a state, according to sociologist Max Weber's classic formulation, is the institution that possesses a monopoly on violence.[48] But Weber's theory offers little in the case of civil conflicts. The Civil War happened because the US government did not have a monopoly on the use of force. Secessionists, usually at the helm of Southern state governments, marshaled state resources and appropriated Federal resources such as forts and weapons (which they then renationalized as Confederate property) that enabled them to present an alternative force to the US government. We are lucky that the state that (eventually) committed to emancipation and union won the US Civil War. But that outcome should not blind us to the unpleasant reality that those progressive political changes relied on destruction and death meted out by the US Army.

Few people who lived through the nineteenth century could profess such innocence. The imperative of maintaining national sovereignty, whether for a republic such as the United States or an empire such as Britain, required military force and the willingness to use it. British historians drew from their past a cynical realist view of international relations. James Froude explained English rule of Ireland without apology: "The right of a people to self-government consists and can consist in nothing but their power to defend themselves." "On the whole," Froude concluded, "and as a rule, superior strength is the equivalent of superior merit."[49] Many Americans agreed. Rather than condemn Britain's brutal suppression of the 1857 Indian Rebellion as colonial violence, the *Atlantic Monthly* applauded it in language that anticipated how Theodore Roosevelt would later marshal men into war against Spain in the 1890s. "The terrible, but glorious, experience of the Indian Rebellion showed that Englishmen still possessed in as full measure as ever those noble characteristics on which they justly pride themselves, and of which a nation of kindred blood would be the last to deny them the praise. When the heroic qualities found their occasion, they were not wanting." The British punished the leaders of the insurrection with gross public violence (tying rebel leaders to the mouths of cannon and discharging the weapons). The public spectacle was intended to deter future resistance to British rule. This made British critiques of Northern purpose in the Civil War all the more frustrating. "England professes not to be able to understand the principles of this wicked, this unholy war, as she calls it. Yet she was not so slow to understand the necessity of putting down the Irish Insurrection of 1848, or the

Indian Rebellion ten years later," complained the journal.[50] Even so gentle a soul as Charles Sumner saw the equivalency, as he noted in an 1862 letter to John Bright: "I should not be astonished to see the whole rebellion crumble like your Sepoy Rebellion, which for awhile seemed as menacing to your Indian empire as ours has been to our republic."[51]

When feeling querulous (as they usually were when Britons critiqued Union war strategies), Northerners responded with sharp readings of British history. Responding to the London *Times*' criticism of the Northern blockade, one widely shared article reminded the world, "No nation has ever existed which punished rebellion with more severity than England. The dungeons of the Tower; the fleshless and grinning skulls which of old formed the appropriate ornaments of Temple Bar [in Dublin;] . . . the massacres of Drogheda and Glencoe . . . all bear witness to the murderous revenge with which England visits rebellion against her authority."[52] Britain had pioneered the use of military violence to establish sovereignty over noncontiguous territory. "She thinks it impossible for the Government of the United States to subdue and hold provinces so vast as the Cotton States of America; yet she neither foreboded nor as yet has found any impracticability in renewing and retaining her hold on the vaster provinces of British India,—provinces inhabited, all of them, by races alien in blood, religion, and manners, and many by a population greatly exceeding that of our Southern States." With this prelude, the *Atlantic Monthly* asked, "Is this, then, to be a commonplace war, a prosaic and peddling quarrel about Cotton? Shall there be nothing to enlist enthusiasm or kindle fanaticism? Are we to have no Cause like that for which our English republican ancestors died so gladly on the field, with such dignity on the scaffold?—no Cause that shall give us a hero, who knows but a Cromwell?" This was not the valorization of Oliver Cromwell that inspired abolitionists to a hard war against slavery. Instead, it was a moderates' plea that the nation needed heroes. "To our minds, though it may be obscure to Englishmen who look on Lancashire as the centre of the universe, no army was ever enlisted for a nobler service than ours. Not only is it national life and a foremost place among nations that is at stake, but the vital principle of Law itself, the august foundation on which the very possibility of government, above all of self-government, rests as in the hollow of God's own hand."[53]

THE WHIGGISH AMERICAN CIVIL WAR

The distemper Americans manifested when they quarreled with Britons about the Civil War itself did not diminish their respect for Britain's history or America's relationship to that history. One of the most penetrating recent assessments of British nineteenth-century historical consciousness, Priya Satia's *Time's Monster*, critiques historians of that era (and later) for wedding a racist imperialism to liberalism. "Liberal theories of history," she writes, "envisioned 'progress' brought about by the will, usually, of great men (chosen and guided by Providence).... Such theories of history, carried around in a nineteenth-century Briton's mind were motivating—galvanizing the exercise of agency—and exonerating insofar as they invoked higher ultimate ends or 'context'—the way circumstances or the *needs* of history constrained agency and thus personal responsibility."[54] Satia offers a devastating indictment of the people who built Britain's empire and those who valorized it under the aegis of progress's worthy ends. Civil War Americans were nearly as wedded to the idea of progress as the nineteenth-century Britons Satia chronicles, and historical thinking shaped the relationship between liberalism and nation- and empire-building in North America just as it did for Britain's empire.[55]

In the American context, conservatives, radicals, and moderates in the North disagreed about what constituted "progress." They all professed to believe in it, though they disagreed about whether progress allowed or required slavery and about the appropriate scale of industrial and urban development.[56] They also disagreed about the nature of liberalism itself. Lincoln and Northern moderates placed great faith in process; they believed in majoritarian democracy, even (perhaps especially) when it changed over time.[57] The experience of war and the great sacrifices made by African Americans encouraged Lincoln to advocate first the end of slavery and then the gradual incorporation of Black men as voters. Lincoln did not imagine our modern democratic electorate (including, for instance, female voters), but his faith in process proved well placed. Thanks to the efforts of generations of activists, starting with Black and white abolitionists in the 1830s and extending into the twenty-first century, the "circle of we" continued to expand. Northern conservatives, in contrast, opposed an open-ended liberalism. They supported a proscriptive democracy, in which power remained in the hands of white men.

As Satia shows, nineteenth-century Britons generated an intoxicating blend of national destiny, racial supremacy, military violence, and economic power to justify and compel their empire. Americans read the same history and philosophy that energized British imperialists. In addition to providing analogies that guided people through the Civil War, readers developed a theory of national development that braided the English and American Civil Wars together. They did this by anchoring the Northern effort to deny secession and preserve self-government within the long trajectory of English history. The first step was to establish the cultural and historical links that bound America and Britain, as when *Harper's Weekly* explained that "America is the child of England. The child left the ancestral home with indignation and violence, but she is none the less of the same blood, of the same sympathy, of the same hope. . . . The glory of England was our glory." Historians, poets, and novelists provided the raw material and served as links themselves. "Carlyle and Macaulay, Wordsworth and Tennyson, Dickens and Thackeray, they were ours as they were England's," proclaimed *Harper's*.[58] John Greenleaf Whittier, one of the country's most popular poets, made this argument in his wartime critique of English neutrality in the Civil War:

> O Englishmen!—in hope and creed,
>   In blood and tongue our brothers!
> We too are heirs of Runnymede;
> And Shakespeare's fame and Cromwell's deed
>   Are not alone our mother's.[59]

Another journal agreed: "No two nations are bound together by so many bonds of sympathy and interest as England and America. England is our mother."[60] John Bright celebrated the joint pride of the two countries, "the two greatest nations who speak the English language, and from their origins are alike entitled to the English name."[61]

The second step endorsed the whiggish view that for English-speaking people, history was a continuous striving for constitutional freedom. Recasting Jefferson Davis's condemnation of the Puritans' humble origins ("gathered from the bogs and fens of Ireland and Scotland"), one author argued, "The first germ of republican liberty sprang into life amid the sedges and savage marshes of uncultivated ages, far remote even from the discovery of America, and [we can] trace it through successive rebellions, both of a political and religious character, from and before the times of Wycliffe, down to Oliver Cromwell and George Washington."[62] The seventeenth-century conflicts established the bedrock for this tradition. According to an Ohio newspaper, "The middle classes rose in their strength, and, under Cromwell, hurled a despotic king from his throne which he or his counsellors endeavored to convert into an altar on which all the religious and civil liberties of his people were to be sacrificed."[63] A minister writing to *The Liberator* adopted a similar framing. "The war of the Revolution under Hampden and Cromwell redeemed England," he argued, "because it was waged for the overthrow of an intolerable tyranny, and the establishment of constitutional liberty."[64]

The third step described Americans as the inheritors of this tradition. In the words of the Ohio paper, "Again, a free people rose under Washington, and from the colonies of America made this great Nation the pillar and champion of freedom."[65] Or, in another telling: "Political and religious liberty are the two sides of the democrat idea, and have always marched hand in hand together. They culminated in England during the Commonwealth, and became thenceforth the base and dome of popular government. The republic of America was born of this idea."[66] A genealogy of heroes provided human form for this interpretation, as a Minnesota journal explained to its Northern readers: "You stood side by side with Milton and Cromwell, Lafayette and Garibaldi, Washington and Kosciusco [sic], in the old conflict between Liberty and Despotism, renewed."[67] The connections among these historical figures were personified in real time during the war. When Confederate diplomat James Mason arrived in London, the *Richmond Examiner* bragged, "We are glad to be able to contrast such a gentleman with Charles Francis Adams," the US ambassador to Britain during the Civil War whom the Virginia paper described as "the Puritan representative of freedom at the Court of St. James." The intended slur—"Puritan"—rebounded as an honorific for *Harper's* editors. "What American," they proudly noted, "who loves Milton and Hampden, and honors Oliver Cromwell, who fought Charles Stuart for the same great cause in which we are fighting Jefferson Davis, will not cry with all his heart, Amen!"[68]

The final step was to crown the US Civil War itself as the last stage in this process.[69] The same Ohio paper that captured the Anglo-American bonds and the role of the Revolution as the second great moment concluded by contextualizing the current conflict: "A third time to complete the work undone by the Fathers of the Country, to maintain inviolate the Constitution and the Union intrusted to our keeping—the people of America have arrisen [sic] with extraordinary unanimity."[70] Part of connecting these two conflicts was interpreting them within the shared framework of whiggish liberty.[71] In a widely reprinted article, the *Monthly Religious Magazine* explained, "The great civil war of England, known as 'the Great Rebellion,' was also a conflict between the oligarchs and the commons; called again the Cavaliers and the Roundheads. ... It divided England horizontally—the king and lords and the bishops on one side, the commons on the other; and it decided a question forever, whether constitutional government was a possible boon to the English race."[72] Lincoln's secretary of state, William Henry Seward, carried this interpretation abroad in his postwar travels, where he advocated "nationalism to be a progressive historical force inextricably entwined with the progress of 'civilization.'" In particular, Seward, once an Anglophobe and now an Anglophile, "conceived of the

Civil War as the pivotal event in the transatlantic struggle pitting advocates of republican government against their monarchical and aristocratic enemies."[73]

The whiggish interpretation of the American Civil War took root as wartime rhetoric but outlived the conflict. By the early twentieth century, it could be found in the leading histories of the conflict.[74] James Ford Rhodes, author of a leading history of the United States, adopted an optimistic and encouraging tone in his explanation of the war. He celebrated the war's gentle conclusion—"Nobody was hanged for a political crime, no land of the vanquished Confederates confiscated"—while lauding Lincoln as "the great man of the Civil War" precisely because he had resisted the despotism of Caesar.[75] Later generations of historians left Rhodes's party-based interpretation of political conflict behind for a more holistic social and cultural analysis of the country's sectional divisions, but his positivist reading of the role of the Civil War in making a modern and more democratic United States remained central to historical writing until the most recent generation of outright critics of the war's outcomes.[76] Even among historians skeptical of celebratory history, the impulse to square ourselves with Lincoln can produce strongly whiggish histories.

Contemporary English liberals, who created the whiggish interpretation that emphasized the inevitable growth of liberty, also connected their history to the American experience. In an 1862 speech, Henry Vincent, a Chartist and antislavery activist, summarized the classic telling of English history. "All nations have their particular difficulties," Vincent explained. "England has been severely tried by many combats . . . through the war of the Roses, through the stupendous struggle between the Parliament and King Charles, in the days of gigantic Cromwell, through the vile reigns of the second Charles and James, to the glorious revolution of 1688—she has marched in the upward career of freedom and glory, shaking all her difficulties, by God's great mercy, like dust from her feet." Despite the seemingly inevitable nature of that progress, by the 1860s the reform project had stalled in England. The state retained property qualifications for voting and for office-holding, and Parliament functioned as a bulwark of conservative power in a country wracked by class inequities created by rapid industrialization. Reformers such as Vincent looked across the Atlantic, because they regarded the American experience as an extension of England's and because they hoped that experience would inspire further change in their country. "Who will dare to talk of the failure of English institutions?" Vincent concluded. "America is a part of ourselves."[77]

Goldwin Smith, the Regius Professor of History at Oxford University, published several pamphlets during the conflict. Like Vincent, Smith expounded on the link between English and American political histories. "English liberties, imperfect as they may be,—and as an English Liberal of course thinks they are,—are the source from which your liberties have flowed, through the river may be more abundant than the spring." This common origin tied the two nations together: "England by her eight centuries of constitutional progress has done a great work for you, and the two nations may yet have a great work to do together for themselves and for the world."[78] "England bore you," Smith proclaimed, "and bore you not without a mother's pangs. For the real hour of your birth was the English Revolution of the seventeenth century at once the saddest and the noblest period of English history." Smith deliberately recast American history as starting not with the Revolution but with the English Civil Wars. "This is not the official version of your origin," he admitted. "The official version makes you the children of the revolutionary spirit which was abroad in the eighteenth century and culminated in the French Revolution. But this robs you of a century and a half of antiquity, and of more than a century and a half of greatness."[79]

In this telling, shared aspirations connected the conflicts despite the two centuries separating them in time. In fact, the nature of the American conflict enabled British liberals to reinterpret their own conflict by emphasizing its political radicalism. Seen in the new light of what Americans were accomplishing, British thinkers could advance readings of their history hardly imaginable even thirty years earlier. Smith lamented that "the Revolution of the seventeenth century failed . . . at least as an attempt to establish social equality and liberty of conscience." Despite the temporary break from hereditary aristocracy, Cromwell could not permanently remake the state. "The Revolution failed in England. Yet in England in the party of Cromwell and Milton still lives. It still lives; and in this great crisis of your fortunes, its heart turns to you. On your success ours depends. Now, as in the seventeenth century, the thread of our fate is twined with the thread of yours."[80] Many histories of Civil War diplomacy focus on Secretary of State William Seward's Anglophobia and the real tensions that arose between the United States and the United Kingdom during the war.[81] At the same time, the deeper cultural continuity described by Smith, Vincent, and their American counterparts reassured Northerners that they stood on the side of progress.

Any conflict on the scale of the US Civil War—involving 30 million people, 3 million soldiers, and over 1 million casualties and occurring over a space larger than continental Europe—leaves a complex, multifaceted legacy. Abolitionists, celebrating emancipation, claimed a radical one. Conservatives, with reunion and the effective defense of existing land policies, claimed a contrary one. Moderates, with their abstract arguments over the relationship between war and nationhood, won as well. The moderate Northern reading of the war also had the virtue of deescalating the rhetoric, common in the North, that demanded Confederates be punished for the war. The famous diarist George Templeton Strong recorded a story he heard of a senator visiting Lincoln "and suggesting a parallel between secession and that first rebellion of which Milton sang. Very funny interview. Abe Lincoln didn't know much about *Paradise Lost* and sent out for a copy, looked through its first books under the Senator's guidance, and was struck by the coincidences between the utterances of Satan and those of Jefferson Davis. . . . 'Yes,' said Uncle Abraham, 'I always thought the Devil was *some* to blame!'"[82] Lincoln may have recognized the "coincidences," but he never made them central to his rhetoric or his policies. In that respect, the moderate insistence on the inevitability of national conflict encouraged Lincoln's late-war call for charity toward the enemy. Assimilating the Civil War into a continuous story of American nation-building did not require villains.

The moderate Northern meaning-making that I have emphasized here contradicted the strong exceptionalist strain in American thought. The belief that America possessed a virtue unique in the world and was obligated to share its values and institutions emerged most fully in the post–World War II era. Allied victory in that conflict followed forty-five years later by the collapse of the Soviet Union made it seem possible that capitalist democracy represented a kind of inevitable end point of political and economic development.[83] Theorists of American exceptionalism recast the country's history, from its beginnings in the Puritans' "city on a hill" to the "Pax Americana" of the twentieth century.[84] This interpretation carries little weight with historians today, though it remains an article of faith in America's national story. In many respects, nineteenth-century Americans can be viewed as the original progenitors of American exceptionalism. Most white Americans considered the country morally and politically superior to any other.[85] Nonetheless, they also understood American history as inexorably bound up with European and other world histories. It was only in the post–World War II era that American historians pursued theories of exceptionalism with vigor, and they did so, as Daniel Rodgers persuasively argues, as a way to explain "in the face of traditional Europe's collapse . . . how it had come about that the United States seemed to have skated past the disasters of the mid twentieth century."[86] The answer to that question does not lie in the nineteenth century. As this chapter has shown, Americans understood their fate following tracks laid down by other people. Whether they linked Union victory to a whiggish procession of liberty or naturalized civil conflict as a routine part of national development, Northerners identified the Union experience with others around the world. Rather than exceptional, the United States was ordinary.

This moderate Northern interpretation of the Civil War did not provide solace to widows or orphans, did not valorize the sacrifices of men who served, and did not speak the emotional language of memorials. Instead, it dwelt in abstractions, such as states and nationalism and destiny. Nonetheless, by identifying civil war as a likely, even perhaps necessary, feature of national development, it reassured Civil War Americans that the sacrifices of war possessed value. Definitions and connotations may seem small consolation for the death and destruction wrought by military conflict, but words and concepts order the world in peacetime. They provide the structure to contain our disagreements and manage our politics. The historian David Armitage, in his global intellectual history of the changing definitions of civil war, identifies the American conflict as a key moment. "During the U.S. Civil War," he writes, "the category of civil war came firmly under the authority of the lawyers for the first time."[87] It also came under the authority of historians and ministers and ordinary people. In the act of measuring the meaning of the Civil War, people were not overmastered by language or swept by rhetoric past their worst intentions, as had happened during the conflict. Instead, people wrestled language to meet their needs, to accommodate the trauma of war within legal, religious, and historical frameworks.

CONCLUSION

Past and Present

> Analogy and metaphor are also constitutive of our cognitive processes: without them there is no possibility of producing theory, no production of thought. The question is not whether analogy should be allowed, but what constitutes a good analogy as opposed to a bad one: to what extent does an analogy *work*.
>
> JESSE McCARTHY, *Who Will Pay Reparations on My Soul?*

The preceding narrative executed (successfully, I hope) a two-step dance. First, I showed that throughout the US Civil War, Americans analogized their experience to the English Civil Wars. The second step involved analyzing how they used those analogies. Northerners and Southerners disagreed with each other, and Northerners disagreed among themselves. History served as a primary language of disagreement. This practice had real consequences. Because Confederates anchored themselves in the Royalist world of the 1640s, they exacerbated class dissension in a society at war and already divided by race. Northern radicals' attachment to Oliver Cromwell led them to see hard war as a tool for remaking society. Northern moderates navigated between these positions, endorsing the Parliamentarian defense of popular rights but seeking to end the war on terms that would enable a rapid reunion. Analogies and metaphors led people into unpredictable and sometimes more violent positions in the 1860s (as they can today), but calling out inaccurate or misleading metaphorical language hardly suffices as useful history. In my case, I hope that parsing participants' views of the past can explain how rhetorical conflict both reflected and shaped the meaning of the Civil War.

In our contemporary world, national memory often serves to buttress rather than redistribute power, to stabilize rather than upset the status quo. Was the same true during the American Civil War? Did appealing to the past support a conservative or a progressive habit in American thought? In some places and times, history served liberal ends. For instance, in seventeenth-century England, Englishmen appealed to an ancient constitution in order to put the law beyond the reach of the monarch, to identify certain fundamental practices that even he could not change.[1] They took history seriously and, in this case, as a force for the protection of the common people. Like the English, Americans believed the past shaped the future. Unlike the English, the American case reveals deep divisions. Americans' loyalty to the Anglo-American past established boundaries for the conflict. Analogies broaden our thinking by enabling comparison of dissimilar things but like all language analogies also confine us. In the case of the US Civil War, participants' frequent references to the English Civil Wars ensured a public conversation bounded by faith in constitutional change and individual property rights and a deep suspicion of using military violence to enact social change. In other words, Americans' uses of the English past shaped their thinking in ways that favored established power. Northern radicals proved an exception; they used history to challenge the status quo, although the history they privileged had ended in failure. Because history restricts our range of vision to what has preceded us, it can produce less radical blueprints than what some communities (particularly historically oppressed ones like the freed people) might feel is necessary to create lasting change.

Historical thinking, alongside literary, religious, and philosophical speculations, was one of the ways that Americans made sense of their world, a method they used to navigate their path. What difference did it make? A skeptic might object that knowing that Americans referenced the English Civil Wars in different ways only reveals what we already know: that Confederates opposed Federals and that Northerners were divided over the purposes and practices of the US Civil War. Even recognizing analogies used by the war's participants does not prove that these conceptions shaped wartime behavior. Does the evidence in these cases reveal that history shapes attitudes or merely signal them? Is history a motive force? Many historians, myself included, might prefer an airtight case that reveals how the past shaped the present, but no one thinks, or explains their thinking, in one-to-one ways. We have to content ourselves with circumstantial proof, but I find the evidence persuasive. Civil War Americans recalled the English Civil Wars to rally and inspire, to demonize and degrade, to justify and explain. Both Northerners and Southerners sought refuge in an analogical world culled from a past one step removed. The past mattered.

It mattered because marshaling the past as evidence and argument enabled the war's participants to push their claims. The cultural distinctions that Southerners conjured by identifying themselves with their seventeenth-century heroes offered an argument for secession, one predicated on the importance of national autonomy for distinct ethnic and cultural communities. During the war itself, Northerners drew on the historical debate over legitimate rebellion to empower the side of established power against insurgents. Because Confederates aspired to establish a conservative political and social order, they did not derive much from the claims of historical rebels. The class distinctions that formed the basis for memories of the English Civil Wars allowed this aspect of the conflict to assume greater importance between North and South, again to Confederates' detriment. Confederates' use of English Civil War analogies raised the stakes of their own conflict and decreased the possibility of a negotiated peace.[2] Within the North, partisan uses of the same analogies sharpened the political divide and show the ways that war energizes political disputes as the stakes and pace of change escalate. The slipperiness of historical thinking also led people to surprising positions, such as abolitionists advocating hard war and Confederates endorsing monarchy.[3] For Northerners who identified with the Parliamentarian cause against King Charles, the model of ordered liberty encouraged a moderation in Lincoln that enabled him to suppress the Confederates while resisting the calls of radicals in his own section.

This study joins others over the last decade that analyze how memories of the Civil War shaped racial, ideological, and partisan battles in America. For a long time, scholars have focused on the contest over national memory.[4] My approach departs from previous studies by considering not just national memory but transnational ones. How did people in one place deploy or exploit the memories of other people's conflicts? Such borrowing might seem to lend itself to even more convoluted and partisan interpretations of the past, but this was not necessarily the case. Given the increasing interconnectedness of the nineteenth-century world, there were limits to the elasticity of global memories and history, just as in national traditions. At the same time, borrowing other peoples' experiences gave Civil War Americans access to a greater range of possibilities than by confining themselves to American ones.[5] Because they looked back two centuries, the analogies never offered precise models for behavior, but that ambiguity provided crucial flexibility. It enabled participants in the conflict to interpret the past in ways that served their needs.

The prevalence of seventeenth-century history in the language and thoughts of nineteenth-century Americans begs the question of how Americans conceptualized history itself. Northerners celebrated their victory as continuing the noble tradition of British liberty. They assured themselves that America's destiny followed a linear trajectory, that progress demanded the extinguishment of slavery and the expansion of freedom. Still, they protested too much. Alongside the claims to the inevitability of national greatness, many Northerners also recognized the pull of cyclical history.[6] Samuel Cox, the Ohio Democrat, endorsed this perspective. "Truly, there are fixed laws for the events of history," he told Congress in 1864. "Society revolves in an orbit."[7] The English Civil Wars ended, finally, in the Restoration, which returned England to a monarchy, one still visible today. The echoes of the British conflicts that reverberated through North America in the 1860s encouraged an approach to the past that emphasized cycles and repetition. Perhaps America's destiny was not like a comet, which would blaze a path across the heavens, but some more humble object whose path describes a predictable ellipse? This orientation toward the past was reinforced by the Civil War's ambiguous legacy—of slavery's end and white supremacy's persistence, of the Union's triumph and the reification of sectionalism—which encourages us to see both continuity and change in the era.

Perhaps history does not move in either an exclusively linear or cyclical fashion. From our position today, especially as we consider the long history of military conflict and the rhetoric that sustains war, we might envision a third pattern, one more attentive to the differences in scale between the long *durée* and history as experienced during people's lives. Wars generate eddies or whorls in the flow of time. People who use history as explanation or justification enter these disruptions, and when they spin free, like leaves carried by a current, the recirculation they experience alters their trajectory. Deliberately invoking history as rhetoric or unintentionally summoning historical parallels alters the course of contemporary events, though not always in predictable ways. The use of historical analogies makes it appear that the same history has come again, even as historians insist that no two eras are alike.

The problem of linear versus cyclical conceptions of history is nowhere more acute than in the field of military history and in public conversations about wars, which draw heavily upon precedents. Since 1975, every military operation conducted by the United States has occurred in the shadow of the Vietnam War. Still today, words such as "quagmire" and "military adviser" resurrect the perils of that conflict in all their immediacy; invoking them imbues the writing with a prophetic power. World Wars I and II generated their own corpus of concepts. Late twentieth-century military planners strove to avoid "needless wars" or to presume that war itself could end armed conflict. Instead, obedient to the false memory of a "good war," they framed half a century's worth of conflicts with the Soviet Union as an existential demand.[8] In the same way, the wars of the English-speaking world that preceded the US Civil War shaped that conflict even as the fighting of the Civil War compelled participants to revise their understanding of those past wars.

A common saying is that we always fight the last war. This saying misrepresents how our memories of war actually work. We do not just fight the last war. In important ways, we fight all the previous wars. The history of military conflict might be thought of as an iceberg. The last conflict is the visible part protruding from the water. But beneath the surface lies the inheritance of previous conflicts. Depending on the clarity of the water and the sophistication of our imaging equipment, we sometimes catch glimpses of these deeper legacies, but too often they appear only as politicized analogies. As the rhetoric of the American Civil War makes clear, past conflicts surface, bidden and unbidden. Like ship captains on a dark night, we would do well to watch for ice. We would benefit from a greater understanding of past conflicts—their political roots, their military operations, their social consequences—and a deeper appreciation of the many ways people have conceptualized and deployed those histories. We need to recognize that just as we inherit the legacies of wars, we inherit the legacy of writing and thinking about wars. The difference between actual events and the historical record is real, but the latter carries the former through time. We may see war's results on a landscape, or in migration patterns, or in the missing members of a family, but for most people, we understand the meaning of past conflicts through what we read about them. In other words, we cannot escape the currents that carry old experiences back into the present. Indeed, sometimes we generate those currents deliberately, even if they sometimes sweep us beyond our intended goal.

Another common saying is that history repeats itself, but this phrasing misrepresents the nature of historical change. History does not operate autonomously, repeating when it feels like playing a cruel joke on unsuspecting people. Rather, historical change happens as a result of the actions we take, magnified by deliberate collective action and by structural forces bigger than any one person. It would be more accurate to say that we repeat history by using historical examples to understand our experiences. The repetition that we perceive is a product of how we think about the relationship between past and present, not a reflection of some objective parallelism that recurs over time.

Civil War Americans' habit of referring to the English Civil Wars marks them as typical rather than exceptional. In moments of crisis, people often, perhaps inevitably, compare themselves and their experiences to those of the past. This practice can illuminate and inspire its practitioners, historians among them, but it comes with costs. The rhetorician I. A. Richards argues that the process of bringing disparate things together subtly changes both of them.[9] When we use metaphorical language—for instance, drawing chronological or geographic comparisons—the act of joining alters them. We do not alter the past itself, of course, but we change the meaning of the past by connecting it to the present. We think differently about that past by identifying it alongside something contemporaneous. Just like nineteenth-century people interpreted the seventeenth century in ways that enabled them to gain advantage in their worlds, we do the same in the twenty-first century with nineteenth-century history. And with the same results. Every time we invoke the US Civil War in conversations about our current political landscape or in conversations about military conflicts around the world, we change what the past means. What was important to the generation that experienced the English Civil Wars was not the same as it was to those who experienced the American Civil War. Similarly, what is important to us today about the US conflict is not the same as it was to the people who lived through the war. This does not reveal disloyalty or violate some tenet of historical thinking. It is historical thinking.

Some people think that by acknowledging the contingency of history itself, the degree to which it is "invented," we nullify its value. The most extreme version of this argument, more prevalent among theorists than ordinary people, is that history may take a more uniform narrative shape than traditional fiction, but they are both, fundamentally, invented and arbitrary.[10] The uses to which Civil War Americans put the seventeenth century and the uses to which we put nineteenth-century history today, instead, reveal the dynamism of history. The reciprocal relationship between past and present is precisely what makes history a living tradition, one anchored where all the humanities are—in our needs and lives today.

NOTES

INTRODUCTION

1. William C. Harris, "Hampton Roads Peace Conference," 54; Stephens, *Constitutional View*, 2:613; Hunter, "Peace Commission of 1865," 175.

2. Sheehan-Dean, *Reckoning with Rebellion*.

3. This is a study of Americans' history and memory of seventeenth-century England. It does not consistently compare the two experiences as the work of a historical sociologist might, nor does it trace the actual historical connections between the two places. Some studies of English colonial settlement take up this topic. See, e.g., McIlvenna, *Very Mutinous People*. Also, in my analysis, I am not including the routine or neutral invocation of historical actors or moments. These occurred with some frequency but rarely carried any ideological charge beyond a cursory awareness of great man history. For example, Henry Ward Beecher proclaimed, "There are two kinds of heroes: those that provoke admiration, and those who can invoke our admiration. Napoleon and Cromwell we can admire, but never revere." "Berkeley Association Lectures," *Boston Daily Advertiser*, January 23, 1861.

4. Ryan, "Bait Goat," 5.

5. Nineteenth-century Americans usually referred to the "English Civil War," singular. By adopting the plural form throughout (English Civil Wars), I am recognizing the modern scholarship that sees a much broader conflict.

6. My summary here draws in particular on Braddick, *God's Fury, England's Fire*; Worden, *English Civil Wars*; Ó Siochrú, *Confederate Ireland*; and Healy, *Blazing World*.

7. That said, the fusion of providential and nationalist thinking in both eras would have made them mutually intelligible, an interpretive thread I emphasize most fully in chapter 8.

8. "Despite its centuries-old tradition and the heightened expectations many had for its success, even as late as 1642 Parliament was without executive or administrative capacities," historian Mark Kishlansky notes. "The Houses had no formal leaders and most of those

who had directed legislative programs in the past departed with the King.... Although the concept of 'representative' was expanding, Parliament had no institutional means for carrying the will of the Houses to the communities of the nation. Local government, despite the presence at Westminster of leading justices, Lords, and Deputy Lieutenants, was the still the King's government." Kishlansky, *Rise of the New Model Army*, 5.

9. For an invigorating recent challenge to the importance of nineteenth-century political parties, see Shelden and Alexander, "Dismantling the Party System."

10. John Brewer argued that the English state, even the military wing, remained weak and disorganized up to the 1640s. "The creation of what I call the 'fiscal-military state' was the most important transformation in English government between the domestic reforms of the Tudors and the major administrative changes of the first half of the nineteenth century." Brewer, *Sinews of Power*, vxii. Michael Braddick's assessment offers similar credit to the civil wars for producing a "modern" state: "What is clear is that a consequence of the civil wars was to break these constraints [to legitimate specialized administrative systems] and in the long run this produced more modern forms of office." Braddick, *State Formation*, 435. As Charles Tilly has argued, it was not that the state expanded in order to fight war but that war compelled the organization of the state. That also described the pattern in the United States. See, e.g., Nevins, *War for the Union*; and Bensel, *Yankee Leviathan*.

11. A valuable introduction to the distinction (about which there is an extensive, interdisciplinary body of writing) can be found in Lowenthal, *Past*, 378–82.

12. The historian Daniel Rodgers observes, about a (supposedly) foundational text in American history, that "no words or text can be insulated from time. Their occasions change, the possibilities others see in them change, sometimes radically. Every subsequent use is by necessity a rewriting, a reinvention for new hopes, new conditions, and new contentions." Rodgers, *As a City*, 6, 280.

13. The rhetorician I. A. Richards offers a useful analysis of the way metaphors operate on our minds. "Let us consider," he writes, "more closely what happens in the mind when we put together—in a sudden and striking fashion—two things belonging to very different orders of existence. The most important happenings—in addition to a general confused reverberation and strain—are the mind's efforts to connect them. The mind is a connecting organ, it works only by connecting and it can connect any two things in an indefinitely large number of ways." Richards quoted in Donoghue, *Metaphor*, 93; Richards, *Philosophy of Rhetoric*, 124–25.

14. Pollan, *Botany of Desire*, 1–58.

15. Janney, "Civil War Memory"; Gaines M. Foster, "What's Not in a Name."

16. Gaines M. Foster, *Ghosts of the Confederacy*; Blight, *Race and Reunion*; Gannon, *Won Cause*; Janney, *Remembering the Civil War*.

17. This book explores only one strand of that memory—we also need a clearer sense of Americans' understanding of classical history, the French Revolution (and Napoléon in particular), and the American Revolution, among other topics. An excellent take on the uses of the classical past can be found in Sutton, "'We Died Here.'" Sarah Gardner's forthcoming study of Civil War Americans' uses of Shakespeare represents another imaginative way to understand the cultural and intellectual history of the era. See Gardner, "Shakespeare Fights."

18. Waldstreicher, *In the Midst of Perpetual Fetes*; Purcell, *Sealed with Blood*; Messer, *Stories of Independence*.

19. Herbert Butterfield's foundational text retains a still precise formulation of whiggishness: "To praise revolutions provided they have been successful, to emphasise certain principles of progress in the past and to produce a story which is the rarification of the glorification of the present." Butterfield, *Whig Interpretation*, v. In the text, I capitalize the word "Whig" when it refers to the political party but use lowercase "whiggish" or "whig" to refer to the historical interpretation.

20. I am revising Louis Menand's powerful argument about the rise of pragmatism by arguing that this account captured an essential but sectionally distinct truth. Menand, *Metaphysical Club*; Thomas, "Romantic Reform in America."

21. Marx, *Eighteenth Brumaire*, 16–17.

22. Marx, *Eighteenth Brumaire*, 18.

23. Pocock, *Machiavellian Moment*, xxiii–xxiv.

CHAPTER 1

1. Writing about the 1750s, historian Michael Hattem concludes, "It seems likely that the average colonist would have had enough exposure to historical information to understand a basic outline of the major events of the seventeenth-century British past: the Civil Wars, Restoration, and Glorious Revolution." Hattem, *Past and Prologue*, 47. This was even more true 100 years later.

2. Reynolds, *Beneath the American Renaissance*.

3. Sutton, "'We Died Here,'" 168–74; Bishop, "Different Kind of Tie"; Winterer, *Culture of Classicism*; Gilbert, "Leopold von Ranke."

4. Colbourn, *Lamp of Experience*, 21; McConville, *King's Three Faces*, 93–94.

5. Alert youthful readers would have encountered Cromwell in the *McGuffey's Sixth Eclectic Reader*, where he is described as "the leading character in the Great Rebellion in England. He was Lord Protector the last five years of his life, and in many respects the ablest ruler that England ever had."

6. Donald, *Charles Sumner*, 10.

7. Gardner, "Shakespeare Fights."

8. Trela, "Cromwell," 128–29.

9. Brontë, *Jane Eyre*, 66.

10. Stowe, *Sunny Memories*, 244.

11. By 1850, 90.4 percent of white Americans over the age of twenty could read. Zboray, *Fictive People*, 96, 83.

12. Michael O'Brien, *Conjectures of Order*, 2:591; Fox-Genovese and Genovese, *Mind*, 125–28.

13. "The shelves of our great reading clubs and libraries are crowded . . . with the history of Carlyle, Froude, Macaulay." "There Can Be No Doubt," *Daily Evening Bulletin*, May 6, 1861.

14. Nixon, *Samuel Rawson Gardiner*.

15. "'Primal Cause' of Secession," *National Intelligencer*, March 8, 1862; review of Clarendon, *History of the Rebellion and Civil Wars in England*, in *Mercersburg Review*, October 1861, 631; "Two Years of American History," *New York Evangelist*, December 1862, 1; Literary Notices, *North American*, September 9, 1863; "History of Civilization in England," *Southern*

Literary Messenger, October 1858, 282; Hattem, *Past and Prologue*, 100. The English also used Clarendon as a way to understand the American conflict. "If Any Person Conversant," *Times*, February 14, 1863.

16. Trela, "Cromwell," 128.

17. Carlyle, *Oliver Cromwell's Speeches*; Gradert, *Puritan Spirits*, 19–24.

18. According to one biographer, "There was, however, a core of Puritanism that Carlyle thought was highly significant for the moral and social wellbeing of his contemporaries and made it eminently worthy of the historian's attention." Morrow, *Thomas Carlyle*, 171.

19. Vaughan, *Revolutions in English History*, 396. Historian Sarah Covington observes, "If the name 'Cromwell' retained its spark throughout the eighteenth century, it reached an altogether higher voltage in the politics of the century after." Covington, *Devil*, 112.

20. Cheng, *Plain and Noble Garb*, 47; Headley, *Life of Oliver Cromwell*.

21. Headley, *Life of Oliver Cromwell*, viii–ix.

22. Hall, *Puritans*, 349.

23. Carlyle, *On Heroes*.

24. Carlyle, *On Heroes*, 5.

25. Carlyle, *On Heroes*, 270–312.

26. Upon Macaulay's death in February 1860, *Frank Leslie's Illustrated Newspaper* offered a lavish editorial, describing his *History of England* as "universally read, more especially in America," which "fine work at once stamped the author as the greatest rhetorical historian of the age." "Lord Macaulay," *Frank Leslie's Illustrated Newspaper*, February 4, 1860.

27. Gooch, *History and Historians*, 280; Koditschek, *Liberalism*, 143–44.

28. Trevor-Roper, introduction to *History of England*, 24. A traveler to Australia recorded that "the three works he found on every squatter's shelf were the Bible, Shakespeare and Macaulay's Essays." Gooch, *History and Historians*, 280; Cheng, *Plain and Noble Garb*, 28.

29. Bray, "What Abraham Lincoln Read."

30. Mycock, "Very English Affair?," 52; Burrow, *Liberal Descent*, 14.

31. Macaulay, *History of England*, 1:97, 112.

32. The classic academic critique of this approach can be found in Butterfield, *Whig Interpretation of History*. John Clive offers a nuanced explanation of Macaulay's whiggish disposition in particular. Clive, *Macaulay*, 77–83.

33. Gooch, *History and Historians*, 277, 278. This represented a sharp about-face. Brendan McConville argues persuasively that "before 1750, disdain for Cromwell ran deep and wide in America. The label of 'Cromwellian' was primarily attached to those accused of extreme political behavior." McConville attributes the rehabilitation to the need for a strong leader against Catholics and other threats to English hegemony and then, during the Revolution itself, as a symbol of "legitimate resistance to imperial authority." McConville, *King's Three Faces*, 94–95, 270. Nelson's *Royalist Revolution* offers a more critical reading of American attitudes toward Cromwell.

34. Trevor-Roper, introduction to *History of England*, 37.

35. Scarborough, *Diary of Edmund Ruffin*, 2:428; "Carlyle and Macaulay," *Southern Literary Messenger*, August 1848, 476–80.

36. "The extent to which [John Stuart] Mill's moral ideal involved an extraordinarily close coincidence of *feelings* among all members of the human race can also be documented from *Utilitarianism*." Collini, *Public Moralists*, 69.

37. Collini, Winch, and Burrow, *That Noble Science*, 192; Koditschek, *Liberalism*.

38. Readers included, famously, John Adams and Thomas Jefferson, who both cherished Milton's writings, his poetry especially but also his prose. Tanner and Collings, "How Adams and Jefferson."

39. One of Milton's admirers, Thomas Hollis V, published and distributed Milton's works across Europe and the American colonies in the mid-eighteenth century. His "liberty books" resided in public and private libraries across the United States in the wake of the Revolution. Tanner and Collings, "How Adams and Jefferson," 207–10; Eaton, *Freedom-of-Thought Struggle*, 59; Bailyn, *Ideological Origins*, 34. For examples of routine uses of Milton's poetry, see Douglass, "American Apocalypse," 127; Garrison, *Letters*, 3:407, 438, 478, 565, 592; and Blum and Matsui, *War Is All Hell*, 6, 26–28.

40. "One great figure after another in the Whig tradition drew on Milton for inspiration and instruction. James Tyrrell, John Locke, Algernon Sidney, John Toland, John Dennis, Daniel Defoe, the Third Earl of Shaftesbury, Joseph Addison: these and many less-remembered Whigs read Milton's works with interest and often with approval." Maltzahn, "Whig Milton," 229.

41. "Freedom of Public Opinion," *Daily Register* (Wheeling, WV), September 17, 1863.

42. Davies, "Borrowed Language," 255.

43. Richard White, "Creative Misunderstandings."

44. Davies, "Borrowed Language," 256.

45. Novick, *That Noble Dream*.

46. Iggers, *Historiography*, 23.

47. Cheng, *Plain and Noble Garb*, 2; Hattem, *Past and Prologue*, 21.

48. Hattem, *Past and Prologue*, 5.

49. Webster, *American Dictionary*, 554.

50. Cheng, *Plain and Noble Garb*.

51. My effort here is similar to Claire Arcenas's study of John Locke's reception in America. Arcenas writes, "This, then, is not a book about John Locke, the seventeenth-century English philosopher, but rather a book about how Americans over time have understood and made sense of him, his work, his ideas, and his relevance. I present interpretations of Locke's life, ideas, and works through the eyes of my subjects—not the lenses of modern scholars." Arcenas, *America's Philosopher*, 4–5.

52. Hattem, *Past and Prologue*, 26.

53. Dorothy Ross, "Historical Consciousness," 919.

54. Throughout the text, I emphasize the ways that mid-nineteenth-century Americans interpreted the English Civil Wars. As a result, I do not engage at a historiographical level with the modern literature on the conflict, which is tremendously rich and multifaceted. Interested readers will find valuable historiographical direction in Braddick, *Oxford Handbook*.

55. Braddick, *Common Freedom*, 283.

56. "Speech of Wendell Phillips," *The Liberator*, April 25, 1862.

57. Cox, *Eight Years in Congress*, 392. Historian Robert Bonner observes that Cox's critique of Puritanism garnered wide applause in the South during the war. Bonner, "Roundheaded Cavaliers?," 49–50.

58. One of my inspirations in privileging thought and language is Elizabeth Varon's effort "to elucidate the war of words" that brought on the conflict. Varon's brilliant analysis of

sectional division attended, as she notes, to "what the participants said, what they believed, and how they expressed their own passions, and agonies." Varon, *Disunion!*, 15, 2.

59. "Shall General M'Clellan Be Called into Service?," *Harper's Weekly*, April 16, 1864.

CHAPTER 2

1. For a sophisticated interpretation that emphasizes growing regional distinctiveness grounded in both reform work and the authority of state power, see Brooke, "Cultures of Nationalism."

2. William Taylor's 1961 study of the cultural expression of Cavalier and Puritan addressed only the antebellum era and treated the distinction as a literary phenomenon rather than a practice of history, as signaled by his title, which replaced the seventeenth-century moniker with its nineteenth-century equivalent, "Yankee." William Taylor, *Cavalier and Yankee*.

3. Wendy Warren, *New England Bound*.

4. Tise, *Proslavery*; Faust, *James Henry Hammond*.

5. Watson, *Normans and Saxons*, 19–46; Hobsbawm and Ranger, *Invention of Tradition*. Previous historians of the South have rooted this identity in different origin points. In *Political Economy of Slavery* Eugene Genovese emphasizes medieval Europe, while Michael O'Brien emphasizes modern Romanticism in *Conjectures of Order*.

6. Editor's Table, *Southern Literary Messenger*, February 1864, 124. Twain discusses Scott and the Civil War in *Life on the Mississippi*, chap. 46.

7. Alexander H. Stephens, "Corner Stone Speech," March 21, 1861, Teaching American History, accessed August 23, 2023, https://teachingamericanhistory.org/document/cornerstone-speech.

8. "This Is a War of Races," *Daily Richmond Whig*, January 30, 1861; "The Puritans," *Richmond Daily Dispatch*, January 24, 1861; "A People of Extremes," *Richmond Daily Dispatch*, October 4, 1864.

9. "Sidney and His Compatriots," *DeBow's Review*, September 1853, 291–97; "The North, the South, and the Union," *DeBow's Review*, August 1854, 173–84; "Bonaparte, Cromwell, and Washington," *DeBow's Review*, August 1860, 139–54; "Milton and Macaulay," *DeBow's Review*, December 1860, 667–80; "Southern Civilization or, The Norman in America," *DeBow's Review*, January–February 1862, 1–19. These pieces were preceded by an important essay identified by Michael O'Brien as the "most formal echo in historical literature" to advance the Cavalier hypothesis. Michael O'Brien, *Conjectures of Order*, 1:315–16, 309–20, 2:647, 981.

10. "Southern Civilization," 6. Rollin G. Osterweis interprets this framing as reflective of white Southerners' investment in the "cult of chivalry," a regional variant of the Romantic movement. See Osterweis, *Romanticism and Nationalism*, 78–79. One of the many ironies entangled in this theory was that the English (from whom white Southerners supposedly descended) rejected the imposition of what they called the "Norman Yoke" from as far back as the seventeenth century. Hill, "Norman Yoke."

11. "Southern Civilization," 8.

12. "Southern Civilization," 8–9; "The Anglo-Saxon Mania," *Southern Literary Messenger*, November 1863, 667–88.

13. Wood, *Radicalism*; Shade, *Democratizing the Old Dominion*.

14. James Henry Hammond, "Mud Sill Speech," March 4, 1858, Teaching American History, accessed September 20, 2023, https://teachingamericanhistory.org/document/mud-sill-speech.

15. See, e.g., Robert Toombs to Stephens, February 10, 1860, in Ulrich B. Phillips, *Annual Report*, 460–62.

16. Watson, *Normans and Saxons*, 152–54. My argument here also challenges the substantial literature built around the idea of a "Herrenvolk democracy" at work within the antebellum South, where white men enjoyed relative equality. Although elites operated within the expanding democratic two-party system, their rhetoric in this period suggests that many saw this as more performative than genuine. George Frederickson introduced the term and offered a still influential and valuable comparative argument to buttress it. Frederickson, *White Supremacy*.

17. "The Cavalier and the Puritan," *Richmond Daily Dispatch*, May 1, 1863.

18. "Late Southern News," *Chicago Daily Tribune*, January 13, 1863; "Address of President Davis," *True Democrat*, January 28, 1863; "Anglo-Saxon Mania," 671, 686; Rable, *Damn Yankees*, 10–11.

19. "The Difference between the Northern and Southern People," *Southern Literary Messenger*, June 1860, 404.

20. "Anglo-Saxon Mania," 683. Florid rhetoric infiltrated even some of the more neutral assessments: "As the Cavalier of the Cromwellian era was a horror to the pharisaical Puritan, and the Puritan in his turn a contempt and an abomination to the reckless, pleasure-hunting Cavalier, so to-day is the 'psalm-singing, clock-peddling Yankee' a foul order to the fastidious nostrils of the lordly Southerner, and the reckless prodigal, dissipated and soul-selling planter a thorn in the flesh of Puritan morality." Egbert Phelps, "The Causes and Results of the War," *Continental Monthly*, May 1863, 622; Michael O'Brien, *Conjectures of Order*, 1:250–51; Quigley, *Shifting Grounds*, 139–40.

21. Bonner, "Roundheaded Cavaliers?," 45. Bonner is more skeptical about the degree to which Confederates believed their own rhetoric, arguing that many regarded it as "make-believe." Historians recognize that the inventedness of these lines of descent was apparent well before Britons arrived in North America. "Most persistent of all the anti-Norman myths was the romantic identification of the English with the defeated Saxons and the Normans with the ruling class. The elements of truth in this were soon submerged in the social, linguistic and legal changes of the later Middle Ages, and transformed out of all recognition, first in the constitutional and social struggles of the seventeenth century, and then in the romantic novels and nationalist movements of the nineteenth." Chibnall, *Normans*, 124. Readers familiar with the later nineteenth-century race language may be surprised to find that this version was explicitly anti-Saxon, rather than lauding the "Anglo-Saxon" as many late-century writers did.

22. "The Puritans at Work," *Richmond Daily Dispatch*, September 11, 1861; "The Difference of Race," *Southern Literary Messenger*, June 1860, 403–4, 406–7; "Anglo-Saxon Mania," 676–77, 679.

23. "Revolutions of 1776 and 1861 Contrasted," *Daily Richmond Whig*, May 7, 1863.

24. *Congressional Globe*, 37th Cong., 2nd Sess., 1715 (1862).

25. Dawson, "Puritan and the Cavalier."

26. "Liberty of Speech, of the Press, and Freedom of Religion," *Richmond Enquirer*, June 3, 1865; "Brown's Foray," *Times-Picayune*, November 8, 1859; Watson, *Normans and Saxons*,

84–86. An important and telling exception came in Confederates' celebration of the fanaticism of Stonewall Jackson, the Confederate general. As Charles Royster observes, both Northerners and Southerners regarded Jackson as a Cromwellian figure of war. Royster, *Destructive War*, 44–45.

27. "Bonaparte, Cromwell, and Washington," 142; "Northern Mind and Character," *Southern Literary Messenger*, November 1860, 343–49.

28. *Congressional Globe*, 36th Cong., Special Sess., 1398 (1861).

29. "The Cause of Southern Superiority," *Richmond Daily Dispatch*, September 18, 1862; "Thomas Carlyle—His Philosophy and Style," *Southern Literary Messenger*, May 1862, 293.

30. "This Is a War of Races"; Dawson, "Puritan and the Cavalier," 601. Northern conservatives disliked the Puritans as well, though their critique made room for the legitimacy of resistance to Charles I. Samuel Cox rejected the nineteenth-century argument (made by Northern writers) that American democracy came from the Puritans. Instead Cox argued, "The [Puritans] left England, because they had not the stamina to remain and contend, like the Hampdens, Sydneys, and Miltons, for their English privileges." Cox, *Puritanism in Politics*, 9.

31. "Difference of Race," 405.

32. "Revolutions of 1776 and 1861 Contrasted."

33. A good study of the continental aspirations of the Confederacy can be found in Brettle, *Colossal Ambitions*.

34. Dzelzainis, "Milton's Classical Republicanism," 3.

35. Dzelzainis, "Milton's Classical Republicanism," 4.

36. Johnson, *Toward a Patriarchal Republic*; Sinha, *Counterrevolution of Slavery*.

37. Tanner and Collings, "How Adams and Jefferson," 214–15.

38. Eaton, *Freedom-of-Thought Struggle*, 29.

39. Milton, *Tenure of Kings*, 10.

40. Milton, *Tenure of Kings*, 78.

41. Dzelzainis, "Milton's Classical Republicanism," 20. Another recent author observes, "It is a landmark argument in the history of modern representative government." Dobranski, *Reading John Milton*, 79.

42. Dzelzainis, introduction to Milton, *Political Writings*, xvii.

43. "Milton and Macaulay," 667.

44. "Milton and Macaulay," 667.

45. "Milton and Macaulay," 676.

46. "About Anti-Slavery Bugle," Chronicling America, accessed July 18, 2023, https://chroniclingamerica.loc.gov/lccn/sn83035487. The *Bugle* hoped to purge slavery from the United States by splitting the nation itself. Cirillo, *Abolitionist Civil War*, 10.

47. "A Northern Plea for the Right of Secession," *Anti-Slavery Bugle*, March 23, 1861.

48. McCurry, *Confederate Reckoning*.

49. McCurry, *Confederate Reckoning*, 301–8.

50. Durden, *Gray and the Black*, 184.

51. The historian James McPherson labels this fixation among white Southerners "ethnic nationalism," as distinct from the broader "civic nationalism" promulgated by Northerners. McPherson, *Is Blood Thicker*, 47–51.

52. Bernard Lewis, "The Roots of Muslim Rage," *Atlantic Monthly*, September 1990, 47–60; Huntington, *Clash of Civilizations*.

53. "Puritans at Work"; "Has the War Vindicated Yankee Heroism?," *Richmond Daily Dispatch*, September 13, 1863.

54. *Congressional Globe*, 36th Cong., Special Sess., 1393–1408 (1861). Concern with regicide does not indicate a pro-monarchy position but does show Confederates' investment in hierarchy, which is at the center of their conservatism. This point is reinforced in their willingness to accept a French monarch in Mexico—better a stable king than an unstable (and antislavery) republic. Kelly, "North American Crisis"; Pani, "Juárez v. Maximiliano," 179–96; Doyle, *Cause of All Nations*.

55. "Anglo-Saxon Mania," 687–88.

56. Recent scholarship that informs my account here includes Winship, *Hot Protestants*; and Hall, *Puritans*.

57. Everett, "Anecdotes," 119.

58. Motley, "Polity of the Puritans," 486.

59. Lepore, *Name of War*.

60. Malcolm X, "Audubon Address," March 29, 1964, Documents for the Study of American History, accessed July 21, 2025, www.vlib.us/amdocs/texts/malcolmx0364.html. Malcolm X may have been inspired by Cole Porter's 1934 take in his song "Anything Goes."

61. Gradert, *Puritan Spirits*, 2, 201n3. Gradert's book offers the most sophisticated and comprehensive treatment of how abolitionists drew strength from their image of their Puritan ancestors.

62. Gradert, *Puritan Spirits*, 6.

63. Walzer, *Revolution of the Saints*, vii, 3.

64. Hall, *Puritans*, 49–50.

65. Oakes, *Scorpion's Sting*; Brooks, *Liberty Power*; Thomas, "Romantic Reform in America."

66. Donald, *Charles Sumner*, 4–5. Although Donald notes that Sumner was reluctant to identify himself with this lineage because his father had been born out of wedlock, it is also clear that he found a deep intellectual affinity there. Donald observes that Sumner "liked to fancy himself the descendant of the Separatists of the English Revolution who uncompromisingly contended 'for religious, intellectual, and political emancipation'" (227). Sumner, "Slavery and the Rebellion," 99.

67. Editor's Table, *Knickerbocker Magazine*, September 1861, 266–67. James McPherson argues that "the Norman-Cavalier thesis, on the face of it, seems little short of ludicrous. Indeed, modern scholars have shown it to have scarcely any foundation in fact. Few Southerners in 1860 were descended from Cavaliers, and even fewer Cavaliers could claim unmixed descent from the Norman barons of William the Conqueror." McPherson, *Is Blood Thicker*, 51.

68. Sumner, "Slavery and the Rebellion," 106.

69. Sumner, "Slavery and the Rebellion," 110.

70. W. H. Whitmore, "The Cavalier Theory Refuted," *Continental Monthly*, 1863, 60–71; Watson, *Normans and Saxons*, 176–77.

71. Whitmore, "Cavalier Theory Refuted," 71.

72. Varon, *Armies of Deliverance*, 2, 4–5, 9–15; Paludan, *"People's Contest,"* xxv, 10–16.

73. "The Great Civil Wars—a Historical Review and Contrast," *Milwaukee Daily Sentinel*, February 15, 1865.

74. "The New England Confederacy," *Harper's New Monthly Magazine*, October 1862, 633–34. Bancroft, catching the revisionist spirit of the mid-nineteenth century, also praised Cromwell. Karsten, "Cromwell in America," 213.

75. Reynolds, "Oliver Cromwell," 445.

76. Stewart, *Wendell Phillips*, 24.

77. Stewart, *Wendell Phillips*, 10.

78. Stewart, *Wendell Phillips*, 28. Phillips was no more consistent than the rest in his use of history—the men he lauded here hardly shared a common mind when it came to politics.

79. Phelps, "Causes and Results," 618; "The Abolitionists," *The Liberator*, January 2, 1863; Watson, *Normans and Saxons*, 221.

80. "How Old John Brown Wasn't Captured," *Douglass's Monthly*, March 1859, 38.

81. "Who Taught John Brown?," *New York Tribune*, November 12, 1859.

82. Stewart, *Wendell Phillips*, 205. Gradert observes that "nearly all of the writers who rose to Brown's defense—Lydia Maria Child, Ralph Waldo Emerson, Henry David Thoreau, Frederick Douglass, and many others—praised him as a Puritan reincarnate." Gradert, *Puritan Spirits*, 3; Bonner, "Roundheaded Cavaliers?," 39.

83. Seelye, *Memory's Nation*, 276, 330–34.

84. Vowell, "John Brown's Body."

85. "The Kansas John Brown Song," *Continental Monthly*, June 1862, 735–36.

86. Reynolds, "Oliver Cromwell," 440.

87. Reynolds, "Oliver Cromwell," 436. In his biography of John Brown, Reynolds argues that Brown's links to Puritanism distinguished him from other abolitionists, who did not necessarily embrace the identity in the antebellum era. Reynolds, *John Brown, Abolitionist*.

88. Susan Howe, in her study of Emily Dickinson, describes the Puritans' "profound conception of obedience to a stern and sovereign Absence that forged the fanatical energy necessary for survival." Howe, *My Emily Dickinson*, 39.

CHAPTER 3

1. Perhaps most obvious (to us today), most Northerners sided with seventeenth-century Parliamentary rebels but nevertheless found ways of delegitimizing rebellion, while Confederates sided with seventeenth-century Royalists yet found ways of legitimizing their rebellion. Ironically, Northerners and Southerners attached themselves to historical role models that harmonized with their respective beliefs about the source of civil authority—the people or a monarch—but were on the "wrong" side when it came to the response of the state to rebellion.

2. Nineteenth-century Americans respected the Scottish Rebellion, especially if they viewed it within the context of the pursuit of freedom of religion, but the public conversation focused more on the English and Irish dimensions, so those receive most of my attention here.

3. Tucker, *First Born*; Fleche, *Revolution of 1861*; Kelly, "North American Crisis," 344.

4. Tim Harris, "Did the English Have," 37.
5. Gallagher, *Union War*; Paludan, "Civil War Considered"; Paludan, *"People's Contest."*
6. Robert Ross, *Outlines of English History*, 136.
7. Collier, *History*, 206.
8. Brodie, *Constitutional History*, 1:236–37; Macaulay, review of *Constitutional History of England*, 112, 120; Brougham, *British Constitution*, 220–25.
9. Macaulay, *History of England*, 1:86. Thomas Carlyle reached a similar conclusion. See Morrow, *Thomas Carlyle*, 182.
10. "Forecasting," *Harper's Weekly*, June 21, 1862.
11. Hope, *Popular View*, 20–21.
12. "The Old Sophistry," *Harper's Weekly*, March 18, 1865; "Between Ourselves and Others There Are Two Kinds," *Times*, January 5, 1863; Forster, "Civil Wars," 275.
13. "A History of Rebellions," *Advocate of Peace*, September–October 1867. As an earlier *Harper's* piece clarified, hindsight alone was not sufficient: "It was not the success of their rebellion that justified it. If the English government had succeeded in quelling it, and Washington, Adam, and Franklin had hung separately, as Franklin jocosely remarked, their rebellion would still have been as noble in its aim as it was complete in its success." "Why We Talk about England," *Harper's Weekly*, June 22, 1861.
14. Ohlmeyer and Ó Siochrú, *Ireland 1641*, 1.
15. Ohlmeyer and Ó Siochrú, *Ireland 1641*, 7.
16. Ó Siochrú, *Confederate Ireland*, 11.
17. "One dominant rumour was near universal: the rebellion was not against the king but for him in support of the royal person against evil counsellors." Raymond Gillespie, *Seventeenth Century Ireland*, 145.
18. "1641," *Irish People*, December 19, 1863.
19. "Mr. Forster on the Reign of Charles I," *Littel's Living Age*, December 31, 1864, 688–89.
20. Macaulay, *History of England*, 1:106.
21. Robert Ross, *Outlines of English History*.
22. "Communicated. St. Patrick's Day," *Freedom's Champion*, March 24, 1864.
23. Kerby Miller, *Emigrants and Exiles*; Gleeson, *Irish in the South*. I am persuaded by Damian Shiels's recent analysis that Civil War soldiering enabled Irish Americans to reconcile their ethnic and national identities. Shiels, "Recovering the Voices."
24. Additionally, the reasons for the relative obscurity of the Irish past bear on observations that Michel-Rolph Trouillot has made in his history of writing on the Haitian Revolution. The willful blindness that prevented generations of French historians from recognizing the Haitian Revolution had a kind of analog in English and, later, American thinking about the Irish experience. They presented the Irish as persistently, even naturally, rebellious. The result was a self-induced myopia, which found expression as an inability to think seriously about the example of the Irish. Trouillot, *Silencing the Past*.
25. Brodie, *Constitutional History*, 2:354.
26. Brodie, *Constitutional History*, 2:388–89.
27. Collier, *History*, 213; James White, *Landmarks*, 130.
28. Temple, *Irish Rebellion*. Temple's conclusions were later amplified in Borlase, *History*.
29. McDonnell, *Light of History*, 28.

30. Canny, *Making Ireland British*, 463; Froude, *English in Ireland*, 83–114.

31. Robert Ross, *Outlines of English History*, 139; Cattermole, *Great Civil War*, 33. Irish historians approached British memory as a mendacious lie that demanded precise rebuttal. John Haverty made this clear in his history, which he wrote in response to Froude's *English in Ireland*, a book he described as "a most mischievous production, which is solely calculated to exasperate the Irish by the calumnious virulence of its anti-Irish spirit, and to persuade Englishmen and Scots that the oppression which the Irish savages had suffered was only too mild for their deserts." John McDonnell angrily quotes David Hume's endorsement of Temple's history of innocents slaughtered with no warning in his standard eighteenth-century history of England. McDonnell, *Light of History*, 1–2.

32. Sheehan-Dean, *Calculus of Violence*, chap. 3.

33. Robert Penn Warren, *Legacy*, 74.

34. The full text of the depositions, along with contextual and editorial information, is available online at 1641 Depositions, Trinity College Dublin, accessed February 12, 2022, https://1641.tcd.ie.

35. Some nineteenth-century historians read the sources with more skepticism and saw even prewar sources as compromised by biases. "The traditions respecting [the Earl of Strafford's] violence and oppression, contain the most exaggerated tales of cruelty, bloodshed and robbery, more like the anecdotes of a leader of banditti in the eleventh century, than of a civil governor in the seventeenth." William Cooke Taylor, *History of the Civil Wars*, 1:251.

36. Darcy, *Irish Rebellion*, 100.

37. Darcy, *Irish Rebellion*, 132.

38. The closest Civil War Americans came to a deposition-like body of evidence happened in 1864. First, there was a congressional report about the Fort Pillow Massacre. Second, the Northern public was exposed to the horrors to which their soldiers had been exposed in Confederate prisons. Woodcuts illustrating the emaciated bodies of Northern prisoners of war stirred outrage of the sort that Temple's book generated. For a brief period in early 1865, the US Senate debated a retaliation measure that would have forced equal suffering on the Confederate prisoners held in Northern hands. Sheehan-Dean, *Calculus of Violence*, 267, 334–37; Neely, "Retaliation." The Southern Claims Commission produced a body of evidence about material property seized, but only from loyal citizens, and even that process was deeply complicated by postwar politics, when testimonies and evidence were gathered. Lee, *Claiming the Union*.

39. Rable, *Damn Yankees*, 5–6; Sheehan-Dean, *Calculus of Violence*, 44–81.

40. Paludan, "Civil War Considered."

41. "Why We Talk about England."

42. "E Pluribus Unum," *Atlantic Monthly*, February 1, 1861; Motley, "Causes," 36–37.

43. "Letter from Cassius M. Clay to the Editor of the *London Times*," *Sun*, June 7, 1861 (but reprinted in Philadelphia and elsewhere); Goldwin Smith, *Letter to a Whig*; Goldwin Smith, *Right, or the Wrong*, 22.

44. Motley, "Causes," 42.

45. "President Lincoln," *Princeton Review*, July 1865, 435–58.

46. Sumner, *Works of Charles Sumner*, 4:73–74.

47. Colley, *Britons*.

48. Kumar, *Making*, 129.

49. Orville Browning, *Congressional Globe*, 37th Cong., 2nd Sess., 1141 (1862).

50. Sumner, *Works of Charles Sumner*, 7:16.

51. Grimsley, *Hard Hand of War*, 78–80; Varon, *Armies of Deliverance*, 87–88.

52. "The Return of the Rebellious States to the Union," *Brownson's Quarterly Review*, October 1863, 484.

53. Grimsley, *Hard Hand of War*; Dilbeck, *More Civil War*; Sheehan-Dean, *Calculus of Violence*. Looking for a proper footing, even one Confederate paper early in the war explicitly embraced the Cromwellian strategy of hard war. "We will stop the effusion of blood," the *Memphis Avalanche* explained, "we will arrest the horrors of war, by terrific slaughter of the foe, by examples of overwhelming and unsparing vengeance." The paper made recourse to Cromwell's famous justification for his refusal to allow surrender during the battle at Drogheda. "When Oliver Cromwell massacred the garrison of Drogheda, suffering not a man to escape, he justified it on the ground that his object was to bring the war to a close—to stop the effusion of blood, and that it was, therefore, a merciful act on his part. The South can no longer afford to trifle—she must strike the most fearful blows—the war cry of extermination must be raised." "The Black Flag in Kentucky," originally in *Memphis Avalanche*, reprinted in *New York Herald*, December 19, 1861.

CHAPTER 4

1. Jason Phillips, *Looming Civil War*.

2. Robert E. Lee to "Rooney" Lee, January 29, 1861, in Lee Family Digital Archive, accessed March 20, 2022, https://leefamilyarchive.org/history-reference-essays-rachal-index.

3. The same tension pervaded the debate over how participants framed the consequences of the seventeenth-century conflicts. Historian Michael Braddick observes about the start of the seventeenth-century conflicts that "both sides claimed to be acting defensively; the war was defined in terms of what it was intended to prevent, rather than what it was hoped it would achieve." Braddick, "History, Liberty, Reformation," 118.

4. "Bonaparte, Cromwell, and Washington," *DeBow's Review*, August 1860, 141.

5. "Southern Civilization or, The Norman in America," *DeBow's Review*, January–February 1862, 7.

6. Fernando Wood, *Congressional Globe*, 38th Cong., 1st Sess., 2077 (1864).

7. Louis T. Wigfall, *Congressional Globe*, 36th Cong., Special Sess., 1398 (1861).

8. Tucker, *First Born*; Eyal, "Romantic Realist."

9. "An Irish Journal on the American War," *Daily Register* (Raleigh, NC), July 6, 1861; "Letters from English Abolitionists on the War in America," *The Liberator*, February 21, 1862. William Lloyd Garrison responded directly to this assertion in a letter to British abolitionist George Thompson. "The charge is cruelly false, that the Government 'is simply fighting for empire.' . . . It is contending, not for 'empire' in itself considered, but for its right to exist over the territory embraced by the republic, with those limitations and prerogatives which are so carefully defined by the Constitution for the promotion of the general welfare and for the common defence." Garrison to Thompson, February 21, 1862, in Garrison, *Letters*, 5:69.

10. Lingard, *History of England*, 41.

11. Dew, *Apostles of Disunion*.

12. Haverty, *History of Ireland*, 512; McGee, *Popular History of Ireland*, 487.

13. For excellent introductions to the massive literature on secession, see Woods, "What Twenty-First-Century Historians"; and Towers, "Partisans."

14. McDonnell, *Light of History*, 31.

15. Yokota, *Unbecoming British*, 9.

16. Michael O'Brien, *Conjectures of Order*, 1:4.

17. Yokota, *Unbecoming British*, 167–91.

18. Braddick, "History, Liberty, Reformation," 118.

19. Barnes, Schoen, and Tower, *Old South's Modern Worlds*; Karp, *This Vast Southern Empire*.

20. Just because rebellion looked rational at the time does not mean it was (in either place). "The outrage among the Catholic leaders in Ireland that resulted from their many disappointments meant that some Catholic landowners were at the brink of rebellion at any given time, and the principal consideration that held them back was the conviction of the more politically astute among them that the insurrection would inevitably fail once it was confronted by government forces. Insurrection, as they saw it, would thus merely provide their Protestant adversaries with the opportunity to accelerate their programme of plantation, thereby enriching themselves at the expense of those who remained Catholic." Canny, *Making Ireland British*, 535.

21. Raymond Gillespie, *Seventeenth Century Ireland*; Goldwin Smith, *Irish History*, 105–6.

22. Robert Ross, *Outlines of English History*, 139.

23. Despite recognizing the numerous factors driving the Irish toward rebellion, M. Perceval-Maxwell has offered the most careful counterreading, arguing that "until the Anglo-Scottish conflict began, Ireland under Charles I had enjoyed a period of relative prosperity.... It has also been shown that the various political components of the island had begun to work together.... In other words, the trend up to 1638 was toward accommodation and away from conflict." This included sectarian relations; he argues that both Protestants and Catholics adopted an attitude of "live-and-let-live before the rebellion." Perceval-Maxwell, *Outbreak*, 48, 285–86.

24. Perceval-Maxwell, *Outbreak*, 4.

25. McDonnell, *Light of History*, 7–8.

26. "The Fate of Conquered Nations," *Fayetteville Observer*, January 11, 1864.

27. Darcy, *Irish Rebellion of 1641*, 3.

28. Lenihan, *Confederate Catholics at War*, 19.

29. William Cooke Taylor, *History of the Civil Wars*, 1:258.

30. Lenihan, *Confederate Catholics at War*, 22.

31. Robert Ross, *Outlines of English History*, 123.

32. McDonnell, *Light of History*, 24.

33. Morrison, *Slavery*; Potter, *Impending Crisis*.

34. Tait, Edwards, and Lenihan, *Age of Atrocity*, 9–10.

35. David Edwards, "Out of the Blue?," 109.

36. "Speech of Hon. S. S. Cox," *Newark Advocate*, January 29, 1864; Howard, *Congressional Globe*, 37th Cong., 1st Sess., 1714–15 (1862).

37. Notwithstanding the still common stereotypes of pugnacious Irishmen and except for those scholars who believe America's violent habits were inherited from Scots Irish settlers in the eighteenth century. McWhiney and Jamieson, *Attack and Die*; McWhiney and McDonald, *Cracker Culture*.

38. It is hard to imagine an analog to Richard Roth's excellent study *American Homicide* in Ireland, where the murder rate in 2023 was 0.7 per 100,000 people, compared to the US rate of 5.8 per 100,000. Wikipedia, "List of Countries by Intentional Homicide Rate," last modified March 13, 2025, 17:17 (UTC), https://en.wikipedia.org/wiki/List_of_countries_by_intentional_homicide_rate.

39. Grimstead, *American Mobbing*; Harrold, *Border War*; Etcheson, *Bleeding Kansas*.

40. Covington, *Devil*, 301.

41. William Cooke Taylor, *History of the Civil Wars*, 1:260.

42. Ayers, *In the Presence of Mine Enemies*.

43. Canny, *Making Ireland British*, 535, 550.

44. "The Irish People," *Daily News and Herald*, May 18, 1861; "The Irish in America," originally in *New Orleans Catholic Standard*, reprinted in *Irishman*, June 29, 1861.

45. "The Voice of the South," *The Liberator*, October 9, 1863; "Correspondence—a Word for the South," *Nation*, November 1, 1862.

46. "The Irish in America," *DeBow's Review*, April 1869, 307.

47. Grimsley, *Hard Hand of War*.

48. Brewer, *Sinews of Power*, 5.

49. The seventeenth-century English context for this question differed from the American one. Historian Michael Braddick draws attention to what he calls the "double concentration of power in king and parliament [which] meant that from a very early date political conflict in England was highly centralized. Serious rebellions, though they might be regional in origin, were not separatist in intent." Braddick, *State Formation*, 9–11. The federalist nature of the American Constitution and the divergent development paths of the North and South over the preceding decades created a much different dynamic.

50. I am deliberately but cautiously echoing the famous historiographical term—a "blundering generation"—that designates a view of the Civil War that blamed the conflict on the incompetence of the politicians of the 1850s. Sternhell, "Revisionism Reinvented?" Ignoring the moral dimensions of slavery, historians of the 1920s and '30s regarded abolitionists and fire-eaters as equally culpable in their extremist rhetoric, which destabilized the political system.

51. Peterson, *Great Triumvirate*.

52. "E Pluribus Unum," *Atlantic Monthly*, February 1, 1861.

53. "Lecture," *Evening Star*, February 19, 1861.

54. Brodie, *Constitutional History*, 2:199.

55. "Historical Parallel—Edgehill and Manassas," *Daily Cleveland Herald*, September 14, 1861.

56. "The Last Ditch," *Hancock Jeffersonian*, September 12, 1862.

57. Burlingame, *Abraham Lincoln*, 152.

58. "A Lesson from History," *Milwaukee Daily Sentinel*, April 22, 1861; "What the Yankee Is," *New Hampshire Statesman*, May 25, 1861; "The Puritan and the Cavalier," *Freedom's*

Champion, November 9, 1861; "Fourth Fraternity Lecture," *The Liberator*, November 8, 1861; "Southern Opinions of Southern Resources," *New York Times*, March 7, 1865.

59. "Soldierly Qualities," originally in *New York Ledger*, reprinted in *Newark Advocate*, October 18, 1861; "Add'd European Intelligence," *Daily Evening Bulletin*, September 10, 1861; Gradert, *Puritan Spirits*, 84.

60. Adams, *Our Masters the Rebels*.

61. Macaulay, *History of England*, 1:118; "The End, and yet Not the End," *Daily Evening Bulletin*, March 13, 1862.

62. Editor's Table, *Harper's New Monthly Magazine*, February 1862, 406.

63. "Rebellion," *Hartford Daily Courant*, April 27, 1861.

64. *Soldier's Pocket Bible*.

65. *Soldier's Pocket Bible*. Advertised for sale in *Richmond Daily Dispatch*, September 11, 1861.

66. Bates, *Brief History*, 5.

67. Orville Browning, *Congressional Globe*, 37th Cong., 2nd Sess., 1141 (1862).

68. "Moderation in War Is Imbecility," *Frank Leslie's Illustrated Newspaper*, October 4, 1862. The paper demonstrated admirable consistency on the question of hard war, quoting Macaulay's "observations . . . which we commend to the attention of the Government at Washington: 'If there be any truth established by the universal experience of nations, it is this: That to carry the spirit of peace into war is a weak and cruel policy.'" "Languid War," *Frank Leslie's Illustrated Newspaper*, January 18, 1862.

69. It is plausible to imagine that the historical legacy of the English Civil Wars should have convinced nineteenth-century readers that civil wars only generate fruitless violence that changes little in the underlying structure of the state or nation. As the scholar John Morrill notes, "The trauma of regicide left few royalists with faith in the providence of God; the much deeper sense of betrayal experienced by the radicals in 1660 largely explains their political quiescence thereafter." Morrill, *Stuart Britain*, 81.

70. Kishlansky, *Rise of the New Model Army*, 222.

71. Matsui, *First Republican Army*; Teters, *Practical Liberators*.

72. Dilbeck, *More Civil War*.

73. Witt, *Lincoln's Code*.

74. Art. 14, General Orders No. 100, available at the Avalon Project, Yale Law School, accessed February 4, 2025, https://avalon.law.yale.edu/19th_century/lieber.asp#art14.

75. "End, and yet Not the End."

76. "A Brace of Traitors," *Western Reserve Chronicle*, January 21, 1863; "The New England Confederacy," *Harper's New Monthly Magazine*, October 1862, 631. I found little evidence that Civil War Americans relied specifically on the writings of seventeenth-century republican thinkers such as James Harrington or Algernon Sidney.

CHAPTER 5

1. Rable, *Damn Yankees*, 26–27, 55, 60–61.

2. Confederates' joy at Lincoln's death still shocks today. See, e.g., Miers, *Diary of Emma Leconte*, 91; and Janney, *Ends of War*, 175.

3. Kellie Carter Jackson has begun a reinterpretation of the role of political violence in the abolition movement. She argues that "the willingness among black abolitionist leaders to embrace violence was not merely a result of frustration but, after years of practicing nonresistance under white leadership, a calculated pivot." Jackson, *Force and Freedom*, 8; Kaufman-McKivigan, *Antislavery Violence*.

4. Frank Cirillo's careful mapping of wartime abolitionist politics shows the emergence of two factions: a prowar "interventionist" camp and an antiwar purist camp. Wendell Phillips joined Frederick Douglass and others who endorsed the interventionist position. Cirillo focuses on the support given to Lincoln; my analysis here emphasizes abolitionists' endorsement of military violence itself, though his argument—that interventionists "fixated upon jump-starting their moral revolution through a sudden, apocalyptic crucible, or golden moment"—suggests that support for a war was not impossible to foresee even in the 1850s. Cirillo, *Abolitionist Civil War*, 2.

5. Gentiles, *New Model Army*, 440, 118–19.

6. Hargroder, "Powerful Auxiliary"; Matsui, *First Republican Army*, 3–6.

7. Williams, *Lincoln and the Radicals*, 71. Williams characterized Radicals as "Jacobins" in a pejorative sense, while more modern studies of the Joint Committee on the Conduct of the War emphasize radicalism with less judgment. Tap, *Over Lincoln's Shoulder*, 19–21, 25–26, 81–82.

8. "Woe to the Vanquished!," *Daily Richmond Whig*, April 7, 1862. The *Richmond Examiner* later echoed the *Whig*, concluding that "Cromwell's confiscations in Ireland, which have always figured as particularly severe, were yet attended with allotments in Connaught, such as the protector deemed sufficient for family support." "The Fate of Conquered Nations," *Fayetteville Observer*, January 11, 1864.

9. "Their Real Purposes," *Richmond Daily Dispatch*, April 14, 1862.

10. "Fate of Conquered Nations."

11. "Letter of Major-General Sherman," *Daily Richmond Examiner*, May 30, 1864.

12. "The Idea Has Been," *Daily Richmond Examiner*, June 30, 1864.

13. "The Late United States," *Richmond Daily Dispatch*, March 6, 1863; "Arbitrary Arrests at the North," *Daily Richmond Whig*, May 23, 1863.

14. "The Life of Oliver Cromwell," *Richmond Daily Dispatch*, December 25, 1863; "Cromwell, Lincoln and Virginia," *Richmond Daily Dispatch*, January 25, 1865. Edmund Ruffin, always the contrarian, proclaimed Cromwell "the greatest king, if not the greatest man that England has produced—the most virtuous of usurpers, & the most moderate, just, & benign of despots." Scarborough, *Diary of Edmund Ruffin*, 2:429, 562.

15. "Nothing New," *Richmond Daily Dispatch*, November 23, 1864.

16. Elizabeth Fox-Genovese and Eugene Genovese, in their study of the antebellum South, argue that "Southerners found it difficult to balance the linear and cyclical views of history." Fox-Genovese and Genovese, *Mind of the Master Class*, 152. I believe that the Civil War resolved this tension and led most white Southern thinkers to endorse a more cyclical position.

17. "What Will They Do with Us?," *Richmond Daily Dispatch*, February 13, 1865.

18. Sumner, *Works of Charles Sumner*, 7:466.

19. "Modern Republicanism and Ancient Puritanism," *Plymouth Weekly Democrat*, December 10, 1863.

20. Many years before the war, Charles Sumner established his positivist bona fides, proclaiming, "'The tocsin of monarchy and injustice of all kinds,' progress ordained that indefinite improvement be 'the Destiny of man, of societies, or nations, and of the Human Race.' The lesson of history was 'Onward forever.'" Donald, *Charles Sumner*, 105.

21. Royster, *Destructive War*, 144–45, 191–92.

22. "Terrorism Is Revolutions—Deplorable Excesses of the South," *New York Herald*, January 9, 1861.

23. Kenyon Gradert explores the uses Black abolitionists made of the Puritan past with great care. Gradert, *Puritan Spirits*, 97–98, 157–74. One of the notable absences in their rhetoric, and that of white radicals as well, were references to the Levellers, a movement from the first phase of the English Civil Wars in which a group of reformers advocated for the sovereignty of the House of Commons over the House of Lords and the monarchy and freedom of conscience. Foxley, *Levellers*.

24. Douglas, "Speech at Salem," 93.

25. Douglass, "Fall of Sumter," 443.

26. "Massachusetts Anti-Slavery Society," *New York Times*, January 25, 1862.

27. Dzelzainis, "Milton's Classical Republicanism," 15.

28. Aaron, *Unwritten War*, 343; Gradert, *Puritan Spirits*, 101–2.

29. "Speech of Wendell Phillips," *The Liberator*, August 15, 1861; "Speech of Hon. Isaac N. Arnold," *New York Times*, May 15, 1864.

30. In using the phrase "abolitionist civil war," I am borrowing from Cirillo, *Abolitionist Civil War*; and Wirzbicki, *Fighting for the Higher Law*.

31. Emerson, *Complete Works*, 11:234–35.

32. Braddick, *Common Freedom*, 42.

33. Gentiles, *Oliver Cromwell*, 83.

34. Gregory P. Downs, *Second American Revolution*, 41.

35. Goldwin Smith, *Right, or the Wrong*, 5.

36. Gregory P. Downs, *Second American Revolution*, 13.

37. Nineteenth-century radicals took advantage of the (admittedly ambiguous) legal category of "wartime," as the legal scholar Mary Dudziak characterizes it: "[Americans] tend to assume that wartime is always followed by peacetime, and therefore that an essential aspect of wartime is that it is temporary. The assumption of temporariness becomes an argument for exceptional policies, such as torture. And those who cross the line during war sometimes argue that circumstances deprive them of agency; their acts are driven or determined by time." Dudziak, *Wartime*, 4.

38. "By mid-century towns and counties in the north were being named for the Lord Protector. Abolitionist ministers Theodore Parker, John Wingate Thornton and John Lord praised him, and when the Civil War came, northerners anxious to use his 'heavy hand and fearless grasp' on the erring south invoked his name; some later linked it with that of the Great Emancipator." Karsten, "Cromwell in America," 214. See also Covington, *Devil*, 316.

39. "Mr. Sumner's Speech," *The Liberator*, October 18, 1861; "Speech of Hon. Charles Sumner," *The Liberator*, December 6, 1861.

40. "Rev. J. Sella Martin's Farewell to England," *The Liberator*, February 28, 1862.

41. "Cromwell—on Destructive Conservatism," *The Liberator*, June 5, 1863.

42. "Supporting the Government," *National Intelligencer*, May 14, 1863; "J. C.," letter to the editor, *The Liberator*, August 2, 1861. Phillips's enthusiasm echoes John Milton's lauding of Cromwell, "our chief of men," in poetry, cheering him on to the work yet to do, even after Pride's Purge. John Milton, "Sonnet XVI: Cromwell, our chief of men, who through a cloud," Poetry Foundation, accessed March 21, 2023, www.poetryfoundation.org/poems/44749/sonnet-16-cromwell-our-chief-of-men-who-through-a-cloud.

43. Headley, *Life of Oliver Cromwell*, 339.

44. "J. C.," letter to the editor.

45. Stewart, *Wendell Phillips*, 236–37.

46. "The Duty of Abolitionists," *Pine and Palm*, June 8, 1861; "Letter to General Fremont," *National Anti-Slavery Standard*, September 28, 1861.

47. Gradert writes, "No one was a more fervid student of Puritanism than Phillips, and the pugnacity he drew from this heritage helped enrapture vast crowds and launched him into the role of America's most renowned speaker even as it stoked his delight in war." Gradert, *Puritan Spirits*, 7.

48. Wendell Phillips, "Speech," *National Anti-Slavery Standard*, May 17, 1862; "Speech of Wendell Phillips," *The Liberator*, April 25, 1862.

49. "Mr. Tilton's Lecture—'The One Great Question,'" *Douglass's Monthly*, May 1, 1862.

50. "Sir Walter Scott," *Aegis and Intelligencer*, August 25, 1865.

51. Grimsley, *Hard Hand of War*.

52. Sheehan-Dean, *Calculus of Violence*.

53. Historian John Morrill offers a careful analysis of Cromwell's Irish campaigns, arguing that the violence of Drogheda and Wexford, though significant and unnecessary, was neither exceptional nor driven by a desire to eradicate Catholics. Morrill finds "the principle of executing those held culpable for delaying a surrender and causing the loss of life preceded Cromwell's arrival in Ireland." Morrill, "Drogheda Massacre," 243.

54. Brodie, *Constitutional History*, 3:371.

55. "The Beginning of the End," *Manchester Journal*, September 2, 1862; "The Attacks on the Emancipationists," *The Liberator*, October 25, 1861. On the eve of the 1864 election, an anonymous letter circulated in the Northern press that elaborated still more. Having adopted a hard war policy, which alienated onetime Southern Unionists, the writer believed the North had no choice but to "adopt the policy that Cromwell proposed for Ireland. . . . *We must exterminate the adult population of the South*. Cromwell wanted to depopulate Ireland of its adults and substitute Englishmen and Scotchmen. *He was right*." It was almost certainly a hoax—the letter also eagerly anticipated a thirty-year war to achieve the goal, national bankruptcy, and the death of one-half to two-thirds of the North's population of military-age men—but one written with relish in its critique of radical fanaticism. "A Great Revelation," *Ohio Statesman*, November 1, 1864.

56. "The War: Lecture by Wendell Phillips," *The Liberator*, December 27, 1861.

57. "European Intervention in the United States," *New York Herald*, June 25, 1862.

58. "Confiscation in Ireland," *Daily State Sentinel*, August 2, 1865.

59. Cox, *Puritanism in Politics*, 5.

60. Historians of the English Civil Wars disagree about how to characterize Cromwell's brand of anti-Catholicism. His "phobia of Roman Catholicism" is emphasized throughout

Gentiles, *Oliver Cromwell*: "What drove Cromwell and many other parliamentarians on in this crisis [supporting the Scots in their Ulster campaign in 1642] was a profound sense of righteous indignation against the Irish" (18, 94–95). See also Bennett, *Oliver Cromwell*, 162. On the other hand, on the question of religion, John Morrill argues that "[Cromwell] came to Ireland with a sense of ethnic superiority but not ethnic hatred." Morrill, "Drogheda Massacre," 251.

61. Gentiles, *Oliver Cromwell*, 18, 94–95.
62. Fuller, *From Battlefields Rising*, 42.
63. "Attacks on the Emancipationists."
64. "Mild Measures," *Hartford Daily Courant*, May 28, 1861.
65. Foner, *Free Soil*, 238–60; Gienapp, *Origins of the Republican Party*, 167–237; Holt, *Crisis of the 1850s*, 161–81.
66. Stewart, *Holy Warriors*, 174. Robert H. Abzug's otherwise brilliant *Cosmos Crumbling* does not address attitudes toward Catholicism or the role of nativism as a force in American life.
67. McGreevy, "Catholicism and Abolition," 418; McGreevy, *Catholicism and American Freedom*, 56–66; Beverton, *Exceptionalism in Crisis*, 55.
68. McGreevy, "Catholicism and Abolition," 419.
69. Murphy, *American Slavery Irish Freedom*, 17; Wirzbicki, *Fighting for the Higher Law*, 203–6.
70. Quoted in Murphy, *American Slavery Irish Freedom*, 159.
71. Stewart, *Wendell Phillips*, 111.
72. Edwards, "John Lothrop Motley," 579.
73. Delahanty, *Embracing Emancipation*, 111–17.
74. Keller, *Chancellorsville and the Germans*, 76–91.
75. Ural, *Harp and the Eagle*, 212–19.
76. Ural, *Harp and the Eagle*, 214; Kurtz, *Excommunicated from the Union*, 1–8.
77. In the postwar period, Protestant voters displayed continuing skepticism about the role of Catholics, especially the concern that state funding could be directed toward Catholic education. The Blaine Amendment and the battle over "nonsectarianism" in American education drew on the same distrust about Catholics' role in democratic America as the ugly debates of the 1850s. Feldman, *Divided by God*, 71–85; Kurtz, *Excommunicated from the Union*, 129–43.
78. "Anti-Catholic Crusade," *Dayton Daily Empire*, November 27, 1864.
79. Morrill, *Oliver Cromwell*, 18.
80. "Celebration of the Society for Religious Inquiry," *Burlington Free Press*, August 8, 1862.
81. Hammond, "Inveterate Imperialists."
82. "Three Conditions of Success," *Christian Recorder*, June 15, 1861.
83. Manning, *What This Cruel War*, 84–95; Teters, *Practical Liberators*.
84. The classic account is Rose, *Rehearsal for Reconstruction*. See also Ash, *Firebrand of Liberty*; and Schafer, *Thunder on the River*.
85. Rufus Saxton to Higginson, March 5, 1863, in Higginson, *Army Life*, 108.
86. "Interesting Letter from Major General Hunter," *Green Mountain Freeman*, May 15, 1863.
87. Higginson, *Army Life*, 240.

88. Gentiles, *Oliver Cromwell*, 146.
89. "War Reading," *Christian Recorder*, June 22, 1861.

CHAPTER 6

1. Two important volumes are titled simply *Why the North Won the Civil War* and *Why the South Lost the Civil War*.
2. McPherson, *Crossroads of Freedom*; Stoker, *Grand Design*; Murray and Hsieh, *Savage War*. Edward Ayers has proposed a related concept, "deep contingency," in an effort to put political and military events in relation to the longer time frame of social and cultural change. Ayers, *In the Presence of Mine Enemies*, xix.
3. Oakes, *Freedom National*.
4. Garrett Davis, *Congressional Globe*, 38th Cong., 1st Sess., 25 (1863).
5. "Opposition of the Republican Journals to the Government," *New York Herald*, April 27, 1861; "Caesar, Napoleon, Cromwell, Lincoln," *Holmes County Farmer*, October 27, 1861.
6. George Yeaman, February 18, 1863, *Congressional Globe*, 37th Cong., 3rd Sess., 1012 (1863). Yeaman took some liberties when quoting lines from William Shakespeare's *Julius Caesar*.
7. James A. Bayard, *Congressional Globe*, 37th Cong., 2nd Sess., 71 (1862).
8. Bayard, *Congressional Globe*, 37th Cong., 3rd Sess., 552 (1863).
9. Daniel Vorhees, February 19, 1863, *Congressional Globe*, 37th Cong., 3rd Sess., 1059 (1863).
10. "The President's Proclamation of September 22," *North American*, November 29, 1862.
11. Armitage, "John Milton," 215.
12. Nevins, *War for the Union*; Bensel, *Yankee Leviathan*.
13. Neely, *Lincoln*; Sandow, *Deserter Country*; Jennifer L. Weber, *Copperheads*.
14. Cox, *Puritanism in Politics*, 5.
15. "The Conditions of War," *Harper's Weekly*, September 6, 1862; Powell, *Congressional Globe*, 38th Cong., 1st Sess., 1473–88 (1864).
16. Bennett's *New York Herald* became the voice of War Democrats. Bennett supported the North in the war but opposed emancipation and abolitionists bitterly. Crouthamel, *Bennett's New York Herald*, 117–19, 141–43.
17. The *Herald* had the largest circulation of any newspaper in the United States or the world at the time of the Civil War. Compared to the *New York Tribune*, Horace Greeley's reforming paper that served as a Republican organ, "to read the *Herald* is to gain some insight into the intellectual currency of a portion of the nearly three million who voted against [Lincoln], of those Democrats who supported the war for the Union, and even of the soldiers in the Army of the Potomac, who read the *Herald* more than any other paper." Fermer, *James Gordon Bennett*, 1, 7.
18. "Terrorism in Revolutions Deplorable Excesses of the South," *New York Herald*, January 9, 1861.
19. "The Virginia State Convention," *New York Herald*, April 3, 1861.
20. Macaulay, *History of England*, 1:122; Robert Ross, *Outlines of English History*, 149.
21. McKitrick, "Party Politics"; Neely, *Union Divided*.

22. "Webb on Piety, Puritanism, and a Holy War," *New York Herald*, January 10, 1861. The Wide Awakes were a Republican electoral club that held torchlight parades promoting Lincoln's election. Grinspan, *Wide Awake*. They were occasionally rowdy, but ideologically they aligned with mainstream Republicans, and the prospect of their becoming an abolitionized New Model Army was pure fantasy. James Webb, on the other hand, had attacked Bennett one day in the street, beating him with his cane.

23. "Historical Parallels of Radical Republicanism in England and France," *New York Herald*, March 3, 1861.

24. "Invasion of the South—the Inauguration of Civil War," *New York Herald*, April 8, 1861.

25. Daniel Vorhees, *Congressional Globe*, 37th Cong., 3rd Sess., 1059 (1863).

26. Siddali, *From Property to Person*.

27. Edgar Cowan, *Congressional Globe*, 37th Cong., 2nd Sess., 1049–50 (1862).

28. Howard, *Congressional Globe*, 37th Cong., 2nd Sess., 1714 (1862).

29. Jacob Collamer, *Congressional Globe*, 37th Cong., 2nd Sess., 1810 (1862). Silvana Siddali, the most careful historian of confiscation, concludes that moderate Republicans and War Democrats "softened and weakened punitive legislation," noting in particular the contributions of "Orville Browning, Garrett Davis, and Collamer." Siddali, *From Property to Person*, 125–26. She also notes that "many Democratic editorials also demanded a vigorous prosecution of the war, which usually included harsh measures toward individual southerners" (134).

30. Mark Neely, the closest student of this process, concludes, "A majority of the arrests would have occurred whether the writ [of habeas corpus] was suspended or not. They were caused by the mere incidents or friction of war, which produced refugees, informers, guides, Confederate defectors, carriers of contraband goods, and other such persons as came between or in the wake of large armies. They may have been civilians, but their political views irrelevant." Neely, *Fate of Liberty*, 233.

31. Jennifer L. Weber, *Copperheads*, 95–100.

32. Jennifer L. Weber, *Copperheads*, 96.

33. Untitled article, *Ashland Union*, June 3, 1863.

34. "The Lecture," *Sioux City Register*, March 12, 1864.

35. "What Is to Be Done with the Abolition Traitors?," *New York Herald*, December 23, 1861.

36. Saulsbury, *Congressional Globe*, 37th Cong., 2nd Sess., 2896 (1862).

37. "What Is to Be Done."

38. The *National Intelligencer*, another leading Democratic paper, simply reprinted Phillips's speeches and assumed its readers would see the errors.

39. "Supporting the Government," *National Intelligencer*, May 14, 1863.

40. "The Party of Blood and Brutality—Tribune and Liberator Its Organs," *New York Herald*, March 18, 1862.

41. Woods, *Arguing until Doomsday*, 93.

42. Adam I. P. Smith, *Stormy Present*, 7.

43. Macaulay, *History of England*, 1:137.

44. Wood, *Congressional Globe*, 38th Cong., 1st Sess., 2077 (1864).

45. Nor did his colleague James Bayard, who condemned "the exactions and abuses on the part of the Stuarts." *Congressional Globe*, 37th Cong., 3rd Sess., 552 (1863).

46. Adam I. P. Smith, *Stormy Present*, 7.
47. Fernando Wood, *Congressional Globe*, 38th Cong., 1st Sess., 2077 (1864).
48. Klement, *Dark Lanterns*; Lause, *Secret Society History*.
49. Northern conservatives, in their persistent inflation of the threat the country supposedly faced from the despot Lincoln, overestimated how much power Lincoln exercised and how much control he wielded over the disparate parts of the Northern war machine (a very decentralized contraption). Something similar transpired during the English Civil Wars. "Blair Worden has perceptively documented the essentially conservative nature of the Rump Parliament in which constitutional power was invested in the period between Pride's Purge and its dismissal in 1653: 'The inauguration of the Commonwealth proved to be the end, not the beginning, of the Long Parliament's revolutionary measures.'" In this interpretation, the rebels acted from instinct, not theory—they blundered through the killing of a particular king, not the idea of kingship. They were not motivated by republicanism; rather, later writers fit the ideas of republicanism around the events. Corns, "Milton and the Characteristics," 27.
50. Mason, *Apostle of Union*, 305.
51. Mason, *Apostle of Union*, 302–3.
52. "The Gettysburg Dedication," *Daily Intelligencer* (Wheeling, WV), November 23, 1863. It is also worth noting that Everett's interpretation of the conflict put the Lincoln administration in the role of the Stuart dynasty as a defender of stability and order, a perspective sharply at odds with how Northern radicals interpreted the conflict.

CHAPTER 7

1. Milton, "Readie and Easie Way," 123.
2. "The Harp of Andrew Marvell," *The Liberator*, November 24, 1865.
3. Sumner and others originally drew on John Quincy Adams's argument about the possibility of emancipation in a time of war. Witt, *Lincoln's Code*, 204.
4. Sumner, "Rights of Sovereignty," 12.
5. Sumner, "Rights of Sovereignty," 13.
6. Sumner, "Rights of Sovereignty," 16.
7. Sumner, "Rights of Sovereignty," 17.
8. Sumner, "Rights of Sovereignty," 17.
9. Union general Benjamin Butler, always a contrarian, supported confiscation as well and the sale of confiscated lands in order to fund the Union's war. Nonetheless, he anticipated that this policy would not obstruct peaceful reunion. "Let us go to the teaching of history," Butler proclaimed. "Every considerable estate in the land of England under Cromwell passed through Courts of Confiscation; and yet when the King came to his own again after a time the nation came together again in friendship nevermore to be divided." "Gen. Butler's Speech," *American Citizen*, December 7, 1864.
10. Sumner, "Rights of Sovereignty," 35.
11. Sumner, "Our Domestic Relations," 496–97. One of Sumner's congressional colleagues, Daniel Morris, urged a similarly hardhanded approach with reference to the same analogy. "Wherein do the rebellious States differ from the ... English usurpers [of the seventeenth century]?" he asked. "These felons [the Confederates] maintain their usurpations by

force, and menace the Government with formidable armies. It is proposed to disperse these armies, capture their leaders, and restore order in these unfortunate States. This being done, what is their position?" Most important, Morris queried, "May they claim a restoration to the places and the power they have forfeited by willful abuse? This is not the usual rule, nor is it just." Morris, *Congressional Globe*, 38th Cong., 1st Sess., 2613 (1864).

12. Sumner, "Our Domestic Relations," 497.
13. Witt, *Lincoln's Code*.
14. Charles Sedgwick, *Congressional Globe*, 37th Cong., 3rd Sess., 630 (1863).
15. Hirst, *Dominion*, 223–24.
16. Darcy, *Irish Rebellion of 1641*, 169.
17. "The Fate of Conquered Nations," *Fayetteville Observer*, January 11, 1864.
18. James White, *Landmarks*, 144.
19. Canny, *Making Ireland British*, 552; R. F. Foster, *Modern Ireland*, 107–14.
20. McDonnell, *Light of History*, 31.
21. Perceval-Maxwell, *Outbreak*, 291.
22. Collier, *History*, 220–21.
23. R. F. Foster, *Modern Ireland*, 78.
24. Darcy, *Irish Rebellion*, 10.
25. Kupperman, *Indians and English*, 212–40.
26. Headley, *Life of Oliver Cromwell*, 300–301.
27. William Cooke Taylor, *History of the Civil Wars*, 2:59–60.
28. Macaulay, *History of England*, 1:130–31.
29. Pocock, "Third Kingdom," 275.
30. Tilly, "War Making"; Bensel, *Yankee Leviathan*.
31. Robert Penn Warren, *Legacy*, 59.
32. Frederickson, *Inner Civil War*, 27.
33. "The Return of the Rebellious States to the Union," *Brownson's Quarterly Review*, October 1863, 481; "Virginia," *Continental Monthly*, December 1863, 690–703.
34. "Return of the Rebellious States," 484.
35. Stewart, *Holy Warriors*, 200–201.
36. Everett, "Anecdotes," 122.
37. Powell, *Congressional Globe*, 38th Cong., 1st Sess., 106 (1864).
38. Powell, *Congressional Globe*, 39th Cong., Special Sess., 65 (1864).
39. Cox also drew from political theory. The epigraph for his collected speeches (published in 1865) featured a quote from Montesquieu on this topic that called for "lenity rather than severity. . . . Under pretense of avenging the republic's cause, the avengers would establish tyranny. The business is not to destroy the rebel, but the rebellion." Cox, *Eight Years in Congress*.
40. "Speech of Hon. S. S. Cox," *Newark Advocate*, January 29, 1864. Cox was consistent in his attitudes. In the travel account he wrote after an 1852 tour across Europe, he bemoaned Ireland's poverty but did not ascribe it to Catholicism. Instead, he critiqued England's persecution of Irish Catholics. "The church of England can gain nothing but must lose much, by its coercive measures towards the Catholics. Persecution will do its old work, by creating devotees around the altars of the persecuted." Cox, *Buckeye Abroad*, 393.
41. Cox, *Congressional Globe*, 38th Cong., 1st Sess., 2099 (1864).

42. Gleeson, *Green and the Gray*, 120, 172; Covington, *Devil*, 301.

43. "Confiscation.—William the Conqueror," *New Oregon Plaindealer*, February 19, 1864.

44. "Butler and Cromwell," *Democrat and Sentinel*, January 18, 1865.

45. "Confiscation in Ireland," *Daily State Sentinel*, August 2, 1865.

46. "Let Us Have a True Peace," originally in *Chronicle*, reprinted in *National Intelligencer*, April 7, 1865.

47. "President Lincoln," *Princeton Review*, July 1865, 435–58.

48. Oubre, *Forty Acres*; Schweninger, *Black Property Owners*, 142–61.

49. As with most aspects of Reconstruction historiography, W. E. B. Du Bois addressed this question of land long before most white scholars gave it the attention it deserves. Du Bois, *Black Reconstruction in America*.

50. Richardson, *Death of Reconstruction*; Perman, *Road to Redemption*; William Gillespie, *Retreat from Reconstruction*.

51. Vaughan, *Revolutions in English History*, 344.

52. S. S. Cox, *Congressional Globe*, 38th Cong., 1st Sess., 2101 (1864).

53. Cox, *Congressional Globe*, 38th Cong., 1st Sess., 2101 (1864); Delano, *Congressional Globe*, 39th Cong., 1st Sess., 425 (1866). "Crossing the English Channel and contemplating Cromwell's famous settlement of Ireland, you behold an extensive scale of plunder and devastation which shocks the sense of justice and fires with indignation the bosom of every honest and philanthropic man; and yet, Mr. Speaker, all that fearful ravage fades into insignificance before the scheme proposed for our adoption in these States lately in rebellion."

54. Douglass, "Our Martyred President," 76.

55. Cox, *Congressional Globe*, 38th Cong., 1st Sess., 2099 (1864); Law, in House, July 4, 1864, *Congressional Globe*, 38th Cong., 1st Sess., 3477–79 (1864).

56. Cox, *Congressional Globe*, 38th Cong., 1st Sess., 2098 (1864).

57. Cox, May 5, 1864, *Congressional Globe*, 38th Cong., 1st Sess., 2098 (1864).

58. "England and America," *Princeton Review*, January 1862, 175.

59. John Clive refers here to the 1832 Reform Bill, but the sentiment was one that animated Macaulay's whole approach to political change. Clive, *Macaulay*, 230, 142–76.

60. Blair, *With Malice toward Some*.

61. Amy Taylor cogently narrates this process. Amy Taylor, *Embattled Freedom*, 211–38.

62. Amy Taylor, *Embattled Freedom*, 214.

63. Burke, "Speech on Conciliation," 350.

64. Macaulay, *History of England*, 1:153.

65. Vaughan, *Revolutions in English History*, 344.

66. "The Meeting in Richmond," *Harper's Weekly*, September 16, 1865.

67. "The Late Abraham Lincoln—His Early Life and Public Character," *Pomeroy Weekly Telegraph*, April 27, 1865.

68. "The Last Address of the President to the Country," *New York Times*, April 17, 1865.

CHAPTER 8

1. Lincoln, "Second Inaugural Address."

2. Noll, *America's God*, 428–32; Rable, *God's Almost Chosen People*, 371–74.

3. The literary scholar Daniel Aaron observed long ago, "One would expect writers, the 'antennae of the race,' to say something revealing about the meaning, if not the cause, of the War.... With a few notable exceptions, they did not." Aaron, *Unwritten War*, xviii.

4. In a study of the relationship among the events of 1641, 1689, and 1776, J. G. A. Pocock explained that by locating "the Puritan Revolution at the beginning rather than the end of a historical series [it enabled] a new perspective" on all three events. Pocock, *Three British Revolutions*, 4.

5. Most works on the Lost Cause focus on the postwar period. Two works that stress wartime creation include Janney, *Burying the Dead*, 15–38; and Broomall, *Private Confederacies*, 108–29.

6. Blight, *Race and Reunion*; Clark, *Defining Moments*.

7. Neff, *Honoring*; Gallagher, *Union War*; Summers, *Ordeal of the Union*.

8. This argument parallels that of Frances Clarke in *War Stories*. Clarke analyzes how people "were engaged in an effort to take control of wartime carnage, invest it with meaning, and turn it to individual, political, and cultural advantage" (6). Her analysis focuses on the value of sentimental stories to provide real emotional sustenance in the face of the war's horrors.

9. As a historian keen to avoid biological metaphors that misrepresent history as the working out of an inevitable sequence, I use the term "naturalized" with reluctance, but it captures the degree to which participants hoped to accomplish precisely that blurring of human agency that modern scholars reject.

10. As many scholars have shown, Northerners regarded the preservation of the Union as the war's supreme achievement. These accounts, rightly, emphasize the emotional and psychological value such interpretation offered. In addition, I hope to show the ways that celebrating reunion projected state sovereignty and American power out into the world. See Neff, *Honoring*; Janney, *Remembering the Civil War*; and Gannon, *Won Cause*.

11. On the former, see Brown, *Civil War Monuments*.

12. "The Union—in the Future," *Harper's Weekly*, June 15, 1861; "Things in General," *Boston Investigator*, May 7, 1862; Robert Ross, *Outlines of English History*; Carlyle, *On Heroes*, 270.

13. "The Lessons of Our National Conflict," *New Englander*, October 1861.

14. Quoted in "Republican Institutions Not a Failure," *New York Times*, September 28, 1861.

15. "Lessons of Our National Conflict"; "The London Times Criticised," *Boston Daily Advertiser*, June 14, 1861. However, this honesty may have dimmed with the war's end. Daniel Aaron argues, "Forgotten in the War's aftermath was the truth Melville and Lincoln saw with their instructed eyes: America could not escape history." Aaron, *Unwritten War*, 330.

16. "On American Secession and State Rights," *Monthly Law Reporter*, May 1864, 363.

17. "A History of Rebellions," *Advocate of Peace*, September–October 1867.

18. "England and America," *Princeton Review*, January 1862, 148; Sheehan-Dean, *Reckoning with Rebellion*, 26–27.

19. "A Letter to England: Not by an LL.D.," *Harper's Weekly*, September 21, 1861.

20. "American Topics Abroad: Mr. John Bright on Our Troubles and the Cotton Question," *New York Times*, August 15, 1861.

21. Goldwin Smith, *Letter to a Whig*.

22. Pierce, *Memoir and Letters*, 4:193, 193n3.

23. Sabato, *Republics*.

24. "Causes of the American Civil War," *Times*, May 23, 1861.

25. Waldstreicher, *In the Midst*; Purcell, *Sealed with Blood*.

26. "E Pluribus Unum," *Atlantic Monthly*, February 1, 1861.

27. "Letter from Cassius M. Clay to the Editor of the *London Times*," *Sun*, June 7, 1861. *Harper's Monthly* concurred, "The principle of Secession aims a deadly blow at all governments. Instead of a nation, claiming the supreme allegiances of every citizen, it would reduce us to a collection of isolated communities." Editor's Table, *Harper's New Monthly Magazine*, February 1862, 405.

28. "Union—in the Future"; Editor's Easy Chair, *Harper's New Monthly Magazine*, April 1862.

29. "Change in Sentiment Abroad," *Frank Leslie's Illustrated Newspaper*, April 8, 1865. Benjamin Butler used the same history to argue that "there will be no difficulty in the good men of the North and the South coming together again, and letting bygones be bygones." "Reception to Major-Gen. Butler," *The Liberator*, November 25, 1864.

30. Forster, "Civil Wars," 263.

31. "The Discipline of Suffering," originally in *Pittsburgh Christian Advocate*, reprinted in *Green Mountain Freeman*, August 23, 1864.

32. "By mid-century, war, so central to the making of the British nation, became *the* testing ground for ethics for Enlightenment thinkers invested in the idea that reason, rather than violence and emotion, lit the path of progress." Satia, *Time's Monster*, 23.

33. Thomas B. Macaulay, "A Conversation between Mr. Abraham Cowley and Mr. John Milton, Touching the Great Civil War: Set Down by a Gentleman of the Middle Temple," *Knight's Quarterly Magazine*, August 1824.

34. "War. Reply to Mr. Knight," *Boston Investigator*, December 17, 1862; "We of This Generation Have Seen Wonderful," *Times*, May 7, 1861.

35. Cattermole, *Great Civil War*, 67; Brodie, *Constitutional History*, 3:356.

36. Emerson, *Complete Works*, 6:253–55; "Education and Strikes," *Times*, October 24, 1864.

37. Douglass, "Slaveholder's Rebellion," 526. The historian John Lothrop Motley offered a different interpretation. "He was always careful to distinguish between the constructive, Whig type of revolution—the Dutch Revolt, the Glorious Revolution, and the American Revolution—and the destructive, or French type. The former was conservative, in that it sought to maintain established, traditional rights against tyrannical encroachment; whereas the latter was directed against the principle of authority itself." Wheaton, "Motley," 325.

38. Douglass, "Fighting the Rebels," 474.

39. "Causes of the American Civil War."

40. Gaines M. Foster, "What's Not in a Name?"

41. "Abolition of Slavery in the District of Columbia," *Bradford Reporter*, March 20, 1862. The tension between these labels is not semantic—there are identifiable differences between revolutions and civil wars. From a purely practical perspective, we need boundaries between events in order to make sense of the continuous flow of history. Not all conflict is war, not all resistance to established authorities is revolution, and not all domestic opposition is civil war. On the other hand, participants in these conflicts disagreed about what they witnessed and what terms were appropriate. Michael Walzer observes the way that Puritans' emphasis on self-discipline and sin enabled them to accept real war alongside personal spiritual struggle. Puritanism "trained them to think of the struggle with Satan and his allies as an extension

and duplicate of their internal spiritual conflicts, and also as a difficult and continuous war, requiring methodical, organized activity, military exercise, and discipline. These ideas were the underlying themes of the new politics; permanent warfare was the central myth of Puritan radicalism." Walzer, *Revolution of the Saints*, 290.

42. Royster, *Destructive War*.

43. Guizot, *History of the Origins*, 435.

44. Satia, *Time's Monster*, 81–106; Koditschek, *Liberalism*, 4–9, 99–100.

45. On Northerners' embrace of emancipation, see Neff, *Honoring*; Janney, *Remembering the Civil War*; and Robert Penn Warren, *Legacy*.

46. Sternhell, "Revisionism Reinvented?" I refer here mostly to the modern revisionists (John S. Rosenberg, Harry Stout, and David Goldfield) rather than the original generation (Avery Craven and James G. Randall). Rachel Shelden, in "Politics of Continuity," offers a valuable critique of the ways that historians use the term "revisionism."

47. Potter, "Historians' Uses of Nationalism."

48. Max Weber, "Politics as a Vocation."

49. Froude, *English in Ireland*, 2–3, 4.

50. "Self-Possession vs. Prepossession," *Atlantic Monthly*, December 1, 1861.

51. Sumner to Bright, October 28, 1862, in Pierce, *Memoir and Letters*, 4:106. Historian David Cannadine characterizes the nineteenth-century British empire as a curious mix of force and freedom. "It was an empire in which authoritarian modes of government and control co-existed uneasily and paradoxically with ideas of liberty, concern for native peoples, and a growing momentum for reform." Cannadine, *Victorious Century*, 53.

52. Untitled article, *Rutland Weekly Herald*, February 20, 1862; "English versus American Inhumanity in War," *Weekly Pioneer and Democrat*, February 7, 1862.

53. "Self-Possession vs. Prepossession." A similar sentiment can be found in a postwar lament for Lincoln's death published as "Reunion," *The Liberator*, June 16, 1865:

> He saw the end, and fixed "the purer laws."
> May these endure, and, as his work, attest
> The glory of his honest heart and hand—
> The simplest, and the bravest, and the best—
> The Moses and the Cromwell of his land.

54. Satia, *Time's Monster*, 7; Mehta, *Liberalism and Empire*.

55. In their history of American education, Wayne Urban and Jennings Wagoner Jr. emphasize the pervasiveness of Enlightenment-era conceptions of progress. "A fundamental belief that emerged as a cornerstone of Enlightenment ideology was the conviction that progress was inevitable and that, in time, the perfect—or at least, near perfect—society would come into existence." Urban and Wagoner, *American Education*, 58.

56. Adam I. P. Smith, *Stormy Present*, 7–8; Carmichael, *Last Generation*, 19–34; Majewski, *House Dividing*; Chad Morgan, *Planters' Progress*.

57. Although Michael Woods's analysis of the concept of majoritarian democracy focuses on Lincoln's rival Stephen Douglas, the two men shared a deep faith in the concept. Woods, *Arguing until Doomsday*.

58. "Why We Talk about England," *Harper's Weekly*, June 22, 1861.

59. Whittier, *In War Time*, 27.

60. "England and America," 147–77.

61. Quoted in Pierce, *Memoir and Letters*, 4:158.

62. "Our Great America," *Continental Monthly*, October 1864, 446. Kenyon Gradert identifies a prewar form of this genealogy that began with Jesus's birth and culminated in the American Revolution. It was a small step to extend that logic through the Civil War. Gradert, *Puritan Spirits*, 24–26.

63. "Citizen Soldiery," *Xenia Sentinel*, May 12, 1865.

64. "Letter from Rev. Daniel Foster," *The Liberator*, September 21, 1862.

65. "Citizen Soldiery."

66. "Our Great America," 446–47.

67. "Letter from Minnesota," *Portland Daily Press*, October 23, 1863.

68. *Richmond Examiner* quoted in "Reuter's Telegrams and Mason's Commission," *Harper's Weekly*, November 23, 1861.

69. Jan Dawson shows that even many white Southerners saw this connection, arguing that "Southern commentators frequently interpreted the historical significance of the American Civil War as the final act in the drama unfolded in the English Civil War." Dawson, "Puritan and the Cavalier," 607. Around the same time as Dawson, J. G. A. Pocock articulated a lineage that bound the English Civil Wars, the Glorious Revolution, and the American Revolution into "a single sequence" united by a "Whig political culture." Pocock, *Three British Revolutions*, 17.

70. "Citizen Soldiery." The historian Edmund Morgan advances a similar interpretation in his history of popular sovereignty when he observes that the English Civil Wars ended with a confirmation of the role of consent in government. "Unfortunately neither Charles II nor those who engineered his return were able to see the usefulness of popular sovereignty in this light, and the lessons of the 1640s and 1650s had to be learned anew in the 1670s and 1680s, and again in the 1770s and 1780s." Edmund S. Morgan, *Inventing the People*, 93. This can also be found in Bernard Bailyn's ideological history of the Revolution, where he writes that "what shaped the colonists' miscellaneous learning and shaped it into a coherent whole, was the influence of still another group of writers . . . the ultimate origins of [which] lay in the radical social and political thought of the English Civil War and of the Commonwealth period." Bailyn, *Ideological Origins*, 34.

71. Southerners did not endorse a whiggish view of history before and, especially, during the Civil War. Dawson, "Puritan and the Cavalier," 611.

72. "The Great Wars—a Historical Review and Contrast," originally published in *Monthly Religious Magazine*, reprinted in *Nebraska Advertiser*, March 16, 1865. Edward Everett offered a similar interpretation at Gettysburg: "The Puritans of 1640 and the Whigs of 1688 rebelled against arbitrary power in order to establish constitutional liberty." Edward Everett, "Gettysburg Address," November 19, 1863, Voices of Democracy, accessed June 23, 2022, https://voicesofdemocracy.umd.edu/everett-gettysburg-address-speech-text.

73. Sexton, "William H. Seward," 414, 412.

74. Thomas Pressly describes a "nationalist tradition" in Civil War historiography, which concluded that "the Civil War experience had resulted in much more good than evil. The Civil War had destroyed the institution of slavery and had preserved and strengthened the American nation." Pressly, *Americans Interpret*, 221–26.

75. Rhodes, *History of the Civil War*, 438.

76. See, e.g., Jim Downs, *Sick from Freedom*; Emberton, *Beyond Redemption*; and Manjapra, *Black Ghost of Empire*.

77. "Henry Vincent on the American Crisis," *North American*, November 14, 1862; Doyle, *Cause of All Nations*.

78. Goldwin Smith, "England and America," *Atlantic Monthly*, December 1864, 751.

79. Goldwin Smith, "England and America," 752. Smith embodies one of Butterfield's chief criticisms of the whig interpretation: "The total result of this method it to impose a certain form upon the whole historical story, and to produce a scheme of general history which is bound to converge beautifully upon the present—all demonstrating throughout the ages the working of an obvious principle of progress." Butterfield, *Whig Interpretation of History*, 12.

80. Goldwin Smith, "England and America," 753. In another context, Smith emphasized the same point through a negative example: "Of two great efforts to drag the English race back into slavery of body and mind, one found its grave at Marston Moor and the other at Gettysburg." "Prof. Goldwin Smith," *New Hampshire Statesman*, January 15, 1864.

81. Jones, *Union in Peril*; Foreman, *World on Fire*.

82. Nevins, *Diary*, 3:308.

83. Fukuyama, *End of History*.

84. Rodgers, *As a City on a Hill*.

85. "Protestant Americans had long had their own universal history, written in the shared language of eschatology and millennialism, their own basic law of sinward historical motion from which a special people might be chosen out, a national 'elected.'" Rodgers, "Exceptionalism," 23.

86. Rodgers, "Exceptionalism," 27.

87. Armitage, *Civil Wars*, 193. Legal scholar John Witt makes a similar point in describing Lincoln's successful refashioning of the laws of war to accommodate emancipation (something they had not done before the American Civil War). "In managing the fallout from Emancipation, [the Lincoln] administration called forth a new blueprint for the international law of war, one that is with us to this day." Witt, *Lincoln's Code*, 368.

CONCLUSION

1. Pocock, *Ancient Constitution*, 21–22.

2. When Confederates attached themselves to the tragic (historical) persecution of Cavaliers by Parliamentarians, they increased the stakes for what they perceived as their own persecution at the hands of Federals. Martha Minnow quotes Michael Ignatieff about a parallel example: "What seems apparent in the former Yugoslavia is that the past continues to torment because it is not the past. These places are not living in a serial order of time but in a simultaneous one, in which the past and present are a continuous, agglutinated mass of fantasies, distortions, myths, and lies. Reporters in the Balkan wars often observed that when they were told atrocity stories they were occasionally unsure whether these stories had occurred yesterday or in 1941, or 1841, or 1441." The history of the seventeenth century had lain mostly inert, but by resuscitating and identifying with it, white Southerners (and then

Confederates, with even more eagerness) exaggerated their own suffering. Minnow, *Between Vengeance and Forgiveness*, 14.

3. For a more extensive discussion of Confederates' willingness to accept, even embrace, French monarchy in Mexico, see Beverton, *Exceptionalism in Crisis*, chap. 2.

4. An excellent guide to this literature can be found in Janney, "Civil War Memory," 1139–54.

5. In the 1840s, American historian John Lothrop Motley believed that America existed in a permanent present, unmoored from any past. Accordingly, although Americans read histories (mostly of Europe), people treated these as mere fables. "The country without a Past cannot be intoxicated by visions of the Past of other lands." Motley, "Polity of the Puritans," 494.

6. Rovelli's *Order of Time*, a physicist's account, offers a comprehensive account of the various ways people have understood the movement of time.

7. Cox, *Eight Years in Congress*, 388.

8. Bodnar, *"Good War."*

9. Richards, *Philosophy of Rhetoric*, 96–100. "Words, [Richards] believes, gain their effect from the multiple contexts in which they are used, so that they are the means by which different discursive powers exerted in different situations may be brought together." Eagleton, *Critical Revolutionaries*, 112.

10. Hayden White, *Metahistory*.

BIBLIOGRAPHY

PRIMARY SOURCES

Newspapers and Periodicals

England
  Knight's Quarterly Magazine
  London Times
  The Telegraph (London)
  Times (London)

Ireland
  Carlow Sentinel
  Irishman (Dublin)
  Irish People (Dublin)
  The Nation (Dublin)
  Wexford People

United States
  Advocate of Peace
  Aegis and Intelligencer (Bel Air, MD)
  American Citizen (Butler County, PA)
  Anti-Slavery Bugle (New Lisbon, OH)
  Ashland (OH) Union
  Atlantic Monthly
  Bangor (ME) Daily Whig and Courier

Boston Daily Advertiser
Boston Investigator
Boston Pilot
Bradford Reporter (Towanda, PA)
Brownson's Quarterly Review
Buchanan County (IA) Guardian
Burlington (VT) Free Press
Charleston (SC) Mercury
Charleston (SC) Tri-Weekly Courier
Chicago Daily Tribune
Christian Recorder
Cleveland (OH) Morning Leader
Continental Monthly
Daily Cleveland (OH) Herald
Daily Confederate (Raleigh, NC)
Daily Evening Bulletin (San Francisco)
Daily Nashville Union
Daily National Democrat (Marysville, CA)
Daily News and Herald (Savannah, GA)
Daily Ohio Statesman (Columbus)

Daily Register (Raleigh, NC)
Daily Register (Wheeling, WV)
Daily Richmond (VA) Examiner
Daily Richmond (VA) Whig
Daily State Sentinel (Indianapolis, IN)
Daily True Delta (New Orleans, LA)
Dayton (OH) Daily Empire
DeBow's Review
Delaware Journal and Statesman (Wilmington)
Democrat and Sentinel (Ebensburg, PA)
Douglass's Monthly
Eclectic Magazine of Foreign Literature
Evening Star (Washington, DC)
Fayetteville (NC) Observer
Frank Leslie's Illustrated Newspaper (New York)
Freedom's Champion (Atchison, KS)
Green Mountain (VT) Freeman
Hancock Jeffersonian (Findlay, OH)
Harper's New Monthly Magazine
Harper's Weekly
Hartford (CT) Daily Courant
Hillsdale (MI) Standard
Holmes County Farmer (Millersburg, OH)
The Independent (New York)
Knickerbocker Magazine
Lancaster (OH) Gazette
Leavenworth (KS) Times
The Liberator (Boston)
Literary and Catholic Sentinel (Boston)
Littel's Living Age
Lowell (MA) Daily Citizen
Manchester (VT) Journal
Memphis (TN) Avalanche
Memphis (TN) Daily Appeal
Mercersburg (PA) Review
Milwaukee (WI) Daily Sentinel
Monthly Law Reporter
National Anti-Slavery Standard (New York)
National Intelligencer (Washington, DC)
National Republican (Washington, DC)
Nebraska Advertiser (Brownville)
Newark (OH) Advocate
New Englander (New Haven, CT)
New Hampshire Statesman (Concord)
New Oregon (IA) Plaindealer
New York Evangelist
New York Herald
New York Times
New York Tribune
North American (Philadelphia)
North American Review
Ohio Statesman (Columbus)
Pine and Palm (Boston)
Plymouth (IN) Weekly Democrat
Pomeroy (OH) Weekly Telegraph
Portland (ME) Daily Press
Princeton Review
Raleigh (NC) Register
Richmond (VA) Daily Dispatch
Richmond (VA) Enquirer
Richmond (VA) Examiner
Rutland (VT) Weekly Herald
Scioto Gazette (Chillicothe, OH)
Sioux City (IA) Register
Southern Literary Messenger (Richmond, VA)
The Sun (Baltimore, MD)
Times-Picayune (New Orleans)
True Democrat (Little Rock, AR)
Vanity Fair
The Vindicator (Youngstown, OH)
Weekly Perrysburg Journal
Weekly Pioneer and Democrat (Saint Paul, MN)
Western (WV) Democrat
Western Reserve Chronicle (Warren, OH)
Wilmington (NC) Journal
Wisconsin State Register
Xenia (OH) Sentinel
Yorkville (SC) Enquirer

Borlase, Edmund. *The history of the execrable Irish rebellion trac'd from many preceding acts to the grand eruption the 23 of October, 1641*. London: Robert Clavel, 1680.
Brodie, George. *A Constitutional History of the British Empire: From the Accession of Charles I to the Restoration*. Rev. ed., 3 vols. London: Longmans, Green, 1866.
Brontë, Charlotte. *Jane Eyre*, 1847. Reprint, New York: Union Square, 2022.
Brougham, Henry. *The British Constitution—Its History, Structure, and Working*. Vol. 11 of *Works of Henry Lord Brougham*. Edinburgh: Adam and Charles Black, 1873.
Buckle, Henry Thomas. *History of Civilization in England*. Vol. 3. New ed. London: Longmans, Green, 1868.
Burke, Edmund. "Speech on Conciliation with America." In *A Philosophical Enquiry into the Sublime and Beautiful and Other Pre-Revolutionary Writings*, edited by David Womersley. 1757. London: Penguin, 2004.
Carlyle, Thomas, ed. *Oliver Cromwell's Speeches and Letters: With Elucidations*. New York: Wiley and Putnam, 1845.
Carlyle, Thomas. *On Heroes, Hero-Worship and the Heroic in History*, 1841. Reprint, London: George Routledge and Sons, 1897.
Carrel, Armand. *History of the Counter-Revolution in England, for the Re-Establishment of Popery*. London: H. G. Bohn, 1857.
Cattermole, George. *The Great Civil War of the Times of Charles I. and Cromwell*. London: Fisher, Son, 1846.
Collier, Francis. *History of the British Empire*. London: T. Nelson and Sons, 1866.
Cox, Samuel S. *A Buckeye Abroad*. Columbus, OH: Follett Foster, 1860.
Cox, Samuel S. *Eight Years in Congress, from 1857–1865: Memoir and Speeches*. New York: D. Appleton, 1865.
Cox, Samuel S. *Puritanism in Politics: Speech of Hon. S. S. Cox, of Ohio before the Democratic Union Association*. New York: Van Evrie, Horton, 1863.
Crist, Lynda, Mary Seaton Dix, and Kenneth M. Williams, eds. *Papers of Jefferson Davis*, 14 vols. Baton Rouge: Louisiana State University Press, 1971–2015.
Douglas, H. Ford. "Speech at Salem, OH, 23 September 1860." In *The United States, 1859–1865*, vol. 5 of *The Black Abolitionist Papers*, edited by Peter C. Ripley. Chapel Hill: University of North Carolina Press, 1992.
Douglass, Frederick. "The American Apocalypse." In *1855–63*, vol. 3 of *The Frederick Douglass Papers. Series One: Speeches, Debates, and Interviews*, edited by John W. Blassingame, John R. McKivigan, et al. New Haven, CT: Yale University Press, 1985.
Douglass, Frederick. "The Fall of Sumter." In *1855–63*, vol. 3 of *The Frederick Douglass Papers. Series One: Speeches, Debates, and Interviews*, edited by John W. Blassingame, John R. McKivigan, et al. New Haven, CT: Yale University Press, 1985.
Douglass, Frederick. "Fighting the Rebels with One Hand." In *1855–63*, vol. 3 of *The Frederick Douglass Papers. Series One: Speeches, Debates, and Interviews*, edited by John W. Blassingame and John R. McKivigan. New Haven, CT: Yale University Press, 1985.
Douglass, Frederick. "Our Martyred President." In *1864–80*, vol. 4 of *The Frederick Douglass Papers. Series One: Speeches, Debates, and Interviews*, edited by John W. Blassingame, John R. McKivigan, et al. New Haven, CT: Yale University Press, 1985.

Douglass, Frederick. "The Slaveholder's Rebellion." In *1855–63*, vol. 3 of *The Frederick Douglass Papers. Series One: Speeches, Debates, and Interviews*, edited by John W. Blassingame, John R. McKivigan, et al. New Haven, CT: Yale University Press, 1985.

Dowdey, Clifford, ed. *The Wartime Papers of R. E. Lee*. Boston: Little, Brown, 1961.

Dzelzainis, Martin. Introduction to Milton, *Political Writings*.

Emerson, Ralph Waldo. *The Complete Works of Ralph Waldo Emerson*, 12 vols. Boston: Houghton, Mifflin, 1903–4.

Everett, Edward. "Anecdotes of Early Local History." In vol. 2 of *Orations and Speeches on Various Occasions*. 9th ed. Boston: Little, Brown, 1878.

Forster, John. "The Civil Wars at Oliver Cromwell." In vol. 1 of *Historical and Biographical Essays*, edited by John Forster. London: John Murray, 1858.

Froude, James. *The English in Ireland in the Eighteenth Century*. Vol. 1. New York: Scribner, Armstrong, 1873.

Garrison, William Lloyd. *The Letters of William Lloyd Garrison*, 6 vols. Edited by Walter Merrill and Louis Ruchames. Cambridge, MA: Belknap, 1975–81.

Gienapp, William E., and Erica L. Gienapp, eds. *The Civil War Diary of Gideon Welles: Lincoln's Secretary of the Navy*. Urbana: University of Illinois Press, 2014.

Guizot, Francois. *The History of the Origins of Representative Government in Europe*. Translated by Andrew R. Scoble. 1851. Indianapolis, IN: Liberty Fund, 2002.

Hallam, Henry. *The Constitutional History of England, from the Accession of Henry VII to the Death of George II*. 5th ed. 3 vols. New York: W. J. Widdleton, 1867.

Haverty, Martin. *The History of Ireland, Ancient and Modern*. Dublin: James Duffy, 1867.

Headley, Joel T. *The Life of Oliver Cromwell*. New York: Baker and Scribner, 1848.

Higginson, Thomas Wentworth. *Army Life in a Black Regiment*. 1869. New York: Norton, 1984.

Hope, A. J. B. Beresford. *A Popular View of the American Civil War*. 2nd ed. London: James Ridgeway, 1861.

Hunter, Robert M. T. "The Peace Commission of 1865." *Southern Historical Society Papers*, no. 4 (1877): 303–16.

Lincoln, Abraham. "Second Inaugural Address." In *Collected Works of Abraham Lincoln*, edited by Roy Basler. New Brunswick, NJ: Rutgers University Press, 1953.

Lingard, John. *A History of England*. Rev. ed. 10 vols. Boston: Phillips, Sampson, 1860.

Macaulay, Thomas B. *The History of England from the Accession of James the Second*, 5 vols. London: Longman, Green, Longman, and Roberts, 1860.

Macaulay, Thomas B. Review of *The Constitutional History of England, from the Accession of Henry VII to the Death of George II*, by Henry Hallam. *Edinburgh Review*, no. 48 (September 1828): 96–160.

Macaulay, Thomas B. Review of *The Romance of History: England*, by Henry Neele. *Edinburgh Review*, no. 47 (May 1828): 331–67.

Madden, Richard. *The United Irishmen, Their Lives and Times*. 2nd ed. London: Catholic, 1860.

McDonnell, John. *The Light of History Respecting the Massacres in Ireland from about A.D. 1580 to the End of the Civil War of 1641*. Dublin: R. D. Webb, 1886.

McGee, Thomas D'Arcy. *A Popular History of Ireland*. Vol. 2. New York: D. and J. Sadlier, 1863.

McGuffey, William Holmes. *McGuffey's Sixth Eclectic Reader*. Rev. ed. New York: John Wiley and Sons, 1879.

Milton, John. *Paradise Lost*. 1667. New York: Penguin, 2003.

Milton, John. *Political Writings*. 1650. Cambridge: Cambridge University Press, 1991.

Milton, John. "The Readie and Easie Way to Establish A Free Commonwealth." In vol. 4 of *The Works of John Milton*. 1660. New York: Columbia University Press, 1932.

Milton, John. "The Tenure of Kings and Magistrates." In vol. 4 of *The Works of John Milton*. 1660. New York: Columbia University Press, 1932.

Motley, John Lothrop. "The Causes of the American Civil War: A Paper Contributed to the London Times, New York, 1861." In vol. 1 of *Union Pamphlets of the Civil War*, edited by Frank Friedel. Cambridge, MA: Belknap, 1967.

Motley, John Lothrop. "Polity of the Puritans." *North American Review*, no. 69 (October 1849): 470–98.

Nevins, Allan, ed. *The Diary of George Templeton Strong: The Civil War, 1860–1865*, 4 vols. New York: Macmillan, 1952.

O'Hanlon, John. *Catechism of Irish History from the Earliest Events to the Death of O'Connell*. Dublin: John Mullany, 1864.

Phillips, Ulrich B., ed. *Annual Report of the American Historical Association for the Year 1911*. Washington, DC: Government Printing Office, 1913.

Phillips, Wendell. *Speeches, Lectures, and Letters*. 2nd ser. Boston: Lee and Shepard, 1891.

Pierce, Edward L. *Memoir and Letters of Charles Sumner*, 4 vols. Boston, MA: Roberts Brothers, 1877–93.

Ross, Robert. *Outlines of English History for Junior Classes in Schools*. London: Simkin, Marshall, 1860.

Sadlier, [Mary Ann Madden] J. *The Confederate Chieftains: A Tale of the Irish Rebellion of 1641*. New York: D. and J. Sadlier, 1864.

Sanborn, F. B. *The Life and Letters of John Brown*. Boston: Roberts Bros., 1891.

Savage, John. *'98 and '48: The Modern Revolutionary History and Literature of Ireland*. 3rd ed. New York: Redfield, 1856.

Scarborough, William K., ed. *The Diary of Edmund Ruffin*, 3 vols. Baton Rouge: Louisiana State University Press, 1976.

Sermons on Slavery and Civil War, Boston, 1851–1865. Boston: W. M. Crosby and H. P. Nichols, n.d.

Smith, Goldwin. *Irish History and Irish Character*. Oxford: J. H. and Jas. Parker, 1861.

Smith, Goldwin. *A Letter to a Whig Member of the Southern Independence Association*. Boston: Ticknor and Fields, 1864.

Smith, Goldwin. *The Right, or the Wrong, of the American War: A Letter to an English Friend*. New York: Anson D. F. Randolph, 1864.

The Soldier's Pocket Bible: An Exact Reprint of the Original Edition of 1643. Cambridge, MA, 1861.

Stephens, Alexander. *A Constitutional View of the Late War between the States*. 2 vols. Philadelphia: National Publishing, 1870.

Stillé, Charles J. *How a Free People Conduct a Long War: A Chapter from English History*. Philadelphia: Collins, 1862.

Stowe, Harriet Beecher. *Sunny Memories of Foreign Lands.* Vol. 1. Boston: Phillips, Sampson, 1854.
Sumner, Charles. "Our Domestic Relations: Power of Congress over the Rebel States." In vol. 7 of *Works of Charles Sumner.*
Sumner, Charles. "Rights of Sovereignty and Rights of War: Two Sources of Power against the Rebellion." In vol. 7 of *Works of Charles Sumner.*
Sumner, Charles. "Slavery and the Rebellion, One and Inseparable." Speech given on November 5, 1864. In vol. 9 of *Works of Charles Sumner.*
Sumner, Charles. *The Works of Charles Sumner,* 15 vols. Boston: Lee and Shephard, 1870–73.
Taylor, William Cooke. *History of the Civil Wars of Ireland: From the Anglo-Norman Invasion, till the Union of the Country with Great Britain.* 2 vols. Edinburgh: Constable, 1831.
Temple, John. *The Irish Rebellion.* London: R. White, 1646.
Todd, William B., ed. *The Early Writings.* Vol. 1 of *The Writings and Speeches of Edmund Burke.* Oxford: Clarendon, 1997.
Twain, Mark. *Life on the Mississippi.* Boston, 1883. www.gutenberg.org/files/8480/8480-h/8480-h.htm.
US Congress. *Congressional Globe.* 36th–39th Congresses. Washington, DC, 1861–66.
Vaughan, Robert. *Revolutions in English History.* Vol. 3. London: Longman, Green, Longman, Roberts, and Green, 1863.
Webster, Noah. *An American Dictionary of the English Language.* Springfield, MA: George and Charles Merriam, 1857.
White, James. *History of England, from the Earliest Times to the Year Eighteen Hundred and Fifty-Eight.* London: Routledge, Warne, and Routledge, 1860.
White, James. *Landmarks of the History of England.* London: G. Routledge, 1855.
Whittier, John Greenleaf. *In War Time: And Other Poems.* Boston: Ticknor and Fields, 1865.

SECONDARY SOURCES

Aaron, Daniel. *The Unwritten War: American Writers and the Civil War.* 1973. Tuscaloosa: University of Alabama Press, 2003.
Abzug, Robert H. *Cosmos Crumbling: American Reform and the Religious Imagination.* New York: Oxford University Press, 1994.
Adams, Michael C. C. *Our Masters the Rebels: A Speculation on Union Military Failure in the East, 1861–1865.* Cambridge, MA: Harvard University Press, 1978.
Anderson, Benedict. *Imagined Communities: Reflections on the Origin and Spread of Nationalism.* New York: Verso, 1983.
Arcenas, Claire R. *America's Philosopher: John Locke in American Intellectual Life.* Chicago: University of Chicago Press, 2022.
Arendt, Hannah. *On Revolution.* 1963. New York: Penguin, 2006.
Armitage, David. *Civil Wars: A History in Ideas.* New Haven, CT: Yale University Press, 2017.
Armitage, David. *The Ideological Origins of the British Empire.* Cambridge: Cambridge University Press, 2000.
Armitage, David. "John Milton." In Armitage, Himy, and Skinner, *Milton and Republicanism.*
Armitage, David. "The Political Economy of Britain and Ireland after the Glorious Revolution." In Ohlmeyer, *Political Thought.*

Armitage, David, Armand Himy, and Quentin Skinner, eds. *Milton and Republicanism*. New York: Cambridge University Press, 1995.

Armstrong, Robert. *Protestant War: The "British" of Ireland the Wars of the Three Kingdoms*. Manchester, UK: Manchester University Press, 2005.

Ash, Stephen V. *Firebrand of Liberty: The Story of Two Black Regiments That Changed the Course of the Civil War*. New York: W. W. Norton, 2008.

Ayers, Edward L. *In the Presence of Mine Enemies: The Civil War in the Heart of America, 1859–1864*. New York: W. W. Norton, 2002.

Bailyn, Bernard. *The Ideological Origins of the American Revolution*. Enlarged ed. Cambridge, MA: Belknap, 1992.

Banville, John. *Time Pieces: A Dublin Memoir*. New York: Knopf, 2018.

Barnes, Diane, Brian Schoen, and Frank Tower, eds. *The Old South's Modern Worlds: Slavery, Region, and Nation in the Age of Progress*. New York: Oxford University Press, 2011.

Barry, Sebastian. *The Lives of the Saints: The Laureate Lectures*. London: Faber and Faber, 2022.

Bates, Samuel P. *A Brief History of the One Hundredth Regiment: Roundheads*. New Castle, PA: Jas. C. Stevenson, 1884.

Bayly, Christopher A. *The Birth of the Modern World, 1780–1914*. Malden, MA: Blackwell, 2004.

Bayly, Christopher A. "European Political Thought and the Wider World during the Nineteenth Century." In *Cambridge History of Nineteenth-Century Political Thought*, edited by Gareth Stedman Jones and Gregory Claeys. Cambridge: Cambridge University Press, 2011.

Bayly, Christopher A. "The 'Revolutionary Age' in the Wider World, c. 1790–1830." In *War, Empire, and Slavery, 1770–1830*, edited by Richard Bessel, Nicholas Guyatt, and Jane Rendall. London: Palgrave Macmillan, 2010.

Bennett, Martyn. *Oliver Cromwell*. London: Routledge, 2006.

Bensel, Richard. *Yankee Leviathan: The Origins of Central State Authority in America, 1859–1877*. New York: Cambridge University Press, 1990.

Beringer, Richard, Herman Hattaway, Archer Jones, and William N. Still, eds. *Why the South Lost the Civil War*. Athens: University of Georgia Press, 1984.

Beverton, Alys D. *Exceptionalism in Crisis: Faction, Anarchy, and Mexico in the US Imagination during the Civil War Era*. Chapel Hill: University of North Carolina Press, forthcoming.

Bishop, James. "A Different Kind of Tie: The Personal and Political Affinities of America's Leadership Class, 1765–1820." PhD diss., Louisiana State University, 2022.

Blair, William A. *With Malice toward Some: Treason and Loyalty in the Civil War Era*. Chapel Hill: University of North Carolina Press, 2014.

Blight, David. *Race and Reunion: The Civil War in American Memory*. Cambridge, MA: Harvard University Press, 2001.

Blum, Edward J., and John H. Matsui. *War Is All Hell: The Nature of Evil and the Civil War*. Philadelphia: University of Pennsylvania Press, 2021.

Bodnar, John. *The "Good War" in American Memory*. Baltimore: Johns Hopkins University Press, 2010.

Bonner, Robert. "Roundheaded Cavaliers? The Context and Limits of a Confederate Racial Project." *Civil War History* 48, no. 1 (2002): 34–59.

Bourke, Richard, and Ian McBride. *Princeton History of Modern Ireland.* Princeton, NJ: Princeton University Press, 2016.

Boyce, D. George. *Nineteenth Century Ireland: The Search for Stability.* Rev. ed. Dublin: Gill, 2005.

Braddick, Michael. *The Common Freedom of the People: John Lilburne and the English Revolution.* Oxford, UK: Oxford University Press, 2018.

Braddick, Michael. *God's Fury, England's Fire: A New History of the English Civil Wars.* London: Allen Lane, 2008.

Braddick, Michael. "History, Liberty, Reformation and the Cause: Parliamentarian Military and Ideological Escalation in 1643." In Braddick and Smith, eds. *The Experience of Revolution in Stuart Britain and Ireland.*

Braddick, Michael, ed. *The Oxford Handbook of the English Revolution.* Oxford, UK: Oxford University Press, 2015.

Braddick, Michael. *State Formation in Early Modern England, c. 1550–1700.* Cambridge: Cambridge University Press, 2000.

Braddick, Michael J., and David L. Smith, eds. *The Experience of Revolution in Stuart Britain and Ireland: Essays for John Morrill.* Cambridge: Cambridge University Press, 2011.

Bray, Robert. "What Abraham Lincoln Read—An Evaluative and Annotated List." *Journal of the Abraham Lincoln Association* 28, no. 2 (2007): 28–81.

Brettle, Adrian. *Colossal Ambitions: Confederate Planning for a Post–Civil War World.* Charlottesville: University of Virginia Press, 2020.

Brewer, John. *The Sinews of Power: War, Money and the English State, 1688–1783.* Cambridge, MA: Harvard University Press, 1988.

Brinton, Crane. *The Anatomy of Revolution.* Rev. ed. New York: Vintage, 1965.

Bromwich, David. *The Intellectual Life of Edmund Burke: From the Sublime and Beautiful to American Independence.* Cambridge, MA: Harvard University Press, 2014.

Brooke, John L. "Cultures of Nationalism, Movements of Reform, and the Composite-Federal Polity: From Revolutionary Settlement to Antebellum Crisis." *Journal of the Early Republic* 29, no. 1 (2009): 1–33.

Brooks, Corey M. *Liberty Power: Antislavery Third Parties and the Transformation of American Politics.* Chicago: University of Chicago Press, 2016.

Broomall, James J. *Private Confederacies: The Emotional Worlds of Southern Men as Citizens and Soldiers.* Chapel Hill: University of North Carolina Press, 2019.

Brown, Thomas J. *Civil War Monuments and the Militarization of America.* Chapel Hill: University of North Carolina Press, 2019.

Burlingame, Michael. *Abraham Lincoln: A Life.* Vol. 2. Baltimore: Johns Hopkins University Press, 2008.

Burrow, J. W. *A Liberal Descent: Victorian Historians and the English Past.* Cambridge: Cambridge University Press, 1981.

Butterfield, Herbert. *The Whig Interpretation of History.* 1931. New York: W. W. Norton, 1965.

Cannadine, David. *Victorious Century: The United Kingdom, 1800–1906.* New York: Viking, 2017.

Canny, Nicholas. *Making Ireland British, 1580–1650.* Oxford, UK: Oxford University Press, 2001.

Carmichael, Peter C. *The Last Generation: Young Virginians in Peace, War, and Reunion*. Chapel Hill: University of North Carolina Press, 2005.

Cheng, Eileen Ka-May. *Historiography: An Introductory Guide*. New York: Continuum, 2012.

Cheng, Eileen Ka-May. *The Plain and Noble Garb of Truth: Nationalism and Impartiality in American Historical Writing, 1784–1860*. Athens: University of Georgia Press, 2008.

Chibnall, Majorie. *The Normans*. Oxford, UK: Blackwell, 2000.

Cirillo, Frank J. *The Abolitionist Civil War: Immediatists and the Struggle to Transform the Union*. Baton Rouge: Louisiana State University Press, 2023.

Clark, Kathleen. *Defining Moments: African American Commemoration and Political Culture in the South, 1863–1913*. Chapel Hill: University of North Carolina Press, 2005.

Clarke, Frances M. *War Stories: Suffering and Sacrifice in the Civil War North*. Chicago: University of Chicago Press, 2011.

Clive, John. *Macaulay: The Shaping of the Historian*. Cambridge, MA: Belknap, 1987.

Colbourn, H. Trevor. *The Lamp of Experience: Whig History and the Intellectual Origins of the American Revolution*. Chapel Hill: University of North Carolina Press, 1965.

Colley, Linda. *Britons: Forging the Nation, 1707–1837*. New Haven, CT: Yale University Press, 2009.

Collini, Stefan. *Public Moralists: Political Thought and Intellectual Life in Britain, 1850–1930*. Oxford, UK: Clarendon, 1991.

Collini, Stefan, Donald Winch, and John Burrow. *That Noble Science of Politics: A Study in Nineteenth-Century Intellectual History*. Cambridge: Cambridge University Press, 1983.

Corns, Thomas N. "Milton and the Characteristics of a Free Commonwealth." In Armitage, Himy, and Skinner, *Milton and Republicanism*.

Covington, Sarah. *The Devil from over the Sea: Remembering and Forgetting Oliver Cromwell in Ireland*. New York: Oxford University Press, 2022.

Crouthamel, James L. *Bennett's New York Herald and the Rise of the Popular Press*. Syracuse, NY: Syracuse University Press, 1989.

Darcy, Eamon. *The Irish Rebellion of 1641 and the Wars of the Three Kingdoms*. Suffolk, UK: Boydell, 2013.

Davies, Tony. "Borrowed Language: Milton, Jefferson, Mirabeau." In Armitage, Himy, and Skinner, *Milton and Republicanism*.

Dawson, Jan C. "The Puritan and the Cavalier: The South's Perception of Contrasting Traditions." *Journal of Southern History* 44, no. 4 (1978): 597–614.

Delahanty, Ian. *Embracing Emancipation: A Transatlantic History of Irish Americans, Slavery, and the American Union, 1840–1865*. New York: Fordham University Press, 2024.

Dew, Charles. *Apostles of Disunion: Southern Secession Commissioners and the Causes of the Civil War*. Charlottesville: University of Virginia Press, 2001.

Dilbeck, D. H. *A More Civil War: How the Union Waged a More Just War*. Chapel Hill: University of North Carolina Press, 2016.

Dobranski, Stephen B. *Reading John Milton: How to Persist in Troubled Times*. Stanford, CA: Stanford University Press, 2022.

Donagan, Barbara. "Atrocity, War Crime, and Treason in the English Civil War." *American Historical Review* 99, no. 4 (1994): 1137–66.

Donagan, Barbara. "Codes and Conduct in the English Civil War." *Past and Present*, no. 118 (February 1988): 65–95.

Donald, David H. *Charles Sumner and the Coming of the Civil War.* 1960. Chicago: University of Chicago Press, 1981.

Donald, David H., ed. *Why the North Won the Civil War.* Baton Rouge: Louisiana State University Press, 1960.

Donoghue, Denis. *Metaphor.* Cambridge, MA: Harvard University Press, 2014.

Downs, Gregory P. *The Second American Revolution: The Civil War–Era Struggle over Cuba and the Rebirth of the American Republic.* Chapel Hill: University of North Carolina Press, 2019.

Downs, Jim. *Sick from Freedom: African American Sickness and Suffering during the Civil War and Reconstruction.* New York: Oxford University Press, 2012.

Doyle, Don H. *The Cause of All Nations: An International History of the American Civil War.* New York: Basic Books, 2014.

Du Bois, W. E. B. *Black Reconstruction in America, 1860–1880.* New York: Harcourt, Brace, and Howe, 1935.

Dudziak, Mary L. *Wartime: An Idea, Its History, and Its Consequences.* New York: Oxford University Press, 2012.

Durden, Robert F. *The Gray and the Black: The Confederate Debate on Emancipation.* Baton Rouge: Louisiana State University Press, 1972.

Dwan, David, and Christopher J. Insole, eds. *The Cambridge Companion to Edmund Burke.* Cambridge: Cambridge University Press, 2012.

Dzelzainis, Martin. "Milton's Classical Republicanism." In Armitage, Himy, and Skinner, *Milton and Republicanism.*

Eagleton, Terry. *Critical Revolutionaries: Five Critics Who Changed the Way We Read.* New Haven, CT: Yale University Press, 2022.

Eaton, Clement. *The Freedom-of-Thought Struggle in the Old South.* 1940. New York: Harper and Row, 1964.

Edwards, David. "Out of the Blue?" In Ohlmeyer and Ó Siochrú, *Ireland 1641.*

Edwards, O. D. "John Lothrop Motley and the Netherlands." *BMGN: Low Countries Historical Review* 97, no. 3 (1982): 561–88.

Eliot, Thomas Stearns. "Tradition and the Individual Talent." *Perspecta,* no. 19 (1982): 36–42.

Emberton, Carole. *Beyond Redemption: Race, Violence, and the American South after the Civil War.* Chicago: University of Chicago Press, 2013.

Etcheson, Nicole. *Bleeding Kansas: Contested Liberty in the Civil War Era.* Lawrence: University of Kansas Press, 2004.

Eyal, Yonatan. "A Romantic Realist: George Nicholas Sanders and the Dilemmas of Southern International Engagement." *Journal of Southern History* 78, no. 1 (2012): 107–30.

Faust, Drew Gilpin. *The Creation of Confederate Nationalism: Ideology and Identity in the Civil War South.* Baton Rouge: Louisiana State University Press, 1982.

Faust, Drew Gilpin. *James Henry Hammond and the Old South: A Design for Mastery.* Baton Rouge: Louisiana State University Press, 1982.

Feldman, Noah. *Divided by God: America's Church-State Problem—and What We Should Do about It.* New York: Farrar, Straus and Giroux, 2005.

Fermer, Douglas. *James Gordon Bennett and the New York Herald: A Study of Editorial Opinion in the Civil War Era, 1854–1867.* Suffolk, UK: Boydell, 1986.

Fitzgerald, F. Scott. *The Great Gatsby*. 1925. New York: Scribner, 2003.
Fleche, Andre. *The Revolution of 1861: The American Civil War in the Age of Nationalist Conflict.* Chapel Hill: University of North Carolina Press, 2012.
Foner, Eric. *Free Soil, Free Labor, Free Men: The Ideology of the Republican Party before the Civil War.* 1970. New York: Oxford University Press, 1995.
Foreman, Amanda. *A World on Fire: Britain's Crucial Role in the American Civil War.* New York: Random House, 2011.
Foster, Gaines M. *Ghosts of the Confederacy: Defeat, the Lost Cause, and the Emergence of the New South, 1865–1913.* New York: Oxford University Press, 1987.
Foster, Gaines M. "What's Not in a Name: The Naming of the American Civil War." *Journal of the Civil War Era* 8, no. 3 (2018): 416–54.
Foster, R. F. *Modern Ireland, 1600–1972.* London: Penguin, 1988.
Fox-Genovese, Elizabeth, and Eugene D. Genovese. *The Mind of the Master Class: History and Faith in the Southern Slaveholder's Worldview.* Cambridge: Cambridge University Press, 2005.
Foxley, Rachel. *The Levellers: Radical Political Thought in the English Revolution.* Manchester, UK: Manchester University Press, 2013.
Frederickson, George M. *The Inner Civil War: Northern Intellectuals and the Crisis of the Union.* New York: Harper and Row, 1965.
Frederickson, George M. *White Supremacy: A Comparative Study in American and South African History.* New York: Oxford University Press, 1980.
Fukuyama, Francis. *The End of History and the Last Man.* New York: Free Press, 1992.
Fuller, Randall. *From Battlefields Rising: How the Civil War Transformed American Literature.* New York: Oxford University Press, 2011.
Gallagher, Gary W. *The Union War.* Cambridge, MA: Harvard University Press, 2012.
Gallman, Matthew. *The Cacophony of Politics: Northern Democrats and the American Civil War.* Charlottesville: University of Virginia Press, 2021.
Gannon, Barbara. *The Won Cause: Black and White Comradeship in the Grand Army of the Republic.* Chapel Hill: University of North Carolina Press, 2011.
Gardner, Sarah. "Shakespeare Fights the Civil War." Brose Lectures, Pennsylvania State University, 2021.
Gellner, Ernest. *Nations and Nationalism.* 2nd ed. Ithaca, NY: Cornell University Press, 2009.
Gemme, Paola. *Domesticating Foreign Struggles: The Italian Risorgimento and Antebellum American Identity.* Athens: University of Georgia Press, 2005.
Genovese, Eugene. *The Political Economy of Slavery: Studies in the Economy and Society of the Slave South.* New York: Pantheon, 1965.
Gentiles, Ian. *The New Model Army: In England, Ireland, and Scotland, 1645–1653.* Oxford, UK: Blackwell, 1992.
Gentiles, Ian. *Oliver Cromwell: God's Warrior and the English Revolution.* New York: Palgrave Macmillan, 2011.
Ghosh, Amitav. *Flood of Fire.* New York: Picador, 2015.
Gienapp, William E. *The Origins of the Republican Party, 1852–1856.* New York: Oxford University Press, 1987.
Gilbert, Felix. "Leopold von Ranke and the American Philosophical Society." *Proceedings of the American Philosophical Society* 130, no. 3 (1986): 362–66.

Gillespie, Raymond. *Seventeenth Century Ireland: Making Ireland Modern*. Dublin: Gill and Macmillan, 2006.

Gillespie, William. *Retreat from Reconstruction, 1869–1879*. Baton Rouge: Louisiana State University Press, 1979.

Gleeson, David. *The Green and the Gray: The Irish in the Confederate States of America*. Chapel Hill: University of North Carolina Press, 2013.

Gleeson, David. *The Irish in the South, 1815–1877*. Chapel Hill: University of North Carolina Press, 2001.

Gooch, G. P. *History and Historians in the Nineteenth Century*. Rev. ed. Boston: Beacon, 1959.

Gradert, Kenyon. *Puritan Spirits in the Abolitionist Imagination*. Chicago: University of Chicago Press, 2020.

Grimsley, Mark. *The Hard Hand of War: Union Military Policy towards Southern Civilians, 1861–1865*. Cambridge: Cambridge University Press, 1995.

Grimstead, David. *American Mobbing, 1828–1861: Toward Civil War*. New York: Oxford University Press, 1998.

Grinspan, Jon. *Wide Awake: The Forgotten Force That Elected Abraham Lincoln and Spurred the Civil War*. New York: Bloomsbury, 2024.

Hall, David D. *The Puritans: A Transatlantic History*. Princeton, NJ: Princeton University Press, 2019.

Hall, David D. *A Reforming People: Puritanism and the Transformation of Public Life in New England*. New York: Knopf, 2013.

Hammond, John Craig. "Inveterate Imperialists: Contested Imperialisms, North American History, and the Coming of the U.S. Civil War." *American Nineteenth Century History* 22, no. 2 (2021): 117–40.

Hargroder, Andrew. "'A Powerful Auxiliary': The US Army and Slave Revolts in the American South, 1803–1835." PhD diss., Louisiana State University, 2002.

Harris, Tim. "Did the English Have a Script for Revolution in the Seventeenth Century?" In *Scripting Revolution: A Historical Approach to the Comparative Study of Revolutions*, edited by Keith Michael Baker and Dan Edelstein. Stanford, CA: Stanford University Press, 2015.

Harris, William C. "The Hampton Roads Peace Conference: A Final Test of Lincoln's Presidential Leadership." *Journal of the Abraham Lincoln Association* 21, no. 1 (2000): 30–61.

Harrold, Stanley. *Border War: Fighting over Slavery before the Civil War*. Chapel Hill: University of North Carolina Press, 2010.

Hattem, Michael. *Past and Prologue: Politics and Memory in the American Revolution*. New Haven, CT: Yale University Press, 2020.

Hayton, David W. "From Barbarian to Burlesque: English Images of the Irish c. 1660–1750." *Irish Economic and Social History*, no. 15 (1988): 5–31.

Healy, Jonathan. *The Blazing World: A New History of Revolutionary England, 1603–1689*. New York: Knopf, 2023.

Heaney, Seamus. "Squarings, xlviii." In *Seeing Things*. London: Faber and Faber, 1991.

Hesketh, Ian. *The Science of History in Victorian Britain: Making the Past Speak*. Pittsburgh, PA: University of Pittsburgh Press, 2016.

Hill, Christopher. "The Norman Yoke." In *Puritanism and Revolution: Studies in Interpretation of the English Revolution of the 17th Century*. London: Secker and Warburg, 1958.

Hill, Christopher. "Thomas Hobbes and the Revolution in Political Thought." In *Puritanism and Revolution: Studies in Interpretation of the English Revolution of the 17th Century*. London: Secker and Warburg, 1958.

Hirst, Derek. *Dominion: England and Its Neighbors, 1500–1707*. Oxford, UK: Oxford University Press, 2012.

Hobsbawm, Eric. *Nations and Nationalism Since 1780*. 2nd ed. Cambridge: Cambridge University Press, 1992.

Hobsbawm, Eric, and Terence Ranger. *The Invention of Tradition*. Cambridge: Cambridge University Press, 1983.

Holt, Michael F. *The Crisis of the 1850s*. 1978. New York: W. W. Norton, 1983.

Howe, Susan. *My Emily Dickinson*. 1985. New York: New Directions, 2007.

Huntington, Samuel P. *The Clash of Civilizations and the Remaking of World Order*. New York: Simon and Schuster, 1996.

Iggers, Georg G. *The German Conception of History: The National Tradition of Historical Thought from Herder to the Present*. Rev. ed. Middletown, CT: Wesleyan University Press, 1983.

Iggers, Georg G. *Historiography in the Twentieth Century*. Middletown, CT: Wesleyan University Press, 2005.

Innes, Stephen. *Creating the Commonwealth: The Economic Culture of Puritan New England*. New York: W. W. Norton, 1995.

Jackson, Kellie Carter. *Force and Freedom: Black Abolitionists and the Politics of Violence*. Philadelphia: University of Pennsylvania Press, 2019.

Janney, Caroline E. *Burying the Dead but Not the Past: Ladies' Memorial Associations and the Lost Cause*. Chapel Hill: University of North Carolina Press, 2008.

Janney, Caroline E. "Civil War Memory." In vol. 2 of Sheehan-Dean, *Companion to the U.S. Civil War*.

Janney, Caroline E. *Ends of War: The Unfinished Fight of Lee's Army after Appomattox*. Chapel Hill: University of North Carolina Press, 2021.

Janney, Caroline E. *Remembering the Civil War: Reunion and the Limits of Reconciliation*. Chapel Hill: University of North Carolina Press, 2013.

Janney, Caroline E., Peter S. Carmichael, and Aaron Sheehan-Dean, eds. *The War That Made America: Essays Inspired by the Scholarship of Gary W. Gallagher*. Chapel Hill: University of North Carolina Press, 2024.

Jansson, Maija. "Shared Memory: John Hampden, New World and Old." *Journal for Eighteenth-Century Studies* 32, no. 2 (2009): 157–71.

Jenkins, Brian. *The Fenian Problem: Insurgency and Terrorism in a Liberal State, 1858–1874*. Liverpool, UK: Liverpool University Press, 2008.

Johnson, Michael. *Toward a Patriarchal Republic: The Secession of Georgia*. Baton Rouge: Louisiana State University Press, 1999.

Jones, Howard. *Union in Peril: The Crisis over British Intervention in the Civil War*. Chapel Hill: University of North Carolina Press, 1992.

Karp, Matthew. *This Vast Southern Empire: Slaveholders at the Helm of American Foreign Policy*. Cambridge, MA: Harvard University Press, 2016.

Karsten, Peter. "Cromwell in America." In *Images of Oliver Cromwell: Essays for and by Roger Howell, Jr.*, edited by R. C. Richardson. Manchester, UK: Manchester University Press, 1993.

Kaufman-McKivigan, John. *Antislavery Violence in Antebellum America: Essays on Sectional, Racial, and Cultural Conflict.* Knoxville: University of Tennessee Press, 1999.

Keller, Christian B. *Chancellorsville and the Germans: Nativism, Ethnicity, and Civil War Memory.* New York: Fordham University Press, 2007.

Kelly, Patrick J. "The North American Crisis of the 1860s." *Journal of the Civil War Era* 2, no. 3 (2012): 337–68.

Kinealy, Christine. *Repeal and Revolution: 1848 in Ireland.* Manchester, UK: Manchester University Press, 2009.

Kishlansky, Mark. *The Rise of the New Model Army.* Cambridge: Cambridge University Press, 1979.

Klement, Frank. *Dark Lanterns: Secret Political Societies, Conspiracies, and Treason Trials in the Civil War.* Baton Rouge: Louisiana State University Press, 1984.

Koditschek, Theodore. *Liberalism, Imperialism, and the Historical Imagination: Nineteenth-Century Visions of a Greater Britain.* Cambridge: Cambridge University Press, 2011.

Kohn, Hans. "The Genesis and Character of English Nationalism." *Journal of the History of Ideas* 1, no. 1 (January 1940): 69–94.

Kumar, Krishan. *The Making of English National Identity.* Cambridge: Cambridge University Press, 2003.

Kupperman, Karen Ordahl. *Indians and English: Facing Off in Early America.* Ithaca, NY: Cornell University Press, 2000.

Kurtz, Will. *Excommunicated from the Union: How the Civil War Created a Separate Catholic America.* New York: Fordham University Press, 2015.

Lause, Mark. *A Secret Society History of the Civil War.* Urbana: University of Illinois Press, 2011.

Lee, Susanna. *Claiming the Union: Citizenship in the Post–Civil War South.* Cambridge: Cambridge University Press, 2014.

Leerssen, Joep. *Remembrance and Imagination: Patterns in the Historical and Literary Representation of Ireland in the Nineteenth Century.* Cork, Ireland: Cork University Press, 1996.

Lenihan, Pádraig. *Confederate Catholics at War, 1641–1649.* Cork, Ireland: Cork University Press, 2001.

Lepore, Jill. *The Name of War: King Philip's War and the Origins of American Identity.* New York: Knopf, 1998.

Lowenthal, David. *The Past Is a Foreign Country.* Rev. ed. Cambridge: Cambridge University Press, 2015.

Lucan. *Civil War.* Translated by Matthew Fox. New York: Penguin, 2012.

Majewski, John. *A House Dividing: Economic Development in Pennsylvania and Virginia before the Civil War.* New York: Cambridge University Press, 2000.

Maltzahn, Nicholas von. "The Whig Milton, 1667–1700." In Armitage, Himy, and Skinner, *Milton and Republicanism.*

Manjapra, Kris. *Black Ghost of Empire: The Long Death of Slavery and the Failure of Emancipation.* New York: Simon and Schuster, 2022.

Manning, Chandra. *What This Cruel War Was Over: Soldiers, Slavery, and the Civil War.* New York: Knopf, 2007.

Marx, Karl. *The Eighteenth Brumaire of Louis Bonaparte.* 1869. New York: International, 2020.

Mason, Matthew. *Apostle of Union: A Political Biography of Edward Everett*. Chapel Hill: University of North Carolina Press, 2016.

Matsui, John H. *The First Republican Army: The Army of Virginia and the Radicalization of the Civil War*. Charlottesville: University Press of Virginia, 2017.

McBride, Ian, ed. *History and Memory in Modern Ireland*. Cambridge: Cambridge University Press, 2001.

McCarthy, Jesse. *Who Will Pay Reparations on My Soul? Essays*. New York: Liveright, 2020.

McConville, Brendan. *The King's Three Faces: The Rise and Fall of Royal America, 1688–1776*. Chapel Hill: University of North Carolina Press, 2006.

McCurry, Stephanie. *Confederate Reckoning: Power and Politics in the Civil War South*. Cambridge, MA: Harvard University Press, 2012.

McDowell, Nicholas, and Nigel Smith, eds. *The Oxford Handbook of Milton*. Oxford, UK: Oxford University Press, 2009.

McGarry, Fearghal. *Republicanism in Modern Ireland*. Dublin: University College Dublin Press, 2003.

McGreevy, John T. "Catholicism and Abolition: A Historical and Theological Problem." In *Figures in the Carpet: Finding the Human Person in the American Past*, edited by Wilfred McClay. Grand Rapids, MI: Eerdmans, 2006.

McGreevy, John T. *Catholicism and American Freedom: A History*. New York: W. W. Norton, 2003.

McIlvenna, Noeleen. *A Very Mutinous People: The Struggle for North Carolina, 1660–1713*. Chapel Hill: University of North Carolina, 2009.

McKitrick, Eric. "Party Politics and the Union and Confederate War Efforts." In *The American Party Systems: Stages of Political Development*, edited by William Nisbet Chambers and Walter Dean Burnham. New York: Oxford University Press, 1967.

McPherson, James M. *Crossroads of Freedom: Antietam, the Battle That Changed the Course of the Civil War*. New York: Oxford University Press, 2002.

McPherson, James M. *Is Blood Thicker Than Water? Crises of Nationalism in the Modern World*. New York: Vintage, 1998.

McWhiney, Grady, and Perry D. Jamieson. *Attack and Die: Civil War Military Tactics and the Southern Heritage*. Tuscaloosa: University of Alabama Press, 1982.

McWhiney, Grady, and Forrest McDonald. *Cracker Culture: Celtic Ways in the Old South*. Tuscaloosa: University of Alabama Press, 1988.

Mehta, Uday Singh. *Liberalism and Empire: A Study in Nineteenth-Century British Liberal Thought*. Chicago: University of Chicago Press, 1999.

Menand, Louis. *The Metaphysical Club: A Story of Ideas in America*. New York: Farrar, Straus and Giroux, 2001.

Messer, Peter. "From a Revolutionary History to a History of Revolution: David Ramsay and the American Revolution." *Journal of the Early Republic* 22, no. 2 (2002): 205–33.

Messer, Peter. *Stories of Independence: Identity, Ideology, and History in Eighteenth-Century America*. DeKalb: Northern Illinois University Press, 2005.

Miers, Earl S., ed. *The Diary of Emma LeConte: When the World Ended*. Lincoln: University of Nebraska Press, 1987.

Miller, Kerby. *Emigrants and Exiles: Ireland and the Irish Exodus to North America*. New York: Oxford University Press, 1985.

Miller, Perry. "The Marrow of Puritan Divinity." In *Errand into the Wilderness*. Cambridge, MA: Belknap, 1965.

Miller, Perry. *The New England Mind: From Colony to Province*. Cambridge, MA: Belknap, 1953.

Minnow, Martha. *Between Vengeance and Forgiveness: Facing History after Genocide and Mass Violence*. Boston: Beacon, 1998.

Morgan, Chad. *Planters' Progress: Modernizing Confederate Georgia*. Gainesville: University Press of Florida, 2005.

Morgan, Edmund S. *Inventing the People: The Rise of Popular Sovereignty in England and America*. New York: W. W. Norton, 1988.

Morrill, John. "The Drogheda Massacre in Cromwellian Context." In *Age of Atrocity: Violence and Political Conflict in Early Modern Ireland*, edited by Clodagh Tait, David Edwards, and Pádraig Lenihan. Dublin: Four Courts, 2007.

Morrill, John, ed. *Oliver Cromwell and the English Revolution*. London: Longman, 1990.

Morrill, John. *Stuart Britain: A Very Short Introduction*. Oxford: Oxford University Press, 2000.

Morrison, Michael. *Slavery and the American West*. Chapel Hill: University of North Carolina Press, 1997.

Morrow, John. *Thomas Carlyle*. London: Hambledon Continuum, 2006.

Mulligan, William. "Weimar and the Wars of Liberation: German and French Officers and the Politics of History." *European History Quarterly* 38, no. 2 (2008): 266–93.

Murphy, Angela F. *American Slavery Irish Freedom: Abolition, Immigrant Citizenship, and the Transatlantic Movement for Irish Repeal*. Baton Rouge: Louisiana State University Press, 2010.

Murray, Gene. "Abraham Lincoln's Relationship with James Gordon Bennett and Horace Greeley during the Civil War." In *Words at War: The Civil War and American Journalism*, edited by David B. Sachsman, S. Kittrell Rushing, and Roy Morris Jr. West Lafayette, IN: Purdue University Press, 2008.

Murray, Williamson, and Wayne Hsieh. *A Savage War: A Military History of the Civil War*. Princeton, NJ: Princeton University Press, 2018.

Mycock, Andrew. "A Very English Affair? Defining the Borders of Empire in Nineteenth-Century British Historiography." In *The Historical Imagination in Nineteenth-Century Britain and the Low Countries*, edited by Hugh Dunthorne and Michael Wintle. Leiden, Netherlands: Bill, 2012.

Neely, Mark E., Jr. *The Fate of Liberty: Abraham Lincoln and Civil Liberties*. New York: Oxford University Press, 1991.

Neely, Mark E., Jr. *Lincoln and the Triumph of the Nation: Constitutional Conflict in the American Civil War*. Chapel Hill: University of North Carolina Press, 2011.

Neely, Mark E., Jr. "Retaliation: The Problem of Atrocity in the American Civil War." Fortenbaugh Lecture, Gettysburg College, November 19, 2002.

Neely, Mark E., Jr. *The Union Divided: Party Conflict in the Civil War North*. Cambridge, MA: Harvard University Press, 2002.

Neff, John. *Honoring the Civil War Dead: Commemoration and the Problem of Reconciliation*. Lawrence: University Press of Kansas, 2005.

Neiman, Susan. *Learning from the Germans: Race and the Memory of Evil*. New York: Farrar Straus and Giroux, 2019.

Nelson, Eric. *The Royalist Revolution: Monarchy and the American Revolution*. Cambridge, MA: Harvard University Press, 2014.
Neufeld, Matthew. *The Civil Wars after 1660: Remembering in Late Stuart England*. Rochester, NY: Boydell, 2013.
Neufeld, Matthew. "From Peacemaking to Peacebuilding: The Multiple Endings of England's Long Civil Wars." *American Historical Review* 120, no. 5 (2015): 1709–23.
Nevins, Allan. *The War for the Union: The Organized War, 1863–1864*. New York: Scribner, 1959.
Nixon, Mark. *Samuel Rawson Gardiner and the Idea of History*. Suffolk, UK: Royal Historical Society, 2010.
Noll, Mark A. *America's God: From Jonathan Edwards to Abraham Lincoln*. New York: Oxford University Press, 2002.
Novick, Peter. *That Noble Dream: The "Objectivity Question" and the American Historical Profession*. Cambridge: Cambridge University Press, 1988.
Oakes, James. *Freedom National: The Destruction of Slavery in the United States, 1861–1865*. New York: W. W. Norton, 2012.
Oakes, James. *The Radical and the Republican: Frederick Douglass, Abraham Lincoln, and the Triumph of Antislavery Politics*. New York: W. W. Norton, 2007.
Oakes, James. *The Scorpion's Sting: Antislavery and the Coming of the Civil War*. New York: W. W. Norton, 2014.
O'Brien, Edna. *House of Splendid Isolation*. New York: Farrar, Straus and Giroux, 1994.
O'Brien, Michael. *Conjectures of Order: Intellectual Life and the American South, 1810–1860*. 2 vols. Chapel Hill: University of North Carolina Press, 2004.
Ohlmeyer, Jane, ed. *Political Thought in Seventeenth-Century Ireland: Kingdom or Colony*. Cambridge: Cambridge University Press, 2000.
Ohlmeyer, Jane, and Micheál Ó Siochrú, eds. *Ireland 1641: Contexts and Reactions*. Manchester, UK: Manchester University Press, 2013.
Ó Siochrú, Micheál. "Atrocity, Codes of Conduct, and the Irish in the British Civil Wars 1641–1653." *Past and Present*, no. 195 (May 2007): 55–86.
Ó Siochrú, Micheál. *Confederate Ireland, 1642–1649: A Constitutional and Political Analysis*. Dublin: Four Courts, 2008.
Ó Siochrú, Micheál. *God's Executioner: Oliver Cromwell and the Conquest of Ireland*. London: Faber, 2008.
Osterweis, Rollin G. *Romanticism and Nationalism in the Old South*. 1949. Baton Rouge: Louisiana State University Press, 1967.
Oubre, Claude F. *Forty Acres and a Mule: The Freedmen's Bureau and Black Land Ownership*. 1978. Baton Rouge: Louisiana State University Press, 2012.
Paludan, Philip S. "The Civil War Considered as a Crisis in Law and Order." *American Historical Review* 77, no. 4 (1972): 1013–34.
Paludan, Philip S. *"A People's Contest": The Union and the Civil War, 1861–1865*. New York: Harper and Row, 1988.
Pani, Erika. "Juárez v. Maximiliano: Mexico's Experiment with Monarchy." In *American Civil Wars: The United States, Latin America, Europe, and the Crisis of the 1860s*, edited by Don H. Doyle. Chapel Hill: University of North Carolina Press, 2017.
Parker, Geoffrey. "The Etiquette of Atrocity: The Laws of War in Early Modern Europe." In *Empire, War and Faith in Early Modern Europe*. London: Penguin, 2002.

Perceval-Maxwell, M. *The Outbreak of the Irish Rebellion of 1641*. Dublin: Gill and Macmillan, 1994.

Perman, Michael. *The Road to Redemption: Southern Politics, 1869–1879*. Chapel Hill: University of North Carolina Press, 1984.

Peterson, Merrill D. *The Great Triumvirate: Webster, Clay, and Calhoun*. New York: Oxford University Press, 1987.

Phillips, Jason. *Looming Civil War: How Nineteenth-Century Americans Imagined the Future*. New York: Oxford University Press, 2018.

Pincus, Steve. *1688: The First Modern Revolution*. New Haven, CT: Yale University Press, 2009.

Pocock, J. G. A. *The Ancient Constitution and the Feudal Law: English Historical Thought in the Seventeenth Century*. 1957. New York: W. W. Norton, 1967.

Pocock, J. G. A. *The Machiavellian Moment: Florentine Political Thought and the Atlantic Republican Tradition*. Princeton, NJ: Princeton University Press, 1975.

Pocock, J. G. A. "The Third Kingdom in Its History." Afterword to Ohlmeyer, *Political Thought*.

Pocock, J. G. A. *Three British Revolutions: 1641, 1688, 1776*. Princeton, NJ: Princeton University Press, 1980.

Pollan, Michael. *The Botany of Desire: A Plant's-Eye View of the World*. New York: Random House, 2001.

Potter, David. "The Historians' Uses of Nationalism and Vice Versa." In *The South and Sectional Conflict*. Baton Rouge: Louisiana State University Press, 1968.

Potter, David. *The Impending Crisis: 1848–1861*. New York: Harper Perennial, 1976.

Pressly, Thomas J. *Americans Interpret Their Civil War*. 1954. New York: Free Press, 1962.

Purcell, Sarah. *Sealed with Blood: War, Sacrifice, and Memory in Revolutionary America*. Philadelphia: University of Pennsylvania Press, 2002.

Quigley, Paul. *Shifting Grounds: Nationalism and the American South, 1848–1865*. New York: Oxford University Press, 2012.

Rable, George C. *Damn Yankees: Demonization and Defiance in the Confederate South*. Baton Rouge: Louisiana State University Press, 2015.

Rable, George C. *God's Almost Chosen People: A Religious History of the American Civil War*. Chapel Hill: University of North Carolina Press, 2010.

Reiff, David. *In Praise of Forgetting: Historical Memory and Its Ironies*. New Haven, CT: Yale University Press, 2016.

Reynolds, David S. *Beneath the American Renaissance: The Subversive Imagination in the Age of Emerson and Melville*. New York: Knopf, 1988.

Reynolds, David S. *John Brown, Abolitionist: The Man Who Killed Slavery, Sparked the Civil War, and Seeded Civil Rights*. New York: Knopf, 2005.

Reynolds, David S. "Oliver Cromwell as an American Cultural Icon: Transcendentalism, John Brown, and the Civil War." In *American Cultural Icons: The Production of Representative Lives*, edited by Günter Leypoldt and Bernd Engler. Würzburg, Germany: Königshausen and Neumann, 2010.

Rhodes, James Ford. *History of the Civil War, 1861–1865*. New York: Macmillan, 1919.

Richard, Carl J. *The Golden Age of the Classics in America*. Cambridge, MA: Harvard University Press, 2009.

Richards, I. A. *The Philosophy of Rhetoric*. 1936. New York: Oxford University Press, 1965.

Richardson, Heather Cox. *The Death of Reconstruction: Race, Labor, and Politics in the Post–Civil War North, 1865–1901*. Cambridge, MA: Harvard University Press, 2004.

Robbins, Caroline. *The Eighteenth-Century Commonwealthman: Studies in the Transmission, Development and Circumstance of English Liberal Thought from the Restoration of Charles II until the War with the Thirteen Colonies*. 1959. New York: Atheneum, 1968.

Rodgers, Daniel T. *As a City on a Hill: The Story of America's Most Famous Lay Sermon*. Princeton, NJ: Princeton University Press, 2018.

Rodgers, Daniel T. "Exceptionalism." In *Imagined Histories: American Historians Interpret the Past*, edited by Anthony Molho and Gordon S. Wood. Princeton, NJ: Princeton University Press, 1998.

Rose, Willie Lee. *Rehearsal for Reconstruction: The Port Royal Experiment*. New York: Vintage, 1964.

Ross, Dorothy. "Historical Consciousness in Nineteenth-Century America." *American Historical Review* 89, no. 4 (1984): 909–28.

Roth, Randolph. *American Homicide*. Cambridge, MA: Harvard University Press, 2009.

Rovelli, Carlo. *The Order of Time*. New York: Riverhead Books, 2018.

Royster, Charles. *The Destructive War: William Tecumseh Sherman, Stonewall Jackson, and the Americans*. New York: Knopf, 1991.

Rubin, Anne S. *A Shattered Nation: The Rise and Fall of the Confederacy, 1861–1868*. Chapel Hill: University of North Carolina Press, 2005.

Ryan, Kay. "Bait Goat." In *The Best of It: New and Collected Poems*. New York: Grove, 2010.

Sabato, Hilda. *Republics of the New World: The Revolutionary Political Experiment in 19th-Century Latin America*. Princeton, NJ: Princeton University Press, 2018.

Sanderson, John. "Philip Hunton's 'Appeasement': Moderation and Extremism in the English Civil War." *History of Political Thought* 3, no. 3 (1982): 447–61.

Sandow, Robert. *Deserter Country: Civil War Opposition in the Pennsylvania Appalachians*. New York: Fordham University Press, 2009.

Satia, Priya. *Time's Monster: How History Makes History*. Cambridge, MA: Belknap, 2020.

Sato, Sora. *Edmund Burke as Historian: War, Order and Civilisation*. New York: Palgrave Macmillan, 2018.

Schafer, Daniel L. *Thunder on the River: The Civil War in Northeast Florida*. Gainesville: University Press of Florida, 2010.

Schweninger, Loren. *Black Property Owners in the South, 1790–1915*. Urbana: University of Illinois Press, 1990.

Seelye, John. *Memory's Nation: The Place of Plymouth Rock*. Chapel Hill: University of North Carolina Press, 1998.

Sexton, Jay. "William H. Seward in the World." *Journal of the Civil War Era* 4, no. 3 (2014): 398–430.

Shade, William G. *Democratizing the Old Dominion: Virginia and the Second Party System, 1824–1861*. Charlottesville: University of Virginia Press, 1996.

Shalev, Eran. *Rome Reborn on Western Shores: Historical Imagination and the Creation of the American Republic*. Charlottesville: University of Virginia Press, 2009.

Sheehan-Dean, Aaron. *Calculus of Violence: How Americans Fought the Civil War*. Cambridge, MA: Harvard University Press, 2018.

Sheehan-Dean, Aaron, ed. *A Companion to the US Civil War*. 2 vols. New York: Wiley-Blackwell, 2014.

Sheehan-Dean, Aaron. *Reckoning with Rebellion: War and Sovereignty in the Nineteenth Century*. Gainesville: University of Florida Press, 2020.

Shelden, Rachel. "The Politics of Continuity and Change in the Long Civil War Era." *Civil War History* 65, no. 4 (2019): 319–41.

Shelden, Rachel, and Erik B. Alexander. "Dismantling the Party System: Party Fluidity and the Mechanisms of Nineteenth-Century US Politics." *Journal of American History* 110, no. 3 (2023): 419–48.

Shiels, Damian. "Recovering the Voices of the Union Irish: Identity, Motivation and Experience in Irish American Civil War Correspondence, 1861–1865." PhD diss., Northumbria University, 2021.

Siddali, Silvani R. *From Property to Person: Slavery and the Confiscation Acts, 1861–1862*. Baton Rouge: Louisiana State University Press, 2005.

Sinha, Manisha. *The Counterrevolution of Slavery: Politics and Ideology in Antebellum South Carolina*. Chapel Hill: University of North Carolina Press, 2000.

Skocpol, Theda, and Margaret Somers. "The Uses of Comparative History in Macrosocial Inquiry." *Comparative Studies in Society and History* 22, no. 2 (1980): 174–97.

Smith, Adam I. P. *The Stormy Present: Conservatism and the Problem of Slavery in Northern Politics, 1846–1865*. Chapel Hill: University of North Carolina Press, 2017.

Spiers, Edward M. "War." In *Cambridge Companion to Victorian Culture*, edited by F. O'Gorman. Cambridge: Cambridge University Press, 2010.

Sternhell, Yael. "Revisionism Reinvented? The Antiwar Turn in Civil War Scholarship." *Journal of the Civil War Era* 3, no. 2 (2013): 239–56.

Stewart, James Bremer. *Holy Warriors: The Abolitionists and American Slavery*. Rev. ed. New York: Hill and Wang, 1997.

Stewart, James Bremer. *Wendell Phillips: Liberty's Hero*. Baton Rouge: Louisiana State University Press, 1986.

Stoker, Donald. *The Grand Design: Strategy and the US Civil War*. New York: Oxford University Press, 2010.

Stovall, Tyler. "White Freedom and the Lady of Liberty." *American Historical Review* 123, no. 1 (2018): 1–27.

Summers, Mark. *The Ordeal of the Union: A New History of Reconstruction*. Chapel Hill: University of North Carolina Press, 2014.

Sutton, Jase. "'We Died Here Obedient to Her Laws': The Reception of Sparta in the Lost Cause and Confederate Memorialization." *Journal of the Civil War Era* 14, no. 2 (2024): 167–93.

Tait, Clodagh, David Edwards, and Pádraig Lenihan. *Age of Atrocity: Violence and Political Conflict in Early Modern Ireland*. Dublin: Four Courts, 2007.

Tanner, John S., and Justin Collings. "How Adams and Jefferson Read Milton and Milton Read Them." *Milton Quarterly* 40, no. 3 (2006): 207–19.

Tap, Bruce. *Over Lincoln's Shoulder: The Committee on the Conduct of the War*. Lawrence: University of Kansas Press, 1998.

Taylor, Amy. *Embattled Freedom: Journeys through the Civil War's Slave Refugee Camps*. Chapel Hill: University of North Carolina Press, 2018.

Taylor, William. *Cavalier and Yankee: The Old South and American National Character*. New York: George Braziller, 1961.

Teters, Kristopher. *Practical Liberators: Union Officers in the Western Theater during the Civil War*. Chapel Hill: University of North Carolina Press, 2018.

Thomas, John L. "Romantic Reform in America, 1815–1865." *American Quarterly* 17, no. 4 (1965): 656–81.

Tilly, Charles. "War Making and State Making as Organized Crime." In *Bringing the State Back In*, edited by Peter Evans, Deitrich Rueschemeyer, and Theda Skocpol. Cambridge: Cambridge University Press, 1985.

Tise, Larry E. *Proslavery: A History of the Defense of Slavery in America, 1701–1840*. Athens: University of Georgia Press, 1988.

Towers, Frank. "Partisans, New History, and Modernization: The Historiography of the Civil War's Causes, 1861–2011." *Journal of the Civil War Era* 1, no. 2 (2011): 237–64.

Trela, D. J. "Cromwell in the Romantic Period: An Overview." *Wordsworth Circle* 25, no. 3 (1994): 127–29.

Trevor-Roper, Hugh. Introduction to *History of England*, by Thomas Macaulay. Edited by Hugh Trevor-Roper. London: Penguin, 1986.

Trouillot, Michel-Rolph. *Silencing the Past: Power and the Production of the Past*. Boston: Beacon, 1995.

Tucker, Ann. *First Born of All Nations: European Nationalist Movements and the Making of the Confederacy*. Charlottesville: University of Virginia Press, 2020.

Ural, Susannah. *The Harp and the Eagle: Irish American Volunteers and the US Army: 1861–1865*. New York: New York University Press, 2006.

Urban, Wayne J., and Jennings L. Wagoner Jr. *American Education: A History*. New York: Taylor and Francis, 2013.

Varon, Elizabeth R. *Armies of Deliverance: A New History of the Civil War*. New York: Oxford University Press, 2019.

Varon, Elizabeth R. *Disunion! The Coming of the American Civil War*. Chapel Hill: University of North Carolina Press, 2008.

Vowell, Sarah. "John Brown's Body." In *The Rose and the Briar: Death, Love and Liberty in the American Ballad*, edited by Sean Wilentz and Greil Marcus. New York: W. W. Norton, 2005.

Waldstreicher, David. *In the Midst of Perpetual Fetes: The Making of American Nationalism, 1776–1820*. Chapel Hill: University of North Carolina Press, 1997.

Walzer, Michael. *The Revolution of the Saints: A Study in the Origins of Radical Politics*. Cambridge, MA: Harvard University Press, 1965.

Warren, Robert Penn. *The Legacy of the Civil War*. Cambridge, MA: Harvard University Press, 1961.

Warren, Wendy. *New England Bound: Slavery and Colonization in Early America*. New York: Liveright, 2016.

Watson, Ritchie Devon, Jr. *Normans and Saxons: Southern Race Mythology and the Intellectual History of the American Civil War*. Baton Rouge: Louisiana State University Press, 2008.

Weber, Jennifer L. *Copperheads: The Rise and Fall of Lincoln's Opponents in the North*. New York: Oxford University Press, 2006.

Weber, Max. "Politics as a Vocation." In *From Max Weber: Essays in Sociology*, edited by H. H. Gerth and C. Wright Mills. 1919. New York: Oxford University Press, 1946.

Wells, Jennifer. "Taking War Crimes Law Seriously in Revolutionary Ireland: A Legal Analysis." In *Law and Revolution in Seventeenth-Century Ireland*, edited by Coleman A. Dennehy. Dublin: Four Courts, 2020.

Wheaton, Robert. "Motley and the Dutch Historians." *New England Quarterly* 35, no. 3 (1962): 318–36.

White, Hayden. *Metahistory: The Historical Imagination in Nineteenth-Century Europe*. Baltimore: Johns Hopkins University Press, 1973.

White, Hayden. "The Value of Narrativity in the Representation of Reality." *Critical Inquiry* 7, no. 1 (1980): 5–27.

White, Richard. "Creative Misunderstandings and New Understandings." *William and Mary Quarterly* 63, no. 1 (2006): 9–14.

Williams, T. Harry. *Lincoln and the Radicals*. 3rd ed. Madison: University of Wisconsin Press, 1969.

Winship, Michael. *Hot Protestants: A History of Puritanism in England and America*. New Haven, CT: Yale University Press, 2018.

Winterer, Caroline. *The Culture of Classicism: Ancient Greece and Rome in American Intellectual Life, 1780–1910*. Baltimore: Johns Hopkins University Press, 2002.

Wirzbicki, Peter. *Fighting for the Higher Law: Black and White Transcendentalists against Slavery*. Philadelphia: University of Pennsylvania Press, 2021.

Witt, John Fabian. *Lincoln's Code: The Laws of War in American History*. New York: Free Press, 2012.

Wood, Gordon S. *The Radicalism of the American Revolution*. New York: Vintage, 1991.

Woods, Michael. *Arguing until Doomsday: Stephen Douglas, Jefferson Davis, and the Struggle for American Democracy*. Chapel Hill: University of North Carolina Press, 2020.

Woods, Michael. "What Twenty-First-Century Historians Have Said about the Causes of Disunion: A Civil War Sesquicentennial Review of the Recent Literature." *Journal of American History* 99, no. 2 (2012): 415–39.

Worden, Blair. *The English Civil Wars, 1640–1660*. London: Weidenfeld and Nicolson, 2009.

Yokota, Kariann Akemi. *Unbecoming British: How Revolutionary America Became a Postcolonial Nation*. New York: Oxford University Press, 2011.

Zboray, Ronald J. *A Fictive People: Antebellum Economic Development and the American Reading Public*. New York: Oxford University Press, 1993.

INDEX

Aaron, Daniel, 77, 174n3, 174n15
abolitionists, 3, 12, 42, 65–66, 71, 104, 108, 121, 124; and antebellum politics, 55; criticism of, 24–26, 31, 73, 94–100, 110–11, 169n16; and hard war, 7, 80–84, 118, 145, 165n4; historical thinking of, 15–16, 34–37, 50, 75–88, 157n61; and Milton, 29; and nativism, 83–86; political thinking of, 3, 19–20, 131, 136, 140, 161n9, 165n3; and Puritan legacy, 22, 24, 31–33; and Thirteenth Amendment, 70. *See also* Brown, John; Catholicism; Cromwell, Oliver; emancipation; Milton, John; Phillips, Wendell; Sumner, Charles
Adams, John, 43, 131–32, 138, 153n38
Alabama, 73
American Party, 14, 84. *See also* nativism
American Revolution, 10, 27, 66, 106, 150n17, 175n37, 177n62, 177n69
American Tract Society, 64–65
analogical thinking, 3–4, 6–7, 9, 20, 31, 65, 70–73, 98, 117, 143–47, 159n24. *See also* Cavaliers; Puritans
Andrew, John, 87

Armitage, David, 93, 142
Arnold, Benedict, 43
Atlantic Monthly, 48, 62, 106, 128, 134–35

Bancroft, Frederick, 8, 18, 35, 158n74
Barbados, 117
Barebones Parliament, 86
Bayard, James, 92–93
Beecher, Henry Ward, 95, 118, 149n3
Bennett, James Gordon, 94, 169n16, 170n22
Black people: and emancipation, 9, 124, 133, 136; military service of, 30, 87–88, 101; political power of, 114. *See also* abolitionists; emancipation; slavery
Bonner, Robert, 155n21
Braddick, Michael, 18, 56, 66, 150n10, 161n3, 163n49
Brewer, John, 150n10
Bright, John, 128, 135, 137
Brodie, George, 43, 46, 82. *See also* England, history of
Brontë, Charlotte, 12–13
Brown, John, 26, 35–36, 73, 158n82, 150n87
Browning, Orville, 50, 65

203

Brownson, Orestes, 110
Buchanan, James, 59, 61–62
Bull Run, battle of, 62
Burke, Edmund, 35, 119
Burr, Aaron, 43
Butterfield, Herbert, 151n19, 178n79

Calhoun, John C., 14
California, 67
Calvin, John, 26, 110
Canaan, 109
Canny, Nicholas, 47, 59
Carlyle, Thomas, 13–14, 17, 78, 106, 137, 151n13, 152n18
Carrel, Armand, 99
Catholicism, 40, 107, 110, 167n60, 168n77; American Party's opposition to, 14, 84; criticism of, 14, 45–47, 83–86, 152n33; and Ireland, 4, 44–45, 56–59, 82, 108–10, 117, 162n20, 162n23, 167n53, 167n60, 172n40; Puritans and, 32, 83. *See also* Christianity; Ireland
Cattermole, George, 130. *See also* England, history of
Cavaliers, 40, 154n2, 154n9, 155nn20–21, 157n67; fictional treatments of, 12–13; as historical figures, 11, 105, 119; rhetorical use of, by Confederates, 9, 22–26, 30–32, 52, 54, 63, 72, 178n2; rhetorical use of, by radicals, 32–35, 64, 67, 138. *See also* analogical thinking; Puritans
Chancellorsville, battle of, 85
Charles I (king of England), 11, 61, 71, 91, 118, 162n23; criticism of, 40, 41–43, 62; historical memory of, in England, 12–13, 18–19, 45, 82, 95, 139; life of, 4–5, 31, 40, 44–45; rhetorical use of, by conservatives, 2, 22, 23, 26, 31, 73, 96–101, 156n30; rhetorical use of, by moderates, 48–50, 63–64, 120, 126, 130, 132–33, 138, 145; rhetorical use of, by radicals, 76–78, 80, 105. *See also* Cromwell, Oliver
Charles II (king of England), 5, 31, 74, 96, 102, 104, 109, 115, 177n70

Christianity, 32, 65, 67; interpretations of war, 129, 137; ministers, 27, 32, 79, 86 142, 166n38. *See also* American Tract Society; Catholicism; Episcopal Church; Presbyterian Church
Cirillo, Frank, 165n4
civil liberties, 75, 90, 94, 98, 137
Clarendon, Earl of (Edward Hyde), 13, 72, 105, 108, 152n15
class relations, 5; in Confederate states, 25–26, 67, 143, 145; in US, 35, 111, 137
Clay, Cassius, 48, 66, 128, 175n27
Clay, Henry, 61, 98
Cobb, Howell, 25, 30
Collamer, Jacob, 97
colonies, America, settlement of, 26, 31–32, 34, 109, 119, 138, 153n38
compromise, political, 2, 37, 62, 69, 76, 86, 99
Confederacy, Irish, 44–45, 107
Confederates, 43, 61, 65, 81, 89, 91, 95, 103, 112, 118, 124; analogized to Ireland, 44–45, 54, 57, 60–61, 68, 107–8, 110, 113; attitudes toward history of, 18, 23–31, 34, 63, 66, 74–75, 86, 93, 100, 178n2; criticism of, 48–52, 80, 83, 105–6, 127, 131–32, 141, 171n11; paradoxes in thought of, 24, 28, 42, 54, 145, 158n1; perceptions of Charles I of, 2, 40; perceptions of Cromwell of, 69–74, 102, 161n53; rhetorical uses of history by, 3–4, 6, 52–54, 94, 138, 143, 155n21; tolerance of monarchy by, 42, 157n54, 179n3. *See also* Cavaliers; Davis, Jefferson; fatalism; preemptive war; property seizure; Puritans; Stephens, Alexander
Confiscation Act, 97, 101, 104, 106
conservatives, Northern, 124, 144; attitudes toward history of, 6–7, 9–10, 16, 18, 53, 71, 90–93, 110–13, 145; criticism of Lincoln of, 66–67, 100–101; and race, 3, 83, 90, 117; and reunion, 101–4, 140; rhetorical uses of the past by, 20, 75, 81, 83, 94–100 156n30; war policies of, 3, 29, 76, 86–87, 124, 136, 171n49. *See*

also Lincoln, Abraham; moderates, Northern; *New York Herald*; radicals, Northern
constitutions: conflict over, 4, 19, 48, 103; English, 5, 13–15, 18, 42–43, 65, 137, 144, 171n49; Lincoln and, 63, 67, 78, 126–27, 138–40; Northern conservatives and, 3, 91–92, 97, 99, 100–101; Northern radicals and, 6, 29, 33, 77–78, 105–6; US, 75, 118, 144, 163n49. *See also* Thirteenth Amendment
Cooper Union, 80, 99
Cowan, Edgar, 97
Cox, Samuel S., 20, 58, 94, 100–102, 112–18, 146, 153n57, 156n30, 172nn39–40
Cromwell, Oliver, 2, 9, 16, 19, 43, 117, 156n26; historical memory of, in England, 13–15, 47, 108–10, 126, 152n33, 161n53, 168n60, 173n53; life of, 5, 117–20, 151n5; rhetorical use of, by conservatives, 2, 25–29, 53, 59, 63, 70–74, 91–102, 165n8, 165n14, 167n55; rhetorical uses of, by moderates, 6, 67, 111–15, 120–21, 137–40; rhetorical use of, by radicals, 6, 9, 33, 35–36, 49–50, 64–65, 74–88, 104–8, 131–32, 135, 143, 167n42, 171n9. *See also* Cavaliers; Charles I (king of England); Charles II (king of England); Puritans
Crowley, Abraham, 130

Darcy, Eamon, 47, 108
Davies, Tony, 16
Davis, Garrett, 91
Davis, Jefferson, 20, 25, 35, 43, 69, 137–38, 141
DeBow's Review, 24, 53, 61
democracy, 7, 24, 29, 33, 100, 104, 136, 141, 155n16, 156n30, 176n57
Democrats. *See* conservatives, Northern
Dispatch, Richmond Daily, 20, 26, 30, 69, 72–74
Douglas, H. Ford, 75–76
Douglass, Frederick, 30, 76, 116, 131
Drogheda, massacre at, 59, 82, 86, 109, 135, 161n53, 167n53

Dublin, Ireland, 47, 54, 60, 107, 115, 135
Dudziak, Mary, 166n37

Edgehill, battle of, 62
Edwards, David, 59
election of 1860, 25, 28, 51–52, 55, 59–61, 91, 112, 170n22
emancipation, 9, 14, 21, 75, 85, 94, 117, 134; history as argument for, 6, 81, 93, 115, 157; as outcome of war, 124–25, 129, 133, 140; as war policy, 20, 70–71, 80, 89–90, 97–99, 101–2, 118–20, 178n87. *See also* abolitionists; Garrison, William Lloyd; Phillips, Wendell; radicals, Northern; Thirteenth Amendment
Emancipation Proclamation, 93, 97, 99, 101, 120
Emerson, Ralph Waldo, 77, 130–31
England, history of, 4–5, 9–10, 33, 39–41, 43, 45, 57–59, 104, 144, 149n3, 149n5, 163n49, 171n49; as Civil War rhetoric, 2–3, 11–12, 19, 61–63, 109, 143–45, 147–48, 155n21, 158n2, 164n69; connection to American history, 8, 125, 135–42; sources of, 12–19, 46–47, 152n26, 152n33; use of, by Confederates, 22–31, 52–56, 72–74; use of, by Northern conservatives, 6, 20, 90–102, 112–17, 145–46; use of, by Northern moderates, 6, 42–45, 48–50, 63–65, 67, 117–21, 124–31; use of, by Northern radicals, 6, 20, 31–37, 65–66, 70–71, 74–76, 78–83, 105–8, 110–12. *See also* Brodie, George; Cattermole, George; Clarendon, Earl of (Edward Hyde); Charles I (king of England); Charles II (king of England); Cromwell, Oliver; Froude, James; Lingard, John; Locke, John; Milton, John; Ross, Robert; Vaughan, Robert
Episcopal Church, 4, 102, 119
Everett, Edward, 32, 101–3, 111, 171n52, 177n72
exceptionalism, of US, 18, 26, 75, 141–42, 148, 178n85

Index 205

fanaticism, 23, 26, 53, 72, 74, 83, 87, 95, 96, 99–100, 113, 135, 156n26, 158n88, 167n55
fatalism, 8, 18, 23, 74 90
Federal Writer's Project, 47
Fitzgerald, F. Scott, 1
Fitzhugh, George, 29
Foster, Gaines, 132
Foster, R. F., 109
Frémont, John, 81
French Revolution, 116, 140, 150n17, 157n37
Froude, James, 134, 151n13, 160n31. *See also* England, history of

Gardiner, Samuel, 13
Garibaldi, Giuseppe, 88, 138
Garrison, William Lloyd, 29, 33, 77, 161n9
genetics, 34
Gentiles, Ian, 77
German Americans, 85
Germany, 128
Gettysburg, battle of, 9, 101–3, 129, 178n80
Gibbon, Edward, 12
Glorious Revolution, 10, 12, 43–44, 139, 175n37, 177n69
Gradert, Kenyon, 32–33, 157n61, 166n23, 167n47, 177n62
Greeley, Horace, 36, 85, 99
Guizot, François, 133

habeas corpus, 63, 90–93, 96, 101, 170n30
Hallam, Henry, 13, 50, 65, 96, 106
Halleck, Henry, 80
Hammond, James H., 24–25
Hampden, John, 49, 53, 66, 121, 132, 137–38
hard war, 6–7, 50, 65, 70, 81–82, 112, 135, 143–45, 161n53, 164n68, 167n55
Harper's New Monthly Magazine, 34
Harper's Weekly, 43, 48, 49–50, 94, 120, 126, 128, 137–38, 159n13, 175n27
Hattem, Michael, 17–18, 151n1
Hawthorne, Nathaniel, 83
Headley, Joel T., 14, 36, 80, 109
Henry II (king of England), 44, 114
Herald, New York, 20, 75, 91, 94–99, 126, 169nn16–17

Herndon, William, 15
Herrenvolk democracy, 155n16
Higginson, Thomas W., 87–88
historical thinking. *See* analogical thinking; exceptionalism; fatalism; whiggish, historical interpretation
Hobbes, Thomas, 27
Howard, Jacob, 97
Howe, Julia Ward, 36
Hume, David, 12–13, 96, 160n31
Hunter, David, 81, 87
Hunter, Robert, 2
Hyde, Edward (Earl of Clarendon), 13, 72, 105, 108, 152n15

Ignatieff, David, 178n2
Illinois, 50, 61, 65, 85
India, 74, 133, 135
Indian Rebellion of 1857, 3, 45, 118, 127, 134–35
Indigenous peoples, 32, 58, 110
Iowa, 98
Ireland, 4, 25 52, 97, 110, 128, 134, 137, 163n38, 172n40; 1641 Rebellion, 44–47, 160n31, 162n20, 162n23; Cromwell's campaigns in, 6, 82, 109; nineteenth-century history of, 55, 59, 106; rhetorical uses of, in US, 40, 48, 60, 67, 71–74, 82–84, 111–16, 127, 165n8, 167n55, 173n53; seventeenth-century history of, 5, 54, 56–59, 104, 107–8, 168n60. *See also* analogical thinking; Charles I (king of England); Cromwell, Oliver; Drogheda, massacre of; population expulsion; property seizure
Irish Rebellion of 1641, 44–47

Jefferson, Thomas, 9, 23, 27–28, 131–32, 153n38
Joint Committee on the Conduct of the War, 71, 165n7

Kansas, 36, 45, 59
King Philip's War, 32
Know-Nothings, 14, 84. *See also* nativism

Landon, George, 132–33
Laud, William, 4, 11, 31, 61–62
Lee, Robert E., 52
Levellers, 99, 166n23
Liberator, The, 32, 78–79, 83, 137
Lieber Code, 67, 106, 128
Lincoln, Abraham, 2, 20, 25, 48, 51, 59, 82, 85, 88, 111, 128; analogized to Cromwell, 59, 70–75, 95–96, 106, 176n53; and causes of Civil War, 21–22, 50, 170n22; criticism of, 28, 55, 58, 90–94, 97–99, 171n49; management of war by, 61–67, 83, 112, 129–30, 165n4, 178n87; as political moderate, 18, 42, 52, 76, 78–80, 101, 116–21, 123–24, 136, 139, 145, 171n52; reading habits of, 13, 15–16; use of history by, 9–10, 127, 141. *See also* abolitionists; conservatives, Northern; emancipation; moderates, Northern; radicals, Northern; Union, preservation of
Lingard, John, 54, 57. *See also* England, history of
Lochrane, O. A., 60
Locke, John, 9, 27, 56, 153n51
Long Parliament, 4, 15, 27, 80, 92, 95, 102, 171n49. *See also* Charles I (king of England); Cromwell, Oliver
Lord, John (Lord Acton), 127
Lost Cause, 57, 124, 174n5

Macaulay, Thomas B., 109, 117, 119–20, 130; reception of, in US, 13–17, 137, 151n13, 152n26, 156n28; rhetorical uses of, 43, 45, 64–66, 95, 100, 164n68. *See also* Carlyle, Thomas; England, history of
Magna Carta, 96
Malcolm X, 32
Marston Moor, battle of, 105, 130, 178n80
Marvel, Andrew, 104
Marx, Karl, 9, 16
Mason, James, 76, 138
Massachusetts, 12, 19, 30, 33, 36, 65, 85, 87, 104, 111
Mather, Cotton, 26

Maximilian (Austrian archduke), 42, 157n54, 179n3
McClellan, George B., 81, 86
McConville, Brendan, 152n33
McDonnell, John, 108, 160n31
McGreevy, John T., 84
McGuffey Readers, 8, 151n5
McPherson, James, 156n51, 157n67
Mendel, Gregor, 34
metaphorical thinking. *See* analogical thinking
Mexican-American War, 70, 90
military governors, 106, 111–12, 118
Mill, John Stuart, 116, 152n36
Milton, John, 16, 28–30, 93, 104, 130, 153nn38–40; *Paradise Lost*, 16, 81, 93, 141; rhetorical use of, by conservatives, 81; rhetorical use of, by radicals, 49, 76–77, 105, 138, 140, 167n42; *The Tenure of Kings and Magistrates*, 28–29, 77
Minnesota, 138
Mitchel, John, 113
moderates, Northern, 3–4, 80; attitudes toward history of, 18, 40, 70, 90, 136; rhetorical uses of the past by, 6, 9–10, 124–25, 129–35; and reunion, 52, 88, 141–42; war policies of, 50, 66, 98, 143–44, 170n29. *See also* conservatives, Northern; Lincoln, Abraham; radicals, Northern
Moore, J. Quitman, 24
Morgan, Edmund, 177n70
Motley, John L., 32, 48, 85, 131–32, 175n37, 179n5
Murphy, Angela, 84

Napoléon, 16, 94, 149n3, 150n17
Naseby, battle of, 77, 105
nativism, 60, 83–86, 168n66; and American Party, 14, 84. *See also* Catholicism
New English, 57, 109
New Model Army, 5, 66, 71, 87, 91, 170n22
New York Herald, 20, 75, 91, 94–99, 126, 169nn16–17

Index 207

Normans, 24–26, 34, 44, 154n10, 155n21, 157n67

O'Brien, Michael, 55, 154n5, 154n9
O'Connell, Daniel, 84
Ohio, 20, 29, 67, 71, 84, 94, 112, 137–38, 146
Old English, 57

pacifism, 70
Paradise Lost (Milton), 16, 81, 93, 141
Pennsylvania, 65, 85, 132
Perceval-Maxwell, M., 108, 162n23
Phillips, Wendell, 19, 26; attitudes toward Irish people of, 84–85, 107; Civil War activism of, 76, 99, 111, 165n4; rhetorical use of history by, 20, 35–36, 77, 80–83, 158n78, 167n47. *See also* abolitionists; Cromwell, Oliver; Puritans
plantations, 24, 57–58, 73, 108–9, 162n20
Plymouth Rock, 26, 32
Pocock, J. G. A., 10, 110, 174n4, 177n69
Poland, 72, 74, 114
Pollan, Michael, 7
population expulsion, 73, 111, 113–14, 167n55
Potter, David, 133
Powell, Lazarus, 111–12
Powhatan Confederacy, 109
preemptive war, 52–55, 58, 67
Presbyterian Church, 4, 6, 40, 45, 63, 76–77, 99, 119
Pride, Thomas, 91–92, 167n42, 171n49
Pride's Purge, 91–92, 167n42, 171n49
property seizure, 42, 52, 58, 61, 72–73, 90, 95–97, 101, 109, 112–14, 118, 124, 134, 160n38
Puritans, 40, 45, 83, 85, 141, 154n2, 155n20; in English history, 5, 11–14, 86, 95–96, 105, 108–9, 152n18, 174n4, 175n41, 177n72; and revolution, 174n4, 175n41; rhetorical use of, by conservatives, 24–31, 53–54, 66, 72–73, 87, 94, 99, 115, 156n30; rhetorical use of, by radicals, 6, 22, 32–37, 63, 65, 77, 106–7, 137–38, 157n61, 158n87, 166n23, 167n47. *See*

also analogical thinking; Cavalier; emancipation; nativism

racism, 90, 94. *See also* Stephens, Alexander
Radical Republicans, 19, 71, 85, 94, 99, 110, 112, 114–15. *See also* Republicans
radicals, Northern, 29, 40, 50, 64, 91, 114, 124, 129; attitudes toward history of, 3, 18–19, 74, 136, 171n52; criticism of, 53, 71–72, 85–86, 94–95, 99–100; and reunion, 103–4, 140; rhetorical uses of the past by, 6, 9–10, 32–33, 35–36, 75–82, 107, 111, 143, 166n23; war policies of, 15, 70–71, 76, 78, 83–84, 86–88, 98, 110, 112, 144, 165n7. *See also* abolitionists; emancipation; Garrison, William Lloyd; nativism; Phillips, Wendell; Sumner, Charles
Ramsay, David, 8
rebellion, 11, 52, 63, 113, 117, 141, 145; Civil War as, 7, 28, 34, 48–49, 57, 66, 86, 105–6; history of, 2, 34, 40, 58–59, 61, 134–35; punishment for, 107–11; theories of, 43–45, 53, 97, 123, 126–32, 158n1, 159n13, 163n49, 172n39. *See also* American Revolution; Indian Rebellion of 1857; Irish Rebellion of 1641
reconciliation, 4, 119–20
Reconstruction, 6, 104, 110–15
Reformation, 5, 26–27, 75, 100–101
regicide, 40, 78, 95, 118, 157n54, 164n69 171n49. *See also* Charles I (king of England); Cromwell, Oliver
republicanism, 5–6, 10, 16, 19, 27–28, 66–67, 71, 73–74, 93, 104, 135, 139, 164n76, 171n49
Republicans, 3, 75, 85, 91, 95, 102, 114, 169n17; antebellum party, 25, 55, 84, 170n22; criticism of, 75, 96, 99, 116. *See also* abolitionists; Browning, Orville; Collamer, Jacob; Cowan, Edgar; Lincoln, Abraham; moderates, Northern; nativism; Radical Republicans; radicals, Northern; Sedgwick, Charles; Seward, William

Restoration, of Charles II, 5, 14, 27, 102, 107–9, 115, 118–20, 146, 151n1. *See also* Everett, Edward
revisionism, in Civil War historiography, 61, 163n50, 176n46
Rhodes, James F., 139
Richmond Daily Dispatch, 20, 26, 30, 69, 72–74
Richmond Whig, 71–72
Rodgers, Daniel, 141, 150n12, 178n85
rosewater strategy, 61, 65, 81
Ross, Robert, 47, 160n31. *See also* England, history of
Roundheads. *See* Puritans
Royalists. *See* Cavaliers
Royster, Charles, 75, 156n26
Ruffin, Edmund, 15, 165n14. *See also* Confederates
Rump Parliament, 62, 91–92, 171n49
Russell, William H., 62–63
Russia, 48, 52, 74, 128

Satia, Priya, 133, 136, 175n32
Scotland, 4–5, 25, 40–48, 56, 59, 83, 94, 104, 127, 137, 158n2, 162n23
Scott, Walter, 12–13, 23
secession, 3, 7, 10, 28–31, 37, 71, 95, 101, 114, 128, 134, 141; Northern arguments against, 40, 42, 48–51, 62–64, 70, 77–78, 80, 92, 116, 124, 127, 175n27; Southern arguments for, 52–61, 99, 145. *See also* Confederates; preemptive war
Sedgwick, Charles, 107
Seward, William, 2, 22, 30, 98, 138–40
Seymour, Horatio, 98
Shakespeare, William, 92, 150n17, 152n28
Sherman, William T., 66, 72–73
slavery, 2–3, 7, 10, 20–21, 47, 43, 67, 84, 87, 98, 117, 135–36; as cause of Civil War, 4, 28, 55, 62; opposition to, 32–37, 48, 52, 75–76, 81, 83, 89–90, 104, 114, 120, 123–24, 131; Southern defense of, 22–25, 27, 29–31, 56–60, 113; and US Army, 42, 70–71, 97. *See also* abolitionists; democracy; emancipation

Smith, Goldwin, 128, 139, 178nn79–80
Soldier's Pocket Bible, The, 64–65
South Carolina, 24, 59, 65, 87, 114
Southern Literary Messenger, 23, 31
Stafford, Earl of (Thomas Wentworth), 56–58, 61–62
Stephens, Alexander, 23–25
Stevens, Thaddeus, 110, 114
Stowe, Harriet B., 13
Strong, George T., 141
Stuarts, 42, 76, 93, 170n45. *See also* Charles I (king of England); Long Parliament
Sumner, Charles, 19–20, 110, 128, 135; education of, 12, 166n20; historical consciousness of, 33–34, 49–50, 75, 157n66; perspectives on Civil War of, 104–7, 111–12

Taiping Rebellion, 3
taxation, 57, 74, 112
Taylor, Amy, 118, 173n61
Taylor, William C., 58–59, 160n35. *See also* England, history of
Temple, John, 13, 46–47, 82, 159n28, 160n31, 160n38
Tenure of Kings and Magistrates, The (Milton), 28–29, 77
Thirteenth Amendment, 70, 75, 78, 119
Tilton, Theodore, 81, 104
Trouillot, Michel-Rolph, 159n24
Tucker, Ann, 54
Twain, Mark, 23

Ulster, 44–45, 58, 168n60
Union, preservation of, 2–4, 42, 46, 51–53, 61, 70, 80–83, 90, 98–101, 110, 116, 124–25, 138–41. *See also* Lincoln, Abraham; moderates, Northern
US Army, 42, 70–71, 97; treatment of Black people by, 114
US Constitution, 63, 67, 75, 77, 78, 92, 101, 105, 118, 126–27, 138–40, 144, 161n9, 163n49
US-Mexican War, 70, 90

Index 209

Vallandigham, Clement, 90, 98
Vaughan, Robert, 45, 115, 120.
    See also England, history of
Vermont, 82, 86, 96
Vincent, Henry, 139–40
violence, 5–6, 11, 58–59, 75, 91, 113, 116, 160n35, 175n32; abolitionist, 36, 82–83, 165nn3–4; and atrocity, 44–47, 50, 160n38, 167n53; colonial, 109; military, 2, 31, 39, 57, 65–66, 81, 144, 161n53, 164n69; necessity of, 62, 64, 104, 125, 133–37. See also Drogheda, massacre of; pacifism
Virginia, 2, 15, 26, 34, 36, 62, 95, 113, 120, 138
Vorhees, Daniel, 96–97

Wade, Benjamin, 71, 112
Walzer, Michael, 33, 175n41
Warren, Robert Penn, 47, 110
Wars of the Roses, 126, 139
Washington, George, 15, 43, 49, 86, 88, 131–32, 137–38, 159n13
Webb, James W., 95, 170n22
Weber, Max, 134

Webster, Daniel, 98
Webster, Noah, 17
Wentworth, Thomas (Earl of Stafford), 56–58, 61–62
West Point, 65, 80
Wexford, battle of. See Drogheda, massacre of
whiggish, historical interpretation, 8–9, 15, 18, 35, 73, 82, 85, 90, 120, 125, 135, 137–39, 141, 151n19, 152n32, 177n71. See also analogical thinking
Whig Party (American), 87, 101
Whitmore, W. H., 34
Whittier, John G., 137
Wigfall, Louis T., 26, 30–31, 53
William of Orange (king of England), 83, 120
Witt, John, 106, 178n87
Wood, Fernando, 53, 100–101
World War I, 147
World War II, 141, 147

Yokota, Kariann, 55

www.ingramcontent.com/pod-product-compliance
Lightning Source LLC
Chambersburg PA
CBHW021855230426
43671CB00006B/401